SACCO AND VANZETTI:
THE CASE RESOLVED

Other books by Francis Russell

Adams:
    An American Dynasty

The American Heritage Book of the Pioneer Spirit (co-author)

A City in Terror:
    1919—The Boston Police Strike

The Confident Years (1865–1917)

Forty Years On

The French and Indian Wars

The Great Interlude

The Horizon Concise History of Germany

Lexington, Concord and Bunker Hill

The Making of the Nation (1783–1860)

The President Makers:
    From Mark Hanna to Joseph P. Kennedy

The Shadow of Blooming Grove:
    Warren Gamaliel Harding in His Times

Three Studies in 20th-Century Obscurity:
    Joyce, Kafka, & Gertrude Stein

Tragedy in Dedham:
    The Story of the Sacco-Vanzetti Case

World of Dürer

SACCO & VANZETTI

THE CASE RESOLVED

by Francis Russell

HARPER & ROW, PUBLISHERS, New York

Cambridge, Philadelphia, San Francisco, London,

1817 *Mexico City, São Paulo, Singapore, Sydney*

Copyright acknowledgments appear on page 246.

SACCO AND VANZETTI: THE CASE RESOLVED. Copyright © 1986 by Francis Russell. All rights reserved. Printed in the United States of America. No part of this book may be used or reproduced in any manner whatsoever without written permission except in the case of brief quotations embodied in critical articles and reviews. For information address Harper & Row, Publishers, Inc., 10 East 53rd Street, New York, N.Y. 10022. Published simultaneously in Canada by Fitzhenry & Whiteside Limited, Toronto.

FIRST EDITION

Designer: Sidney Feinberg

Library of Congress Cataloging in Publication Data

Russell, Francis, 1910–
   Sacco and Vanzetti.

   Bibliography: p.
   Includes index.
   1. Sacco–Vanzetti case.   2. Trials (Murder)—
Massachusetts—Dedham.   I. Title
KF224.S2R84   1986   345.73'02523   85-45228
ISBN 0-06-015524-8   347.3052523

86 87 88 89 90 RRD 10 9 8 7 6 5 4 3 2 1

For
Ideale Gambera,
who cares about the truth

Most of our ideas are not propagated by reason
but caught by contagion.

—SAMUEL JOHNSON

Contents

1. The Roads of the Sacco-Vanzetti Case   1
2. The Road to Sandwich   11
3. The Road to Boston   19
4. The Road to Friendship   32
5. The Road to Braintree   43
6. The Road to Brockton   55
7. The Anarchist Road   64
8. The Road to Dedham   87
9. The Road to Charlestown   108
10. The Road from Charlestown   124
11. The Path of the Bullet   145
12. The Roads to Providence and Needham   164
13. The Road to Washington   173
14. The Road to Norwood   183
15. The Road to Cambridge   196
16. The End of the Road   203

Appendix A: The Eloquence of Vanzetti   221
Appendix B: The After Years   223
Appendix C: The Perjury of Ramuglia   225
Notes   227
Bibliography   235
Index   239

SACCO AND VANZETTI:
THE CASE RESOLVED

1

The Roads of the Sacco-Vanzetti Case

The holdup in South Braintree on that April afternoon in 1920 was commonplace enough, if brutal. Two gunmen shot down a paymaster and his guard as they carried the weekly payroll money in metal boxes to a local shoe factory. Seizing the boxes, leaving the paymaster and his guard sprawled dying in the gutter, they escaped with three confederates in a stolen touring car. There was no further trace of them.

Three weeks later Nicola Sacco and Bartolomeo Vanzetti, aliens unknown to the police, were picked up in Brockton, nine miles away, as suspected auto thieves. While they were under arrest, several witnesses identified them as participants in the Braintree killings and they were then held on a charge of murder. The editor of a New York Socialist paper, sent by an anarchist friend to Boston to investigate, reported back that "there's no story in it . . . just a couple of wops in a jam."[1]

Such were the beginnings of the Sacco-Vanzetti case, destined to expand to the American case of the century, the transatlantic Dreyfus affair, one of those climactic events that polarize a society. According to received dogma that became a liberal shibboleth, Sacco and Vanzetti were harmless philosophical anarchists arrested during the hysteria of the postwar Red scare. The police, in cooperation with the Department of Justice's Bureau of Investigation, considered a robbery-murder charge a good way of getting rid of two troublesome agitators. Neither the police nor the Bureau of Investigation nor the district attorney who prosecuted them could have considered them guilty. Nor in the trial's aftermath could Massachusetts' Governor Alvan T. Fuller nor Harvard's President A. Lawrence Lowell, who headed a committee appointed by Fuller to review the case. Sacco and Vanzetti died because they were anarchists, their lives snuffed out by Massachusetts reactionaries. Their Dedham trial, little better than a kangaroo court, held in an atmosphere of violent anti-foreign and antiradical prejudice, was presided over by an intemperate narrow-minded judge—"a black-gowned cobra," in Vanzetti's words—already determined to convict the defendants. The jury was made up of nativist bigots, the prosecution corrupt to the point of faking evidence. In the post-trial stages of the case, parvenu Governor Fuller, a bicycle mechanic who had turned to automobiles and made himself rich selling Packards to the rich, was no more than a toady to Beacon Hill Boston. President Lowell, at the governor's request heading a committee to review the case, knew that the two anarchists were innocent but preferred to see them die rather than to disturb the social structure he represented.

That dogma I accepted as self-evident. When, a quarter of a century ago, I began my history of the case, *Tragedy in Dedham,* I took for granted the innocence of Sacco and Vanzetti and the villainy of the prosecution. At the start I saw a straight road stretching ahead of me. Though I thought of myself as impartial, ready to consider any fact however awkward, I had no doubts about my conclusions. Persuaded by the dogma, I identified myself emotionally with the two dead anarchists more than I realized. But as I progressed, the road that had at first seemed straight developed so many bends, twists, reverses, and side paths, so many culs-de-sac and unexpected detours, that in the end I found myself facing in the opposite direction.

Questions that I had first brushed aside as inconsequent returned to trouble me. Why, after their arrest, did Sacco and Vanzetti lie about matters that had no connection with their anarchist beliefs or the Braintree crime? Why were they armed when they were picked up by the police? Both described themselves as men of peace. "I would my blood to prevent the sheeding of blood," Vanzetti wrote. Yet they were carrying on their persons the weapons of violence. Their defenders have tried to explain that they lived in a time of fear; that in any case it was a common custom for Italians to carry weapons. But for me the excuses never quite convinced.

In the spring of 1959, still a believer in their innocence, I sat next to Dr. Ralph Colp, Jr. at a dinner given for one of the more voluble defenders of Sacco and Vanzetti, Judge Michael Musmanno, who had come to Boston as chief speaker at the Massachusetts legislature's

Judiciary Committee hearing on a proposed posthumous pardon. Dr. Colp, a psychiatrist, had gone over the medical records of Sacco and Vanzetti covering the periods when they had suffered mental breakdowns.* During the course of the dinner, I said to him that I could never really understand why Sacco and Vanzetti were armed on the night of their arrest. "Neither can I," he said with an emphatic toss of his head. "Neither can I."

I became more ambivalent about Sacco and Vanzetti when I discovered that, after the trial, their chief counsel, the bohemian radical Fred Moore, had come to question their innocence. Finally my doubts crystallized when I learned that Carlo Tresca, the anarchist leader who brought Moore into the case, had said flatly in 1941 that Sacco at least was guilty. My shift from belief to disbelief did not affect the true believers. Intellectual opinion remained solidly behind Sacco and Vanzetti. In 1948 G. Louis Joughin had written that "prosecutors, judges, and the hostile public majority have not in twenty years found a single literary defender of their position."[2] Not for another decade would this position be challenged.

Some time after *Tragedy in Dedham* was published I happened to be talking about the case with a young woman, an instructor in one of the smaller Ivy League colleges. "Sacco and Vanzetti were innocent," she told me challengingly.

"Have you read my book?" I asked her.

"No," she said, "but they *had* to be innocent."

In intellectual circles generally Sacco and Vanzetti have *had* to be innocent. Their innocence has been taken for granted in the *Dictionary of American Biography*, the *Encyclopedia Americana*, the *Encyclopaedia Britannica*, and other books of reference; in popular histories such as F. L. Allen's *Only Yesterday*, J. J. Hoffman's *The Twenties*, Arthur Schlesinger, Jr.'s *The Crisis of the Old Order*, and Cleveland Amory's *The Proper Bostonians;* in various cultural studies; and in a score of novels and plays. Mass protests against their conviction and impending execution seemed the spontaneous response of men of goodwill all over the globe.

The initial crack in this monolith of opinion came oddly enough—and unintentionally—from Moscow. In 1958 the Dietz

---

* Sacco and Vanzetti, diagnosed as suffering from psychosis of a paranoid character, each spent five months in the Bridgewater State Hospital for the Criminally Insane, though at different times. Colp wrote two articles on their mental state for *The Nation*: "Sacco's Struggle for Sanity" (August 16, 1958) and "Bitter Christmas: A Biographical Inquiry into the Life of Bartolomeo Vanzetti" (December 27, 1958).

Verlag in East Berlin published a Professor Johannes Zelt's *Proletarischer Internationalismus im Kampf um Sacco und Vanzetti* (*Proletarian Internationalism in the Battle for Sacco and Vanzetti*). Zelt had the Moscow archives open to him for his researches and he is at pains to show that the world agitation, the great demonstrations, were Communist-organized and directed. He has a withering contempt for what he considers the ineffectual efforts of the bourgeois liberals with their "milk and pap" respectability. The real force that gave life to the Sacco-Vanzetti protest movement, he points out, was the Communist International Red Aid. But in proving his point, Zelt all unwittingly undermines the myth of spontaneous protest.

I came across Zelt's book in the Harvard library. Later, when I was in East Berlin, I decided to see him. First I called at the Dietz Publishing House, located in some sort of party headquarters on the Wallstrasse near the Spree. Everyone there was most cordial. The girl at the reception desk even gave me a little hammer-and-compass souvenir badge, and the editor explained to me amiably that he was now preparing a twentieth-century edition of Marx's works. Zelt, he said, had an office elsewhere. He looked up the address in his file and gave it to me—a little hesitantly, I thought. Subsequently I discovered it was that of the Institute for Social Studies of the Communist Central Committee.

The street, Taubenstrasse, is one of the smaller thoroughfares parallel to Unter den Linden, the building high, gray, unmarked, and of sinister length. Somehow it reminded me of Goering's Air Ministry. At the entrance were merely the numbers 17–53 and a notice above a push button: KLINGELN (RING). I rang and the door swung open, silently, automatically. As I stepped inside, five men in brown uniforms, wearing belts and pistols and sitting behind a horseshoe-shaped counter, confronted me without speaking.

"I'm looking for Professor Zelt," I said in my rough-edged German, trying to seem as if I took them and all police for granted.

"Yes?" the man in the middle finally said.

"In America I read his *sehr wertvolles* [very worthwhile] book on the Sacco-Vanzetti case and in passing through I wanted to pay my respects to him."

The five seemed to lose something of their sternness; their turned-down mouths relaxed a little.

"His office is upstairs," said the middle man. "You can call him." He dialed a number on his counter telephone and handed it to me.

When I asked for the professor, his secretary answered. "Comrade Zelt is not here today," she told me. "He is at the Congress Against War and Fascism, but he will be back tomorrow."

I made an appointment to see him the next morning at eleven. As I went out, I nodded to the five uniformed men and they briefly acknowledged my nod. But I did not go back. One never knew about East Berlin, and once before I had been arrested there.

The first direct challenge to the dogma of innocence was made two years after Zelt's book when a crusty Boston lawyer, Robert Montgomery, published his acerbic *Sacco-Vanzetti: The Murder and the Myth.* Montgomery, who had spent years probing into the case records, concluded that the two anarchists were indeed guilty and the subsequent proceedings fair, though in his angry defense of the Massachusetts judiciary he could not see that Sacco and Vanzetti, whatever their guilt or innocence, were interesting men. To him they were no more than a couple of sleazy criminals. Nevertheless, his coldly elenctic analysis rends much of the dogma's fabric and undermines many of the long-held assumptions and contentions of Sacco-Vanzetti defenders. A New York liberal lawyer, James Grossman, wrote in *Commentary* that, for believers in innocence, Montgomery's book stood like a lion in the path.[3]

A year after the execution of Sacco and Vanzetti, James Rorty, death-watch street demonstrator and poet of the cause, in a review of Upton Sinclair's documentary novel *Boston* for *The Nation,* wrote of their "seven years of incredible judicial torture," and called their case "as great a tragedy as has been enacted in our time."[4] A third of a century later, in reviewing Montgomery's book in *The New Leader,* Rorty wrote that after "this honest and able reappraisal of the court record" he was forced to accept Sacco's and Vanzetti's guilt and the fact that "the full resources of Massachusetts justice were expended in their behalf."[5]

The second challenge came two years later with the appearance of Grossman's "Sacco and Vanzetti Case Reconsidered" in *Commentary.* Though sympathetic to Sacco and Vanzetti as individuals, Grossman—a New York lawyer—through his examination of the post-trial ballistics evidence had come to doubt Sacco's innocence. In his closely reasoned article he explained why he was now convinced that the automatic pistol found on Sacco at his arrest was the Braintree murder weapon.

Grossman pointed out that while Vanzetti proclaimed his inno-

cence eloquently over the years even to that last moment when he
stood in the death chamber, Sacco's last words were "Long live anarchy!" Unlike Vanzetti, Sacco, once he had been sentenced and made
his defiant speech to the court, did not emphasize his innocence, for
all his attacks on judge, jury, and prosecution. To have admitted
guilt, as Grossman points out, would have betrayed his cause. To
continue to proclaim his innocence would, in Grossman's opinion,
have betrayed his inner self.

My own altered conclusions in *Tragedy in Dedham,* published six
months after Grossman's article, were much like his. Sacco and Vanzetti died for a cause. Sacco was guilty, Vanzetti was not. That was
how I finally came to see the case. But much important information
still remained unknown or unavailable—the FBI files, Harvard President Lowell's papers, certain anarchist documents.

In 1965 Professor David Felix of the City University of New
York, a biographer of Rathenau and Marx, completed his reevalua-
tion of the Sacco-Vanzetti case. [6] He had first become interested in it
through what he considered its illogicalities, and his approach was
coldly rational, with no bias toward either side. His main concern
was with the role of the intellectuals, why they had been drawn into
the case so compulsively. But his painstaking study of the evidence
also convinced him that Sacco and Vanzetti were guilty.

The belated emergence of the revisionists stirred up a dust cloud
of vituperative protest among Sacco-Vanzetti partisans, still adamant
more than thirty years after the executions. In 1969 the last surviving
defense counsel, Herbert Ehrmann, challenged the dissenters in the
special pleading of his *Case That Will Not Die,* a skillful lawyer's
brief, though equivocal and tediously long.

In June 1962, *American Heritage* printed my article on the
Sacco-Vanzetti ballistics evidence with photographs to show that
Sacco's pistol was the murder weapon. But eight years later the
American Heritage History of the 20's & 30's reverted to the dogmatic assertion that Sacco and Vanzetti were convicted "in spite of
copious evidence of their innocence." The editors even repeated the
partisan fabrication that the judge at Vanzetti's earlier robbery trial
had instructed the jury that "although he may not actually have
committed the crime attributed to him he is nevertheless morally
culpable, because he is the enemy of our existing institutions."[7]*

* There is nothing remotely resembling such a statement in the judge's charge, with
which both defense and prosecution lawyers had expressed themselves content.

Inevitably someone was bound to make a Sacco-Vanzetti film. Dino De Laurentiis had planned one in 1962 after the publication of *Tragedy in Dedham* and intended to make that book the framework for his film—though, as I discovered in my one talk with him, with conclusions so opposite that I declined to allow him to use it. He hired a Hollywood writer, Edward Anhalt, to prepare the script he had in mind. Anhalt's version was of Sacco the shoemaker-philosopher with his wife and child in their rose-embowered bungalow. Into this proletarian paradise come the hounds of hell, harriers of innocent Red dreamers and philosophical radicals. Anhalt crossed each *t* and dotted every *i* of the accepted dogma, giving special attention to Sacco's wife, Rosina, since she was to be played by De Laurentiis's wife, Silvana Mangano. For some months De Laurentiis's New York office had meter stamps reading: SEE SACCO AND VANZETTI. Then for some reason the whole project was junked, not to be revived for another eight years, this time with Giuliano Montaldo as director.

Montaldo's Technicolor *Sacco and Vanzetti*, released in 1971, is straight black and white, a melodrama instead of the tragedy the case actually was. The trial itself is an imaginative *tour de force* that bears no relation to anything that took place in the courtroom. Although in Massachusetts judges do not use gavels, the film judge wields one the size of a croquet mallet; the district attorney makes a flag-waving oration that I presume Anhalt or Montaldo must have written, since there is no trace of it in the official transcript; the courtroom is packed with Students for a Democratic Society who boo the judge and pick fights with the police.

It was only two years since the Harvard riots, and the SDS seemed to make up much of the audience when I saw the film in Cambridge. For me it dragged to the point of second-degree tedium. The students did not share my apolitical ennui. At times they even applauded. I suppose that they were attending the lay church of their choice and Monsignor Montaldo was merely preaching to the converted. On my way out, after two hours of overexposed villainy, I heard a student remark to his girl: "Things haven't changed a bit in this country!" Yet in the farrago of film distortions there is one moment of truth. Massachusetts Governor Fuller, after interviewing Vanzetti a few days before the execution, tells him on leaving: "You have the choice of being a myth or a human being." Vanzetti did have that choice.

Montaldo's film was shown on French television in May 1977, as

part of a three-hour program "Dossiers de l'Ecran" that ended with
a discussion panel of a dozen participants, among them Montaldo;
Maurice Lederman, a leading Communist lawyer; Professor Felix;
Vanzetti's younger sister Vincenzina; and Sacco's grandson Spenser
Sacco. Vincenzina and Spenser had nothing more to say than that
their relatives were innocent and that they hoped to see them vindi-
cated. They gave no additional information about the case.

The French program was a prelude to the commemorative ob-
servances marking the fiftieth anniversary of the Sacco-Vanzetti executions. On August 23, Massachusetts Governor Michael Dukakis,
acting on the advice of his legal counsel, created a national sensation
by declaring the anniversary of the executions to be "Nicola Sacco
and Bartolomeo Vanzetti Memorial Day." After signing a proclamation to that effect in the crowded senate chamber, with Spenser
Sacco in tears at his side, Dukakis explained that although he took no
stand on whether the two were guilty or innocent, he wanted to re-
move "any stigma or disgrace from the names of their families and
descendants and so from the name of the Commonwealth of Massachusetts."[8] How that could be done without declaring them innocent
is a politician's secret. Just why Dukakis issued his proclamation remains a mystery. He has been accused of courting the ethnic vote in
a state that had recently elected two Italian-American governors.
State Senator Alan Sisitsky, though a Democratic liberal who
thought Dukakis at least partially right, remarked sardonically that
"if there were a couple of thousand cannibals in Massachusetts and
he could get their votes, he would make some gesture."[9] My own
opinion is that the governor would like to consider himself an intellectual and that his proclamation was meant as a gesture of solidarity
with the liberal academic community, still overwhelmingly tied to
the dogma of innocence betrayed.

The State House ceremony was televised by the networks and
was featured on the "Today" show. With the renewed wave of interest in Sacco and Vanzetti, several earlier books on the case were reissued. Three new books also appeared, one by Katherine Anne Porter,
the two others by unknowns. Miss Porter's sixty-three-page *Never-
Ending Wrong* is a description of her experiences in Boston half a
century earlier as a protester and State House picketer. Her brief
elegiac account reveals nothing new, but she does succeed in captur-
ing the flavor of the turbulent August week before the executions.
Though her mind and thought have not advanced beyond that point,

she has been affected enough by the revisionists to admit the possibility—if not probability—of Sacco's guilt. The shrill and hysterical *Justice Crucified* makes no such admission, its author, Roberta Feuerlicht, being still inwardly engaged in the 1927 picketing of the Massachusetts State House. For her the revisionists do not exist. To the more balanced Sacco-Vanzetti defenders her book has proved an embarrassment. At a 1979 Sacco-Vanzetti conference Professor Nunzio Pernicone of the University of Illinois took her to task as a detriment to the cause he was defending. "The most recent book on the case," he told a Boston audience, "Roberta Feuerlicht's *Justice Crucified*, categorically dismisses every shred of evidence ever produced by the revisionists that suggests that Sacco and Vanzetti might have been something less than 100% pure and innocent. This cannot be. . . . If there are new aspects of the case that threaten traditional assumptions, that's too bad."[10]

Brian Jackson, an Englishman, is a far abler writer than Roberta Feuerlicht, but his Sacco-Vanzetti book, *The Black Flag*—most of it written overseas—is a misfortune that at times verges on the ludicrous, as when he refers to the "North Church where Paul Revere rang the bell" or calls Phi Beta Kappa "si, beta, kappa" or has Americans "playing craps." His study, he claims, is not a text but an experience, and he states "the bare story as fairly as I can."[11] His European experience and background, and his unfamiliarity with the Massachusetts landscape, keep tripping him up, for all his high intentions. In his book Fall River becomes "Falls River," Harvard's Harry Elkins Widener Library appears as the "Charles Weidener Library," and the Ingersoll Lectures are labeled "Ingwell," etc. Of Boston he writes that "it was here that Sacco and Vanzetti were arrested, tried and executed."[12] As any elementary student of the case knows, they were arrested in Brockton, twenty miles from Boston, tried in Dedham, and executed in Charlestown. Felix Frankfurter, though an unofficial adviser to the defense committee, was never—as Jackson claims—a counsel for Sacco and Vanzetti.

Such a proliferation of subsidiary errors casts much doubt on the author's ability to reevaluate this much-evaluated case. Yet he has brought up one profound question that is well worth pondering. With only a "ripple of uncertainty" as to the innocence of Sacco and Vanzetti, he wonders if it might not be possible that they had come to believe in their own innocence even though guilty. "Might you not commit a murder and deny it not only to the court but to yourself?" he asks. "Might you not forge a new identity in that furnace, and emerge a phoenix of our time, . . . that guilt which self-deceives and is purged?"[13]

For the Committee to Vindicate Sacco and Vanzetti, for sympathizers and partisans new and old, Governor Dukakis's proclamation was a moment of triumph. Carey McWilliams, the former editor of *The Nation,* an archetypical Sacco-Vanzetti supporter, wrote that with this proclamation fighting over the case would finally cease because the enemy had been routed. "It now seems unlikely that there will be still another campaign by 'neo-conservative' intellectuals or others, to convict the innocent."[14] Now, with all stigma and disgrace eradicated from the linked names, vindicators could look forward—as they had long anticipated—to having Gutzon Borglum's Sacco-Vanzetti plaster bas-relief cast in bronze and placed on Boston Common. But the lurking question, though seemingly in abeyance, remained. Could Sacco and Vanzetti have been among the five men in the murder car on that April afternoon? Two or three of those men might still be alive. Or their closest relatives might know. Ferris Greenslet, the biographer of the Lowells, wondered quizzically if immortality was really desirable, then decided it was if only to get at the truth of the Sacco-Vanzetti case. One of the more balanced Sacco-Vanzetti advocates, Edmund Morgan, a professor of evidence at the Harvard Law School, doubted that human judgment would ever be able to arrive at absolute certainty.[15] Yet the truth was simple. Who were the five men in the South Braintree murder car and what did each of them do? It needed only one man to come forward and say there must be those somewhere who knew the truth, as I wrote in the foreword to my revised *Tragedy in Dedham,* "elderly people now, still tenaciously prepared to carry the weight of their secret to the grave."[16] But barring a sudden revelation by one of them, I did not see how any more clarity could be reached.

Living remotely in Sandwich, on Cape Cod, I had long given up the hope or even the thought of any such revelation. Those who knew would die with their knowledge. In this seaside village, in this creaky, ancient house built when Charles II was king of North America, the turbulence of the great case that Stalin had called the most important event since the October Revolution had muted for me to less than a seashell echo. Then, in the quiet of an overcast November afternoon in 1982, the revelation came.

2

The Road to Sandwich

On that fading afternoon, as I walked down to the Sandwich post office, I noticed a lacing of ice along the edge of Shawme Pond. Farther out the water was mirrorlike, reflecting two motionless swans on its blank surface. Across the pond the slate headstones in the old cemetery on the point looked dun as the landscape under the pewter sky. Yet the air was extraordinarily clear, no touch of wind, no movement except for the restless coots gathered near the milldam. Because it was to be such a momentous afternoon, I try to recall what I was thinking as I walked along the empty road, past the twin-columned town hall, the United Church with its (supposed) Christopher Wren steeple, the brick library. Nothing very much, beyond wondering why the coots always came in November and where they disappeared to in the spring.

At the post office the woman behind the counter handed me a yellow slip of paper. "You have a registered letter," she said. "Sign here." I signed, and she passed me a brown envelope with the name Ideale Gambera and a San Francisco address on the return sticker. Man or woman, no one I had ever heard of. "Another crackpot letter," I said to the woman.

"Do you get many?" she asked me.

"Enough."

I had indeed received enough. The letter from the Italian was probably another on Sacco and Vanzetti. Ever since I had changed my mind about their innocence, my mail had been cluttered with bristling protests from their sympathizers. Having read the letters of Sacco and Vanzetti, how—I was asked—could I possibly have arrived at such nonbelief? How, in the light of the falsified ballistics evidence, could I consider Sacco guilty? What did I know about guns and bullets anyhow? How dared I say that the stubborn silence of Sacco's son reflected on his father's innocence? What did I know about the Italian community? What did I really know about the case?

In the last few years such letters had tapered off, and I had not received any for several months until this one from San Francisco. I stuck the brown envelope in my duffel-coat pocket and started back. It was spitting snow by the time I reached the pond. A wind had sprung up, ruffling the water. The swans had gone, the headstones on the point were scarcely visible. I turned up the driveway, a storm in prospect. That was what the weather report had predicted.

Before opening the letter I made myself a cup of tea, carried it up to my study. It scarcely seemed worth the trouble of slitting the envelope, but when I finally read the contents I sat for some moments at my desk stunned, staring unseeing at a watercolor of a Harz landscape that my artist friend Else had give me in Hildesheim so many years ago.

Here, in all suddenness and after six decades, was the revelation I had thought would never be made:

My father, Giovanni Gambera, died in June, 1982, at the age of ninety-three. He was one of those "elderly people now still tenaciously prepared to carry the weight of their secret to the grave." Except that he left some of his secret to me. My mother, Signorina Monello, niece to Angelo Monello, still alive and alert, has always substantiated all my father recounted. But my father demanded the strictest secrecy and no one would ever dare challenge his authority.

This letter is based on my appraisal of your work *Tragedy in Dedham* which I consider the definite text about this case. Everyone [in the Boston anarchist circle] knew that Sacco was guilty and that Vanzetti was innocent as far as the actual participation in the killing. But no one would ever break the code of silence even if it cost Vanzetti's life. My father was with the case from its beginnings but is never mentioned simply because that is the way he wished it. He commanded great respect and loyalty amongst the anarchists combined with an aura of deadly intent. He was the head of a family of six and he was involved in so many activities of dubious nature that he made sure that no disgrace or notoriety would touch us.

I think you would appreciate a bit of dramatic irony in this case. Before it all became public, there was a committee of four who represented Sacco and Vanzetti. These four were Aldino Felicani, Professor

Guadagni, Lucia Mancini, and my father. The prime purpose of this committee was to decide what should happen to Sacco and Vanzetti. Katzmann* had proposed that he would guarantee deportation as undesirable aliens back to Italy for Sacco and Vanzetti if he were given $35,000 cash. Felicani and Mancini visited Sacco, and my father and Guadagni visited Vanzetti with this proposal. Both men left it up to the committee to decide. Three members of the committee, excluding my father, voted for the trial. Their argument was that this would bring great publicity for the anarchist movement and that there was every chance that the men would go free. My father was vehemently opposed and stated that they would send these men to their doom. My father was always the most astute and intelligent thinker of them all.

For added color, you may be interested in knowing that Fred Moore was an inveterate cocaine addict and my father kept him going by providing the necessary amount needed. My mother still remembers well the many nights that Moore would call the house at any hour of the night and my father would leave and not return for days at a time. And my mother specially remembers the scandal of Rosina Sacco's affair with another man during the last few years of the case.

I, too, recall vividly the great political arguments with my father, Guadagni, and Felicani—frightening in their intensity and loudness. I still see the two—Felicani very tall for a Sicilian, who had a crush on my mother—and Guadagni, with his distinguished goatee and pot-belly devouring enormous plates of pasta. My father also published an Italian weekly called *Il Pungolo* [*The Spur*] at 6 Beacon Street, an independent journal of some repute to the anarchists.

I do hope this letter brings you some added ease and satisfaction for the research you did. Between you and me, this is the last word.

It was indeed the last word. That Sacco was guilty I had long accepted, but there had never been irrefutable proof with which to confront the embattled partisans. For them Sacco *had* to be innocent. Those few among the anarchists who knew otherwise continued to guard their knowledge. The whole superstructure of the great case was made possible by their silence, a mixture of loyalty and fanaticism. Now the silence had given way to this voice from beyond the grave.† Here, in a single-spaced page, was that proof.

The Boston Public Library's edition of the 1979 Sacco-Vanzetti

---

* Frederick Gunn Katzmann, district attorney for Norfolk and Plymouth counties, chief prosecutor of Sacco and Vanzetti.

† Later I was to hear a tape-recording of Gambera repeating in his cracked old voice: "Sacco was guilty! Sacco was guilty!"

conference includes a snapshot of eight anarchists on a picnic in Philadelphia in 1915. Felicani is in the center. Seven of the group have their names inked in. The eighth, a thin, hawk-nosed young man with a high forehead and a receding hairline, remains unidentified. He is—as I learned subsequently—Giovanni Gambera, even then intent on his anonymity.[1]

Sacco was the key. Once he was fixed as one of the five men in the murder car, the other four, as his known associates, would fall into place like pieces in a puzzle. Gambera, the ultimate insider, knew. Only someone within the closed anarchist circle could have written a letter with such corroborative details: the hastily organized defense committee's first visit to Sacco and Vanzetti after their arrest; the mention of the otherwise unrecorded Lucia Mancini, the one woman on the committee; Moore's drug addiction; the meetings in the Gambera kitchen; the long-forgotten *Il Pungolo*. Even the charge against District Attorney Katzmann becomes a left-handed confirmation, reflecting the set—though erroneous—anarchist belief that Katzmann had been willing to sell the case. Did the letter's ending mean, though, that Gambera's son would say no more, would not come out of his shell?

Who would believe me if that letter was lost or destroyed? Certainly not the remaining Sacco-Vanzetti partisans. The next morning I had it photostated and locked the original in my safety-deposit box. I wrote back, enclosing a copy of the Public Library book, but did not receive a reply.

Within the Boston anarchist circle the belief had never wavered that the district attorney had offered to free Sacco and Vanzetti for a sum variously mentioned as between $25,000 and $50,000. Though one of the graver charges leveled against the prosecution, there happens to be no truth in it. Katzmann, whatever his limitations, had an honest and honorable career both before and after the Sacco-Vanzetti trial. The story came about through the machinations of a Dedham court hanger-on, Angelina De Falco. Four months before the Dedham trial she had gone to Felicani, introducing herself as a court interpreter and a close friend of District Attorney Katzmann. According to Felicani, she told him that

> Sacco could get off . . . if we were interested to secure his freedom by paying a sum of money. . . . Vanzetti is a tough case. He has been sentenced. It's pretty hard. But you can get Vanzetti out provided you are in a position to pay. . . . It will cost a great deal of money. The district

attorney, and his assistants, and the foreman of the jury, will all have to be paid. There will be a mock trial and the men will be acquitted.[2]*

Mrs. De Falco, a dumpy twenty-five-year-old woman with thick eyeglasses, had grown up in Dedham speaking English as well as Italian. Never a court interpreter, she did from time to time interpret for various local lawyers, among them Katzmann's brother Percy and the Dedham clerk of court, Francis Squires. She had met Squires through her husband, who was his gardener, and in small interpretive tasks for him she had met other lawyers. The courthouse, so formidable a symbol of authority to Italian aliens, became familiar to her. She often dropped in at court sessions and meetings, developing a nodding acquaintance with court officers, deputies, and lawyers. Sometimes she could be seen passing the time of day with a group on the courthouse steps, all very impressive to any immigrant Italian.

Dedham had a large Italian population, few of whom knew English, many of whom were illiterate, living in the swampy flatlands between Dedham and West Roxbury. Dedham, for all its nearness to Boston, was not a suburb. It lacked a middle class. Old Yankee families of staid respectability occupied the gracious eighteenth-century houses along High—not Main—Street and the wooded estates with their long driveways. Their money derived from the previous century—railroads, cotton mills, real estate. Old Dedham children started their education with the Misses Hewins, never in the public schools. The golf club was the Country *and* Polo Club. Old Dedham lawyers—who scorned the word *attorney*—had offices on Boston's State Street and concerned themselves chiefly with corporations, trusts, and estates.

Yankee Dedham hired the flatlands Italians as gardeners and odd-job men. When the Italians ran afoul of the law, they turned to those like Mrs. De Falco who acted as go-betweens and who expected a finder's fee for their services in bringing them to the local attorneys with their upstairs offices in the town center. Squires and Percy Katzmann were among those to whom Mrs. De Falco brought clients, in return for which she hoped to receive favors consequent on their goodwill. Small-town lawyers, they were respected and respectable members of the bar, knowing little or nothing of the finder's fees that the Italians took for granted.

In later meetings Mrs. De Falco told Felicani and other commit-

---

* At the time Mrs. De Falco talked to Felicani, Vanzetti had already been convicted for an earlier holdup attempt.

tee members that to get Sacco and Vanzetti acquitted they would have to discharge their other lawyers and retain Squires and Percy Katzmann.* As for Moore, he could stay on in a secondary role. Moore, with his quick legal mind, saw through the shallow trickery at once. While the committee members were discussing Mrs. De Falco's offer, he had her arrested, though all she could be charged with was attempting to solicit law business, not being an attorney. She was tried before Judge Michael Murray in Boston's municipal court. Squires testified that she had merely told him the Sacco-Vanzetti Defense Committee wanted to retain him as counsel. Nothing more. Percy Katzmann said he had never spoken with her about the Sacco-Vanzetti case. Occasionally he had employed her as an interpreter, but "not as much as she made out." His brother, the district attorney, said he had never even heard of her until her arrest. She herself said she had merely wanted to get good lawyers to help free Sacco and Vanzetti.

Judge Murray found her not guilty of soliciting law business but called her conduct "imprudent and unwise." He exonerated Squires and the two Katzmanns from any complicity. Ten years later Mrs. De Falco was found guilty on five counts of larceny for taking money from an Annie Caruso on the pretense that she could get Annie's husband freed from state prison. For this she received six months in jail. She was still alive in 1958, still living in Dedham, but when I telephoned and asked to see her she hung up.

If the committee had followed Gambera's advice and agreed to pay a bribe, it is curious to think what might have happened. Possibly something along the lines of the Annie Caruso incident, with adverse reflections on the defense. That is no doubt what Moore tried to scotch by having Mrs. De Falco arrested.

I sent Gambera's son a card at Christmas; by the end of January, when I had almost given up hearing from him again, a second letter arrived:

Though I had not planned to continue communicating with you (shades of my father), your letter and your courteous card awakened my own sense of courtesy. . . . I think if you understood the Sicilian nature and mind, especially the anarchist thinker, then everything would be more

* Mrs. De Falco did approach Squires to ask if he would consider taking the case. He said he would not.

credible. There was a self-discipline and code that was virtually un-breakable—except at the expense of one's life. That is how my father achieved such privacy. He made it clear that he never wanted his name mentioned—and it never was. He had complete anonymity.

The week after I had received Gambera's first letter, I took the photostat to the director of the Boston Public Library, Phil McNiff, whom I had known for years and to whom I had given a number of documents to add to the library's Sacco-Vanzetti collection. McNiff had organized the 1979 conference in connection with the presentation to the library of the Felicani papers. Felicani had died in 1967, but it took a decade of tactful persuasion before his sons would at last agree to turn over the material on Sacco and Vanzetti that their father had so scrupulously and indiscriminately hoarded. Its formal presentation formed the core of the two-day conference. A dozen or so papers, mostly by academics, were read along with briefer personal tributes to Felicani. The conference's general tenor was summed up by its moderator, Professor William Salomone of the University of Rochester, who saw Sacco, Vanzetti, and Felicani as "three unheroic but gigantic fighters for justice and freedom—men unbroken by social calamity and judicial prejudice."[3]

Where the conference did open up new vistas was in dealing with Sacco's and Vanzetti's anarchist background. They were not the harmless philosophical radicals portrayed by their harmless philosophical Yankee-radical supporters, but militants, revolutionaries at heart. Three speakers on "The Anarchist Connection" were clear about this.

Vanzetti's surviving sister Vincenzina had been brought from Italy especially for the conference, a mild, blue-eyed woman with white hair and the manner of a retired schoolteacher or librarian. She had been nineteen when her brother was executed. "What I hope is to know the truth," she told the conference members. "Sacco and Vanzetti are already rehabilitated in the conscience of millions of men all over the world, but the case is not closed."[4] The case was indeed not closed, but the truth, carried in that photostat in my pocket, was more ironic than she could possibly imagine.

What Phil McNiff really thought about the Sacco-Vanzetti case he never said. Perhaps he deliberately chose not to form an opinion even to himself. To all he came in contact with he remained non-committally gracious, and I am sure he would have been as cordial to the testy and cantankerous Robert Montgomery as he was to Felicani and his sons or, for that matter, to me. He had invited me to take part in the 1979 conference, but I declined. Seven years before, when I agreed to speak at a meeting of the American Italian Historical Association in Boston's Italian North End and tried to explain why I considered Sacco guilty, there were shouts of rage, and I thought for a moment that the meeting was going to be disrupted. I suppose to an audience of Sacco-Vanzetti sympathizers I offered a catharsis of the emotions. No doubt a Public Library audience would be more decorous, but I had had enough of being the devil's advocate. This time I would pull in my horns.

There was one puzzling thing I wanted first to ask Phil about as I walked into his office on that winter morning, a rumor I had recently picked up and that I found too bizarre to credit. Always there had been the question of what had happened to the ashes of Sacco and Vanzetti after their cremation. Some said they were still on the shelf in the Forest Hills Crematory. One story had it that the ashes had been taken back to Italy in copper cylinders. Another cruder and crueller story was that they had been left with the undertaker, who finally lost patience and one winter day scattered them on the icy sidewalk in front of his establishment.

"Well," said Phil as I met him in his office in the library annex, "you said you have something new about Sacco and Vanzetti. I didn't think there could be anything really new, just elaborations of the old."

"It is new," I said, "and it will astonish you. But before I show you anything, I have a question to ask. Is it true that the library now has the ashes of Sacco and Vanzetti in its possession?"

He hesitated, winced slightly. "Yes," he said at last. "It is true."

"It must be the library's least desired acquisition."*

He smiled, a rather sour smile, without replying. I handed him Gambera's letter.

Sitting at his desk, he read it, very slowly it seemed to me, his grave Celtic face immobile. Then he put it aside. "This is it," he said quietly. "Beside this our conference didn't matter.

"But what are you going to do now?" he asked me suddenly.

"I don't know yet," I told him.

"You must go to California."

* The library also has the original death masks of Sacco and Vanzetti.

3

The Road to Boston

In writing *Tragedy in Dedham* I had been helped and encouraged by the Sacco-Vanzetti old guard, particularly by those arch-defenders Tom O'Connor, founder and secretary of the Committee to Vindicate Sacco and Vanzetti, and Aldino Felicani, the printer who had been treasurer of the original defense committee. They looked forward to my book as the vindicating book that would sum up all the others. When it at last appeared, with its contrary conclusion, they regarded me as a renegade, a reactionary, venal, a bad writer, and a worse historian. "How could you dare even *think* that Sacco was guilty?" Judge Michael Musmanno, the most bombastic defender of the two dead anarchists, demanded rhetorically in a florid letter to me. Just for a handful of reviews I had left them. To minimize that handful, Tom and Musmanno organized what they called Operation Assault, a campaign to persuade editors and reviewers to give no space to such a meretricious tract.*

During the time when I still thought Sacco and Vanzetti innocent, I often used to drop in on Felicani at his Excelsior Press on Boston's Milk Street. By then his sons had taken over the business and he spent his days in a little tin-sheathed alcove editing his anarchist journal, *Controcorrente,* which he got out whenever he happened to feel like it. After my book was published he denounced me regularly in its pages. I was a "Maramaldo of the pen."† I was "diabolically hypocritical . . . a self-styled literary critic and historian

---

* I did not learn about Operation Assault until after Tom's death, when I came across references to it in the papers he left to Brandeis University.

† Fabrizio Maramaldo commanded the Italians in the service of the Holy Roman Emperor Charles V besieging Florence in 1530. At Gavinna he stabbed the already mortally wounded Francesco Ferrucci, who exclaimed: "You kill a dead man!" Maramaldo's name has become eponymous for a stab-in-the-back coward.

who makes use of innuendo and malice." I was a charlatan who "proves nothing but works with a fantasy that tears truth to shreds." I was a "so-called historian, a vulgar lout."[1] And so on, issue after issue, my writing compared to, among other things, a gob of stale tobacco juice.

I suppose I might have sued the old man for libel, but I understood. I liked him. I still do. In challenging his core belief I did seem a Maramaldo, just as I did to Tom O'Connor. When I met Tom on the street a few weeks after my book came out, his face reddened and, almost spitting the words, he shouted, "I don't want to have anything more to do with you!"

Unamuno, in his *Tragic Sense of Life*, wrote that at the core of every belief is disbelief. For Felicani and Tom their most intense and cherished belief was the cause of Sacco and Vanzetti. They had to deny any inner doubt even to themselves, but their anger showed it was there. To externalize this doubt, they attacked me. They had to.

It was that bouncy and ebullient Boston politico Clem Norton who finally went to Felicani and told him to stop. Though an obsessive Sacco-Vanzetti partisan, Clem remained friendly to me even after I had lost my belief in the two men's innocence. When he saw my book on the stands, he called up to congratulate me. I mentioned Operation Assault and he gave me a bit of advice. "You got too close," he told me. "When you write, don't get too close."

Clem was one of the last survivors of Boston's gaslight-era politicians: faded legendary figures like Martin Lomasney, the lantern-jawed "Mahatma" of Ward Eight; beringed and flashing "Diamond Jim" Timilty; "Honey Fitz" Fitzgerald, the "Sweet Adeline"–singing grandfather of the Kennedys; rapier-thrust Jim Curley, who had driven Honey Fitz from city hall; the impeached, disbarred, and still effervescent governor's councilor, Dan Coakley; and others still more faded. Clem as a city councilor, chairman of the school committee, and perennial candidate for mayor, had known them all. Edwin O'Connor caricatured him—if it was possible to caricature Clem—as Charlie Hennessey in his Boston political novel, *The Last Hurrah*.

In the days when I knew Clem he had put politics behind him to take on the role of scholar. He had preempted a corner of the Boston Public Library's patent room, an act of squatter sovereignty recognized as such by the library staff. Most days one could find him there hunched behind his typewriter, hemmed in by mounds of books, papers, clippings, files, manuscripts, discarded pages, and crumpled

Baby Ruth wrappers, so enmeshed that it was a puzzle how he got to his desk. A rat's nest, it was known as Clem's Corner. There he squatted, his head scarcely visible, a sagging rumpled figure, oily-haired, his dark and dancing eyes just a little too close together, abstracted yet ready to dart out like a spider if he saw an acquaintance pass.

Whenever I was busy I took care not to pass by, for Clem was a hard man to get away from. If I should run into him in the library corridors, I knew I was buttonholed. A vague urinous scent clung to him, and when he got excited he tended to spit. He talked and talked, exploding words and at the same time jabbing with his forefinger. Brought to a stop by him on occasion, I have backed round the library's courtyard several times, trying to keep out of saliva range as Clem in a fantastic checked suit talked and walked and jabbed, his blunt finger pointing at my chest like a stiletto. He had a lurid collection of tales about most Boston politicians, and his gossip concerning the Kennedys was large and intimate. Some of what he said was uniquely true, some just the offshoot of his erratic mind. I could never be sure which.

Clem had two topics that engrossed him above all others. One was the malign influence of the papacy, the other the villainy of the Sacco-Vanzetti prosecution. I don't know how many times he told me of District Attorney Katzmann's receiving a briefcase stuffed with bills. Clem's story was the same, but the amount kept varying—one time $5,000, another time $10,000, and once even $25,000. Who paid the money, he never mentioned. "Katzmann got it," he would say, jabbing at me, "all tied up in bundles of tens and twenties."

Tucked away in his corner, Clem always seemed to be working at top speed. It was rumored that he was writing his autobiography. He admitted that among his other projects he was preparing the last word on the Sacco-Vanzetti case. But during his lifetime he never attempted to publish anything. After his death there was nothing cohesive in the massed litter of his corner, nothing that could in any way be considered publishable.

Yet it was through Clem that I learned that Fred Moore had finally developed doubts about the innocence of his clients. Back in California after their execution, Moore told Upton Sinclair in the course of a long evening's conversation that he had reluctantly come to the conclusion that Sacco was guilty, Vanzetti possibly guilty.

Much troubled, Sinclair wrote to his friend Robert Minor for advice.* Minor telephoned him from New York in a panic. "Upton, you must not say it, you must not say it!" he repeated. "You will ruin the movement! It will be treason."[2] Sinclair kept the information to himself until 1953 when he let it appear in the relative obscurity of an *Institute for Social Studies Bulletin.* In *Boston,* his novel about the case, he made no mention of Moore's doubts.

Without Moore there would have been no Sacco-Vanzetti affair with its worldwide repercussions. Two obscure immigrants would have been tried as such, convicted, and executed within a year or so of their arrest, their foreign names soon forgotten. But Moore saw Sacco and Vanzetti in a larger role, as intellectuals would not see them for another seven years. The image he shaped and fashioned of the imprisoned anarchists would become the intellectuals' image. His arguments would become their arguments.

Nonconformist by nature, Moore had started out as a young railroad lawyer in a sedate well-established firm, on the path to wealth and a senior partnership. It was not the path he wanted to follow. In 1912, when a casual acquaintance, arrested in a free-speech fight in San Diego, appealed to him for help, he left the corporate world behind him, taking along nothing but a broad-brimmed hat and his revolver. "I'm running over to San Diego to see what I can do for that fellow," he told his associates. "I'll be back soon."[3] They would not see him again for a dozen years. From then on he cast his lot with the underdog, with radical unions, with the emergent Industrial Workers of the World, moving from one labor battle to another, taking on desperate, almost hopeless cases that lacked the money for better-known lawyers. Expecting his adversaries to be unscrupulous, he was ready to fight fire with fire, to turn a blaze into a conflagration. His tense unresolved energy spilled over into his private life. Whatever money came to him, he spent. Never would he stay long in one place. He loved a succession of women, each one more intently than the last. Alcohol gave him relief from his tensions, then drugs. At loose ends in New York, he came into the Sacco-Vanzetti case through his friend Carlo Tresca.

After the 1919 deportation of Luigi Galleani, leading figure of the Italian-American anarchist movement, Tresca remained the most conspicuous anarchist in the United States. His relations with Gal-

* Minor, an anarchist turned Communist, would become editor of the *Daily Worker.*

leani, however, had been distant. Galleani preached the overthrow of predatory capitalism and had nothing but contempt for the ameliorative goals of the trade unions. If his followers cooperated in a crucial strike, as they sometimes did, it was with the intent of furthering revolution. Tresca was prepared to postpone the revolution and work with the more radical unions. Many Galleanisti came to hate and denounce him, but anarchists of all persuasions turned to him when they were in trouble. He was irrepressible, a fixer, with connections everywhere, among union organizers, politicians, the Mafia, even the police. Before coming to America in 1904 he had led an adventurous life as an itinerant radical. Born of an upper-class family in Sulmonia, an ancient hill town in the Apennines, a Socialist before he left school, at twenty-two he was elected secretary of the Italian Railroad Workers' Union. Rapidly he became one of the most popular undesirable citizens of his Apennine region. After being convicted of libeling a political boss, he fled to Geneva. There in a noisy company of café exiles, he met one of the noisiest, a young comrade by the name of Benito Mussolini. They did not take to one another. Mussolini thought Tresca not radical enough. Tresca thought Mussolini talked too much.

The year after Tresca came to America, the one-eyed giant "Big Bill" Haywood and other labor radicals formed the Industrial Workers of the World, soon to be known as the Wobblies. They were syndicalists, their goal not the Socialist one of nationalizing and directing the means of production, but of letting the revolutionary unions take over and run the factories and fields. Tresca, drawn magnetically to Haywood and the Wobblies, considered himself from then on an anarcho-syndicalist. Yet, unlike the purist Galleani, he could not be doctrinaire. Beyond any labels he was himself, an abounding personality. He relished the mere fact of being alive and he loved to the full the smaller personal things life had to offer him—women and wine, talk, food, and song. Even the police who arrested him became his friends—and he had been arrested some thirty-six times on charges varying from blasphemy, libel, disorderly conduct, criminal obscenity, and incitement to riot, to conspiracy, sedition, and murder. The district attorney who in the afternoon had denounced him as an enemy of society would eat and drink with him in the evening. "Big, bearded, boastful, life-loving," Eugene Lyons described him, "and as unlike the embittered anarchist of popular tradition as possible. Priest-baiting and spaghetti were among his chief passions, and his hairbreadth escapes from enemy bullets everywhere from Abruzzi to the copper empire of Montana were ample proof of his charmed life."[4] Suzanne La Follette, who served with him on the Dewey Commission in 1936 investigating the Moscow treason trials, remembered him as

> tall, very heavy, with grey hair and beard and the kindest blue eyes twinkling through glasses (if my memory is correct he wore a pince-nez with a black cord). He always wore a black hat with a rather low crown and wide brim. Altogether a most impressive looking man—warmly affectionate toward his friends, wise and humorous, without a touch of the fanatic about him.[5]

Tresca was brought together with Big Bill Haywood by the 1912 textile workers' strike in Lawrence, Massachusetts, a polyglot company town on the banks of the Merrimack River. Some twenty-five thousand subsistence workers of twenty-eight different nationalities struck spontaneously when the company reduced their wages. Joe Ettor of the IWW executive board and the radical poet Arturo Giovanitti came to Lawrence to give the strike force and direction. In bitter winter weather the Wobblies paraded the streets, flaunting banners that read NO GOD! NO MASTER! Governor Eugene Foss called out the state militia. The violence that followed made IWW a familiar acronym from coast to coast. One afternoon a girl striker was shot and killed. No one knew who fired the shot, but Ettor and Giovanitti were arrested as accessories to the murder.

With the strike leaders in jail, Haywood came on to take charge, accompanied by the slim, dark-haired, blue-eyed "East Side Joan of Arc," Elizabeth Gurley Flynn. Tresca, Giovanitti's friend, arrived to help organize the mass agitation. His notoriously wandering eye found the firebrand young woman's combination of beauty and radicalism irresistible. His grand passion for Gurley—as she was called—outlasted all his other affairs. They lived together for the next eleven years.*

After the strike—which the workers eventually won—Ettor and Giovanitti were placed on trial. The defense strategy was to have their case tried by a well-known local conservative lawyer. To assist him, mostly in selecting witnesses and collecting evidence, Haywood brought in Fred Moore, whom he had known in California. Moore

---

* In after years grown enormously fat, almost rotund, Elizabeth Gurley Flynn would become general secretary of the Communist Party USA.

was indefatigable. Beyond his trial work he and Tresca launched a massive propaganda campaign, and in the end Ettor and Giovanitti were acquitted, as much a triumph for Moore as for their conservative lawyer. Moore's Lawrence comradeship with Tresca would form the genesis of the Sacco-Vanzetti case.

Following the arrest of Sacco and Vanzetti, five witnesses identified Vanzetti as a mustached man with a shotgun, one of four men who had taken part in an abortive holdup in Bridgewater—fourteen miles south of Braintree—the day before Christmas 1919. Vanzetti was tried separately for this a year before the Dedham trial and found guilty.

Tresca was then in New York editing his anarchist paper *Il Martello* (*The Hammer*), which he placed at the disposal of the Sacco-Vanzetti Defense Committee. When he heard of Vanzetti's conviction he was outraged at what he considered the bungling of the Boston comrades and sent Moore to Boston to take over the defense in the coming Braintree murder trial, packing him off with two anarchists on the run from the police. Tresca did not participate in the inner activities of the defense committee, since Emilio Coda, the violent red-headed Galleanisti who would head it, hated him, but his connection with the case was continuous. From 1921 to 1927 he crisscrossed the country denouncing the Dedham verdict and the impending executions, drumming up money for Sacco's and Vanzetti's defense at innumerable meetings, keeping their cause alive. When Vanzetti's sister Luigia arrived in New York in 1927 to see her brother for the last time, it was Tresca who met her as she landed. In the final weeks he was the main speaker at Union Square mass meetings, and when all legal means to save the two convicted anarchists had been exhausted, he waged a last-ditch campaign to organize a general strike.

Tresca's detractors have claimed that he never knew Sacco or Vanzetti. Such is not the case. He knew them both, though he was better acquainted with Vanzetti. After Vanzetti's arrest police found two registered—but still unopened—letters from Tresca in his room. On receiving a copy of *Il Martello* in state prison Vanzetti wrote to Tresca that it was "the unique voice of battle that passes through the cold walls of this jail and warms my heart." Sacco, two months after his murder conviction, wrote Tresca from the Dedham jail—the "Bastille," as he called it—a letter that Tresca reprinted in *Il Martello:*

You cannot realize the joy I feel when I get *Il Martello*. I devour it—it reminds me of the glorious days of your *Avvenire*, the flaming periodical which I learned to love, which was the first to enlighten my mind, urging me to walk in the path toward the ideal of the human family liberated and fraternized. . . . A kiss and a fraternal embrace, to you and to the comrades whom I never forget.[6]

After their deaths, Tresca remained among those intimately concerned in keeping their memory red. Yet shortly before his own death in 1943 he said flatly that Sacco was guilty. I first learned this, incredible as it then struck me, from Rorty's *New Leader* review of Montgomery's *The Murder and the Myth*.[7] Here Rorty made this astonishing reversal public for the first time, though—as I was later to discover—others had known it privately but had kept their silence.

That a kingpin of the defense had come to deny Sacco's innocence was for me overwhelming. I wrote at once to Rorty asking him if he could tell me more of Tresca's turnabout. He replied that he had heard the story from the former Communist writer and publicist Max Eastman and that I should get in touch with him. Later I learned that Rorty had also heard it from Tresca himself, but at this point he had put the Sacco-Vanzetti case, along with his versifications, behind him and apparently did not want to get involved further.

Eastman was then living at Gay Head on Martha's Vineyard. When I telephoned him there, he was open enough, saying he would be glad to talk to me any time I cared to come to the island. Several days later I took the ferry from Hyannis to Oak Bluffs, Martha's Vineyard's little port frozen in time with its rows of bright gingerbread-trim cottages. It was still fourteen miles from those frets and filigrees to the sea change of Gay Head. I rented a bicycle.

I spent the afternoon with Eastman. What he had to tell me was brief. He had talked with Tresca, he said, some months before Tresca had been shot down by a GPU agent as he was leaving his office in lower Manhattan.* Tresca had mentioned Sacco and Vanzetti. "Do

---

* According to those closest to Tresca, the man responsible for his murder was the Italian Communist Vittorio Vidale, who had come to New York from Mexico three weeks earlier for that purpose. Vidale, under the name of Colonel Carlos Contreras, as commissar of the Fifth Brigade in the Spanish Civil War, had conducted the bloodiest of the Communist-directed purges and had personally arranged the execution of the Spanish anarchist leader Andrés Nin. Tresca had denounced Vidale on the front page of *Il Martello* as a "commandant of spies, thieves and assassins."

To the long-standing resentment of the Communists, Tresca was able to keep them out of the Garibaldi Society, the leading organization of Italian anti-Fascists. Even in the hot-you know the real truth, Carlo?" Eastman asked him. "Sacco was guilty but Vanzetti was innocent," Tresca said emphatically. He would have said more but just then someone came into the room and interrupted their conversation—the anarchist from Porlock, I thought afterward.

"I don't know why I never mentioned it before," Eastman went on. "Recently I wrote an article about it. I didn't want the story to appear first in a conservative paper so I sent it to *The Nation* and then *The New Republic*. Both turned it down."*

"If it does come out," I said, "the Sacco-Vanzetti vindicators will say that you are lying, that you have a guilty conscience because you were once a Communist and took part in the October Revolution."

He laughed. "Do I seem a liar?" he asked me.

"Not from the liars I've known," I said. "But of course there'll be others to say that you're crazy."

"Perhaps I am," he said, "but Tresca still said it."

It was late in the afternoon as I left Eastman standing in the doorway waving to me, and the shadows were long on the Oak Bluffs road. By the time I boarded the ferry, the sun had set. From the deck I watched the Victorian-rococo town recede, lights appearing in a few cottage windows, the first stars coming out in a slate-blue sky. An east wind stirred the water slightly as I put the day behind me. The day, I knew, was a turning point. Until now I had managed to thrust my developing doubts aside, but after Eastman had told me about Tresca, they crystallized. Tresca could have said he did not know. He could have said that of course Sacco and Vanzetti were innocent. Instead, bluntly, angrily, he had said that Sacco was guilty. He had no need to say anything at all.

What I had set out to prove had turned into its opposite. I knew then that I must rewrite, reshape as best I could what I had already

---

house period of Russian-American friendship after Pearl Harbor, he continued to bar their way. When the Office of War Information organized the Italian-American Victory Council to arrange overseas broadcasts to Italy, he was able to exclude the Communists as well as former Fascists from the new organization. The Italian Communist leader Pietro Allegra called attention to Tresca's "moral suicide" and demanded the "elimination from society of beings hateful to themselves and society."

Early in January 1943, Tresca learned that Vidale was in New York. "Where he is I smell death," he told a friend. A few days later he was shot down by a paroled convict, Carmine Galante, believed to have been hired by Vidale. Professor Daniel Bell of Harvard, however, with an intimate knowledge of Tresca's life, maintains that his murder was a response by the Mafia to his affair with a Mafia leader's mistress. Given Tresca's amorous nature, this is possible. It is also possible that Vidale turned to the Mafia for a hit man.

* Eastman's article, "Is This the Truth about Sacco and Vanzetti?" appeared in *National Review*, October 21, 1961.

written. The case reversed. An empty feeling as I stood alone on the upper deck.

To Tom O'Connor and Felicani and Musmanno, to the vindicators, to those who had welcomed me as a comrade of the cause, I now had the obligation of telling what I had learned from Eastman before it appeared in print. O'Connor tried to shrug it off. "Thoroughly untrustworthy," he said of Eastman. "He used to write for *The Masses* and now he writes for that Buckley paper. In any case, he stayed away from Boston all those years between the trial and the execution."

Musmanno suggested that Tresca spoke such thick English that Eastman had misunderstood him. A few weeks later he concluded that Tresca had never said it. But after others came forward to corroborate Eastman, he denigrated Tresca as a pornographer who had served a year in the penitentiary for sexual offenses.*

When I dropped in on Felicani in his tin-lined office, he was as usual at his desk, busied with *Controcorrente*. Behind him on a filing cabinet I noticed a small plaster bust of Tresca. I told him what Eastman had said. He dropped his pen, looked up, his face contorted. "Believe me," he said in an anguished voice, "believe me, Tresca never told me that. Never! But," he admitted, "if Eastman said Tresca said it, Tresca did say it." Then I had to tell him. "I can no longer believe," I said. He did not reply, merely bent his head slightly. As I turned to go, I could see the light reflected from his bald skull. I never saw him again.

After Eastman's belated admission I discovered that Tresca in 1941 had told a number of acquaintances that Sacco was guilty, among them Rorty, the author and journalist Isaac Don Levine, Socialist leader Norman Thomas, and John Roche, later dean of the Fletcher School of Diplomacy at Tufts. In 1972 Roche wrote me that

in 1941 (after the Nazi invasion of Russia, before Pearl Harbor) I was at a Youth Committee Against War planning-meeting at Norman [Thomas's] house. . . . Tresca came bounding in enraged about something or other and took over the show. Somehow the subject of Sacco

---

* Tresca had printed a small advertisement for a book on birth control in *Il Martello*. The Italian embassy, long nettled by his attacks on the Duce, complained to the postal authorities. Tresca was prosecuted for sending obscene material through the mail, found guilty, and sentenced to a year and a day in the federal penitentiary in Atlanta. Relatively speaking, he enjoyed himself there. After three months Congressman Fiorello La Guardia persuaded President Coolidge to pardon him.

and Vanzetti came up. . . . I couldn't possibly quote him, but the gist of his vigorous remarks was that Sacco had murdered a good comrade (Vanzetti) because he thought they could beat the rap. Vanzetti was innocent, but Sacco was involved and refused to plead guilty and save Vanzetti. What intrigues me in retrospect is that I can't recall Norman reacting at all; there was no argument. . . .

On the night of the execution of Sacco and Vanzetti, James Farrell, coming from a Union Square deathwatch meeting, could not hold back his tears as he walked along the shadowed New York streets. "The martyred, murdered flesh of Sacco and Vanzetti," he recalled in his 1946 autobiographical novel, *Bernard Clare.* Years later Rorty told him of Tresca's admission. In 1976 Farrell wrote me:

> I can't, as I used to, accept the innocence of Sacco. That hurts. . . . Jim Rorty told me that Carlo Tresca had said that Sacco was guilty and Vanzetti innocent. I was shocked, angry and felt betrayed. . . . I have been indignant ever since, and feel that I was used.

Farrell, who had been close to Tresca in the thirties, continued to wonder why Tresca had never told him. "It is true," he wrote me, "that I never happened to talk to him about the case, and in consequence I can't say that he deliberately lied to me. But someone should have admitted something somewhere along the line."

The inescapable conclusion is that at this point Tresca himself did not know. According to his daughter, Beatrice Tresca Rapport, who had seen much of her father in the twenties, he never wavered in his belief in the innocence of the two anarchists. Giuseppe Popolizio, a member of *Il Martello* staff, told Nunzio Pernicone that he would have been the first to know if Tresca had suspected Sacco's innocence.[8] Another comrade of the twenties, Joseph Ienusco, said that as hopes for Sacco and Vanzetti dimmed, "it was Tresca who encouraged me to keep on stumping in defense of the two martyrs."[9] As late as 1939 Musmanno talked with Tresca, who was "just as devoted to the innocence of Sacco and Vanzetti then as when they were living."[10]

Yet within two years of their talk Tresca was angrily telling his acquaintances that Sacco was guilty. He talked compulsively. But men do not nurse such compulsive anger for years on end. One can only conclude that sometime about 1941 he must have learned suddenly and irrefutably of Sacco's guilt. Like Farrell he felt he had been sold, and he reacted with the devastating statement in front of

Norman Thomas that Sacco had murdered a good comrade. Why would he say it, unless from the realization that the truth he had so long defended was untrue? Efforts of present-day advocates to explain this are involved and—as they are bound to be—makeshift. Jejune attempts like Musmanno's to dismiss Tresca are no longer considered tenable by current, mostly academic, Sacco-Vanzetti partisans. Admitting that Tresca did make the statement, they attribute it to early doubts that Moore had implanted in his mind and that had lain fallow until quickened by the hostility of the Galleani anarchists, who, mostly out of political rivalry, had viciously attacked him in their paper, *L'Adunata dei Refrattari (The Call of the Refractories)*. Pernicone tries to make this conflict account chiefly for Tresca's untoward reversal:

> By the end of the 1930s Tresca would have already concluded that the Galleanisti were perfectly capable of having deceived him about Sacco from the beginning. Therefore, if new speculations concerning Sacco reached him at this time, Tresca would have been more inclined to place credence in them than he would have in the 1920s. Once inclined toward suspicion, Tresca could have been swayed by evidence he would have dismissed as inconsequential a decade earlier. Finally, under the pressures of anger and disillusionment, Tresca's memories of old rumors may have combined with new doubts to create serious belief in Sacco's guilt.[11]

The explanation, though ingenious, fails to explain. What were those new speculations and new doubts? Where did they originate? Why, in contrast to Moore's opinion that Vanzetti was "possibly guilty," did Tresca now see him positively as a betrayed innocent? Why Tresca's sudden anger, his compulsive talk? He was noted for his robust opinions, not a man to be swayed. To those who knew Tresca, Pernicone's hypothesis would appear quite unconvincing.

Pernicone, with a scholar's respect for evidence, is not one willfully to deny facts. Yet, involved as he is in the cause of Sacco and Vanzetti, he must endeavor to make the facts, however awkward, fit the cause. When he wrote me to ask about my interview with Eastman and its aftermath, I told him what I knew and added that someone at the very core of the case must have told Tresca the truth. At the close of the Boston Public Library conference he replied:

> Apprised of the fact that Tresca's closest associates of the 1920s and 1930s attested to his belief in Sacco's innocence, Russell, in a letter to

me, took the position that only someone of absolutely sterling character and with incontrovertible evidence could have been able to make Tresca change his mind. Who was this *deus ex machina?* Russell has no idea. As far as I'm concerned, I doubt that any such person existed. My own suspicion is that the disillusionment and bitterness that resulted from his long fratricidal conflict with the publishers of the anarchist newspaper *L'Adunata dei Refrattari,* may have caused Tresca to believe that the Galleanisti lied to him about Sacco's innocence from the beginning. This is only a hunch, and I may be completely wrong. What can be said for certain, however, is that Tresca had no private pipeline to Mount Olympus through which he obtained absolute truth about the case. Thus there is no guarantee that anything he said regarding Sacco's alleged guilt is of real importance.[12]

For all that Tresca was a friend of Gambera and Felicani, those two were members of the clannish Galleanisti inner circle, while Tresca remained an outsider. From the evidence of Tresca's associates and his daughter, from Musmanno as late as 1939, it is clear that he did not share in the Galleanisti secrets. Pernicone is correct in stating that "the Galleanisti considered open class warfare the only way to fight the government—whether with clandestine publications or with bombs. . . . Thus, if the South Braintree holdup and murders represented one tragic incident in this class war, it is inconceivable that Tresca, above all others, would have had inside knowledge of the affair."[13]

When I wrote Pernicone, I had no idea who Tresca's confidant was. Although I had all but given up hope of ever learning his identity, I remained convinced of his existence. To Pernicone's ironic question of who the *deus ex machina* might be, Gambera supplied the sudden, illuminating answer. In 1941 Gambera was preparing to leave Boston for California, and in leaving his past behind him he must have felt free in meeting Tresca to tell him the bedrock truth about Sacco and Vanzetti. Like Farrell, Tresca felt betrayed. Hence his sudden anger, his compulsive talk. For him the truth was too bitter to bear alone.

4

The Road to Friendship

When in 1958 I spoke from the platform of Boston's Community Church at a Sacco-Vanzetti memorial meeting, I was still convinced that the two Italians were innocent men, railroaded to their death for a crime they knew nothing about. In speaking to the church members I was not telling anyone a thing he had not believed for a long time. Yet such unanimity of opinion had perplexed me ever since I began studying the case. It seemed almost impossible for people to be objective about it, even a generation later. Anyone who joined the undogmatic Community Church accepted the dogma that Sacco and Vanzetti were guiltless persecuted radicals, just as members of the American Legion—at least in Massachusetts—assumed automatically that they were subversive criminals who had got just what was coming to them. My father and my Aunt Amy had reacted in the same automatic way in the late twenties when the case had grown into an international issue. Aunt Amy, a social worker who lived at the Elizabeth Peabody Settlement House, insisted with angry self-righteousness that the two Italians were innocent and that my father was being his usual pigheaded self in maintaining otherwise. My father, a lawyer and a Republican, insisted with equal anger that they were guilty. I don't suppose either one had more than a superficial knowledge of the case, but I can never forget their arguments around the Sunday dinner table.

My father had served as a representative in the Massachusetts legislature when Calvin Coolidge was governor and had then sponsored the bill that created a state police.* For this he was "given the

* The new force was first called the "State Constabulary" to distinguish it from the existing State Police, a minute investigative body. Its police are still called troopers.

quill" by Coolidge. (In those days Massachusetts governors still signed a bill with a quill pen which was then presented to the bill's sponsor—hence the expression.) Some years after the Sacco-Vanzetti trial my father was present in the state ballistics laboratory when new tests were being made of the Sacco-Vanzetti evidence. What he saw then convinced him of the two men's guilt. But whatever his beliefs, he liked to disagree with his sister Amy. Their most explosive quarrel occurred after the publication of Felix Frankfurter's *Case of Sacco and Vanzetti,* a book Aunt Amy accepted as gospel. Later, when I read in James Joyce's *Portrait of the Artist as a Young Man* of the Christmas outburst between Stephen Daedalus's father and his Aunt Dante over Parnell, I thought of my own father and my own aunt arguing about the Sacco-Vanzetti case. "Devil out of hell! We won! We crushed him to death! Fiend!," Joyce had Aunt Dante say. Our Sunday dinner dispute was less literary. "Professor Frankfurter says—" Aunt Amy began.

"I don't give a damn what that man says," my father interrupted, his voice rising several notes. "I've seen the proof. Sacco and Vanzetti are guilty!"

I could see Aunt Amy's prim face distorted in the curved glass of the china cabinet. "You're a liar!" she all but shouted, slapping the round oak table with the flat of her hand.

The six years that I spent at the Roxbury Latin School more or less coincided with the Sacco-Vanzetti case. In that Roxbury backwater we boys accepted as a fact that Sacco and Vanzetti were guilty without thinking much more about it. The father of one of my classmates, Ethelbert Grabill, a reporter of decisions of the Massachusetts Supreme Court, had written a thirty-seven-page pamphlet, *Sacco and Vanzetti in the Scales of Justice,* in which he defended the Massachusetts judiciary as a sacrosanct inheritance that he now saw threatened by such radicals as Frankfurter. Mindful of his Puritan ancestors, he set forth that he had been moved by their spirit to attempt to "bring a wandering citizenry back to confidence in our courts, in their proceedings, and in our Governor, and fortify and strengthen those who have not wandered."[1] This was the sole literary accomplishment of Grabill, who was listed in *Who's Who.* How he got into *Who's Who* remained something of a mystery. "He must have known the editor," our worldly-wise lower-school English master, Mr. Farnham, remarked.

Not until I was at Harvard in the early thirties did I change my

mind about Sacco and Vanzetti. It was then that I read the volume of
their selected letters. Those moving and eloquent letters—particularly Vanzetti's—just did not seem compatible with the sordid rob-
bery-murders for which they had been convicted. I felt, from a quick
reading and without knowing much more about the case, that men
with such a gift of expression had to be innocent.* As to who did
murder the paymaster and his guard on that spring afternoon—if
Sacco and Vanzetti did not—I thought I found the answer in Herbert
Ehrmann's *The Untried Case: The Sacco-Vanzetti Case and the
Morelli Gang.* Ehrmann, a post-trial defense counsel, had worked out
an elaborate hypothesis that demonstrated convincingly—at least to
someone like myself unfamiliar with the case—that the South Braintree crime was the work of the Morelli Gang of Providence, Rhode
Island. The pictures of Sacco and the gang leader Joe Morelli, published side by side in his book, made them look enough alike to be
brothers.

Ehrmann's book struck me like a conversion, turned me into a
Sacco-Vanzetti partisan. At about this time I saw Maxwell Anderson's *Winterset,* with Burgess Meredith and the enchanting Mexican
actress Margo, and this deepened my identification with the two executed anarchists. I felt somewhat as Aunt Amy must have felt when
she was arrested in the last days of the case for picketing the State
House: a glowing sense of belonging to a cause. I suppose this was in
part a delayed adolescent rebellion against my father, in part a reaction against a city that was at the same time a state of mind and that
had always seemed alien to me. It gave me a certain satisfaction to
believe the worst of entrenched Boston—beyond Ehrmann's *parti
pris* that I so uncritically accepted. I then read Frankfurter's incan-
descent special pleading, and this confirmed what I had already
come to believe.

Someday, I promised myself, I was going to sit down and study
the Sacco-Vanzetti trial transcript. But with the coming of the war
my interest lapsed. If I had not been called for a month's jury duty at

---

* I later thought the same thing about Caryl Chessmann, until John Cutler, who had
edited his manuscripts into a printable state, told me he was guilty. William F. Buckley and
Norman Mailer have made similar misjudgments about literary criminals. Buckley helped
arrange the release of Edgar Smith, under life sentence for murder. A few months later
Smith stabbed and robbed a woman, and when he was picked up by the police admitted to
the murder for which he had been originally convicted and of which Buckley had believed
him innocent. Mailer was similarly bemused by the talents of another murderer, Jack
Henry Abbott, who, after being paroled, killed again.

the Dedham courthouse in the spring of 1953, I doubt that I should ever have concerned myself with the case again. I was then living in Wellesley, eight miles away, and when the weather was good I used to walk along the back roads to Dedham. By starting at quarter to eight I could get to the courthouse just before ten o'clock, when the morning session began.

I liked those brisk bright mornings, the earth smelling of spring, the maples in misty shades of mauve and red. From Wellesley the road dipped past the country club, curving down to Needham, a semi-suburb of repetitive three-bedroom houses, commonplace enough, yet—as I was later to discover—singularly interwoven with the Sacco-Vanzetti case.

Spring was late that year. Not until my second week, as I crossed the bridge over the Charles River the other side of Needham, did I hear the creaky notes of the redwings among last year's cattails. A few mornings later I saw a couple of painted turtles still torpid from hibernation. From the bridge I headed up the winding road to Dedham, past much empty land, orchards, stone walls, and the driveways of the discreetly hidden river estates. Then, from Common Street on Dedham's outskirts, I swung into High Street, ahead of me above the still-bare elms the courthouse dome, mosquelike in the early light, crowned by an ornate metal grille and a flagpole. On those placid mornings the flag hung limp.

It was almost a third of a century since Sacco and Vanzetti had been tried, yet the ghost of their trial still seemed to haunt the courthouse. Scarcely a day passed while I was on jury duty but some reference to it came up. It shadowed us all. We served in the same paneled room with the marble-faced clock where Sacco and Vanzetti had been tried and sentenced. There was the same enclosure for the prisoners that Sacco-Vanzetti partisans referred to as a "cage"—as if the two defendants had been exhibited like animals in a zoo. Actually, it was a waist-high metal lattice, slightly higher in the back, with nothing formidable or forbidding about it. Our white-haired sheriff, Samuel Capen, in his blue-serge cutaway, its gleaming brass buttons embossed with the state seal, and his white staff of office that he wielded like a benevolent shepherd, had been sheriff at the time of the great trial. In the overlong lunch hours he would sometimes talk about it, telling of the day Sacco and Vanzetti were sentenced, how Vanzetti made his famous speech, and how Judge Thayer sat

with his head bent and never looked at him. I don't suppose any
doubts had ever crossed the sheriff's mind as to the guilt of the two
Italians or the rectitude of Massachusetts justice.

When the sheriff found I was interested, he took me on a visit to
the jail just down the street and let me see the cells where Sacco and
Vanzetti had been confined. One dull and rainy afternoon I had been
drawn as a juror on an auto accident case. No sooner was I in the jury
box than the counsel for the plaintiff appeared, and I was aware of a
slight buzz in the courtroom. The counsel seemed nothing to buzz
about: a portly, elderly man, quietly dressed, a little pompous but
with a soft voice. The juryman next to me nudged me."That's Katzmann," he whispered. Suddenly I realized. Here a few feet away was
the man who had been district attorney in 1921 and had prosecuted
Sacco and Vanzetti. He seemed the culmination of my days as a
juror. I decided then that once the month was over I should read
through the trial transcript and see what I could learn firsthand
about those summer weeks in 1921. During that month I felt that I
and my fellow jurymen had conscientiously done our best, had tried
with almost exaggerated effort to be fair and unbiased. Could those
Norfolk County jurors of an earlier generation have been so different? How should I have reacted, how should I have felt, if I had been
on the Sacco-Vanzetti jury?

That was something I wanted to discover, so many years after I
had first thought of it, through reading the transcript. Our Wellesley
library had the six massive buckram volumes of *Transcript of the
Record of the Trial of Nicola Sacco and Bartolomeo Vanzetti in the
Courts of Massachusetts and Subsequent Proceedings,* but when I
asked for them the librarian said they had been put in storage among
the books for which there was no longer any demand, and it would
take a day or so to locate them. Before I left for Maine for the summer, she promised to have them ready. "Keep them as long as you
want," she said. "I don't think anyone else will want them."

No one else did. The Sacco-Vanzetti case was then in a period of
dormancy. Scarcely noticed was the memorial service still held each
year by the Community Church. Those dormant fifties would, however, give way to the activist sixties, when the fate of Sacco and Vanzetti would again become a living issue.

I took the volumes with me to the coastal village of Friendship.
There, day after day, as I sat at my desk overlooking Muscongus Bay,
the Massachusetts trial appeared even more remote than it had in

Wellesley. What I tried to envision was a clean slate, as if the transcript before me did not concern a world-reverberating event but merely recorded the murder trial of two unknowns. I then knew little about the background of Sacco and Vanzetti. That even seemed to me an advantage, for neither had the jury known. Nevertheless, as I sat down to read, I could not wholly rid myself of the belief that the trial had been a travesty.

Much those two thousand pages of testimony and countertestimony could not offer—the atmosphere of the court with its tensions, the appearance of the witnesses and the defendants, the subtleties that can be gathered from a tone of voice but cannot be recorded in black and white. Yet the substance of the trial endured, each word spoken during those six and a half weeks preserved between the yellowing pages. As an imagined juror I tried to absorb the words, occupied solely with the question of whether two men had murdered two other men, and judging this by the evidence offered in court.

For me the prosecution's most questionable feature was District Attorney Katzmann's interrogation of the defendants as to their anarchist beliefs, their lack of patriotism, and their running away to Mexico in 1917 to avoid the draft.* Yet from my own experience in Dedham, I could not believe this was primary in the jury's verdict. On the other hand, the judge's charge, which Frankfurter had so assailed, for all its old-fashioned rhetoric seemed reasonable enough. No doubt Judge Webster Thayer had practiced declamation at high school in the post–Civil War era of baroque oratory, but he could scarcely be faulted for that. "Let your eyes be blinded to every ray of sympathy or prejudice," he told the jury, "but let them ever be willing to receive the beautiful sunshine of truth, of reason and sound judgment, and let your ears be deaf to every sound of public opinion or public clamor, if there be any, either in favor of or against these defendants."[2] It was for the court, he said, to decide questions of law. Only the jury could decide the facts. Alibis were always questions of facts.

> The Commonwealth claims that these defendants were two of a party of five who killed the deceased. The defendants deny it. What is the fact? As I have told you the Commonwealth must satisfy you beyond reasonable doubt that the defendants did. If the Commonwealth has

* Katzmann maintained that he was trying to establish whether Sacco and Vanzetti were merely using the anarchist label as a cover for their actions on the night of their arrest. He was hard, as his assistant district attorney admitted—perhaps too hard.

failed so to satisfy you, that is the end of these cases and you will return verdicts of not guilty. This is so because the identity of the defendants is one of the essential facts to be established by the Commonwealth. On the other hand, if the Commonwealth has so satisfied, you will return a verdict of guilty against both defendants or either of them that you so find to be guilty.[3]

"My duties, gentlemen, [he concluded,] have now closed and yours begun. From this mass of testimony introduced you must determine the facts. The law, as I have told you, places the entire responsibility in your hands. . . .

"I have now finished my charge. My duties are now at end. I have tried to preside over the trial of these cases in a spirit of absolute fairness and impartiality to both sides. If I have failed in any respect you must not, gentlemen, in any manner fail yours. I therefore now commit to your sacred keeping the decision of these cases."[4]

Leafing through the transcript pages on those summer days, gradually, and to my surprise, I found myself diverging from the Sacco-Vanzetti dogma that I had once so wholeheartedly and uncritically accepted. The trial, if not ideal in the Platonic sense—and what actual trial ever had been?—was not the kangaroo court of my preconceptions. As a layman with a layman's blinders, I hesitated to dispute Professor Frankfurter's trained legal vision. Yet after I had twice gone back to reread the judge's charge, my conclusion was that it was reasonable and fair. Judge Thayer and District Attorney Katzmann no longer struck me as malevolent. The judge may have been indiscreet off the bench, but, from the record, he seemed to have done his best to conduct the trial fairly. The district attorney was as sharp as most district attorneys out for a conviction. Both judge and district attorney were men whose integrity up until the trial had never been questioned. That I had to admit.

I still accepted Ehrmann's Morelli hypothesis, still believed that Sacco and Vanzetti were innocent men, but I could no longer see Katzmann and Thayer as villains. Believing in the innocence of the two Italian aliens, I now considered them victims of circumstance, their conviction a result of mistaken identity underlined by the inculpatory fact that they were armed. I still retained my villains: the Commonwealth in its blind rejection of such telling post-trial evidence as Ehrmann's; the Department of Justice agents working behind the scenes to get rid of two troublesome radicals, whatever their guilt or innocence; Governor Fuller and President Lowell, who in the last stages of the case, I was sure, must have known that Sacco and Vanzetti were innocent.

For Sacco-Vanzetti partisans the case was a melodrama, with the good and the innocent on one side and evil, conniving men on the other. I could no longer see it that way. For me it seemed not so much a melodrama, with its heroes and villains, as a tragedy. Indeed the case became a tragedy for all the principals concerned in it—for Sacco and Vanzetti, who died; for Thayer, Katzmann, Moore, Lowell, and others who would be haunted by its shadow the rest of their lives.

At about this time I wrote an article giving my subjective impressions of the case, based chiefly on my month as a juror and on my summer's reading of the transcript. I called it "Tragedy in Dedham," because I had come to see the Sacco-Vanzetti case as a Greek drama in modern dress, men brought to ruin by fate and their own weakness. For if Sacco and Vanzetti, professed men of peace, had not been armed on the night of their arrest, it is doubtful that they would have been indicted, much less tried. In my article I claimed that the prosecution never did establish an adequate motive for the crime and failed to account for the other three bandits who had taken part in the Braintree robbery. I added that the report of President Lowell's committee was indefensible. As for Governor Fuller, I wrote that I could never see him swinging into Boston's State Street Trust Building without thinking of the blood on his hands. I did concede that

> I was finally left with the feeling that if I had been on the original jury and heard the evidence that was placed before those men, I should probably have voted with the others. Yet I was not wholly certain.[5]

This was as far as I could then bring myself to go. Being "not wholly certain" was an equivocation that at that point I could not admit even to myself. Inwardly I *was* certain, although, as I wrote in my article, I still did not see how "any reasonable-minded person reading over the literature of the Sacco-Vanzetti case could come to any other conclusion than that the two men were innocent."

I sent "Tragedy in Dedham" to *The Antioch Review,* whose editor had published earlier articles of mine. He accepted it but said that the blood on the hands of the still-living Fuller was too libelous and must come off. The amended article appeared in the 1955 winter issue. Though a magazine highly respected in academic circles, *The Antioch Review* had a circulation of only about fifteen hundred, and my article brought little comment. Those few Sacco-Vanzetti partisans who did read it so approved of my vehement insistence on the two men's innocence that they were willing to overlook my wavering on the trial. A justice of the Massachusetts Superior Court, Reuben Lurie, earlier connected with the defense committee, told me it was the best piece on the case that he had read. But not until three years later, when *American Heritage* reprinted it with Ben Shahn illustrations, did it cause any stir. With its publication in this widely circulated magazine, the Sacco-Vanzetti case emerged from hibernation.

Shortly after it was reprinted, the Reverend Donald Lothrop of Boston's Community Church asked me to be one of the speakers at the next Sacco-Vanzetti memorial meeting. I was glad to accept, looking forward to talking with some of those who had had firsthand contact with the case. Many times I had passed the church's storefront on Copley Square, without ever having been inside, although I had heard my Aunt Amy speak glowingly about it. Facing the Richardson-Romanesque bulk of Trinity, it eschewed such ecclesiastical fripperies. Trinity had the decor of a cathedral without being one. The Community Church, "a church outside the churches," was a cathedral of free thought. Even the immanental liberalism of King's Chapel was regarded by Communityites as subversive of the ultimate values of truth-in-itself. Radicals and free-thinkers of all shades, even atheists, were welcomed to the Community Church's pulpit. It was the first religious institution in America to come to the defense of Sacco and Vanzetti. Canonized at their deaths, they remained its saints.

After a quarter of a century, my memory of that commemorative evening is fragmented. I have a mental Polaroid-print image of Don Lothrop—he did not like to be referred to as Reverend—genial in a white chef's apron as he ladled out goulash to a cafeteria line at the pickup supper before the meeting. With equal clarity I remember my fellow speakers, Aldino Felicani and Tom O'Connor, whom I met there for the first time. But I do not recall any other specific face or figure. The fifty or so congregants seemed cut from the same cloth, determined elderly women for the most part, high thoughts and low heels, their faith in the innocence of Sacco and Vanzetti as fixed as that of Jehovah's Witnesses in the inerrancy of Scripture. Each year they gathered to renew their vows, to revive factitiously the splendid moments of those electric August days before the executions when protesters picketed the State House until the police hauled them off to the Joy Street station. "We hard-bitten liberals," I heard one woman remark to another as I balanced my plate of goulash.

In one corner of that assembly room was a bookshelf. I noticed—and again the impression has remained fixed—several books against capital punishment, Joughin's and Morgan's retrospective *Legacy of Sacco and Vanzetti,* and other books on the case, more books and pamphlets defending the Rosenbergs and Alger Hiss. Apparently, to be a Community Church communicant required believing that Hiss and the Rosenberg couple were as much victims of a frame-up as were Sacco and Vanzetti. Though I still shared the latter belief, I couldn't help wondering about the implacability of the dogma. It wasn't open to discussion or argument.

We three speakers of the evening had been enrolled as evangelists of the cause. Nothing we said wasn't well known to everyone present. But we said it rhetorically. Felicani spoke first, a tall, bald, blue-eyed man who looked more Viking than Sicilian except for the Latin animation of his face. With his warm and smiling manner one couldn't help liking him—I couldn't. There was a friendly, open, and guileless quality about him that nevertheless, as I later discovered, concealed a residue of guile. Whenever he spoke in public he wore the black string tie that, with the wide-brimmed hat, was the anarchist formal dress.

If Felicani looked a Viking, Tom O'Connor looked a Firbolg, the primal map of Ireland written into his features. He said himself he looked like Cardinal Spellman. Stubby, with stubby fingers, he had a nose that had grown somewhat bulbous with advancing years. The obverse of his Hibernian birthright was the enmity he shared with Clem Norton toward their inherited Catholicism. For him the Sacco-Vanzetti case had come to be a kind of religion. Vanzetti, at his trial for the Bridgewater holdup, had offered the alibi that he was selling eels that day in Plymouth, and Tom planned to have a solemn memorial banquet each year on the execution date with the eating of eels as a sacrament.

As proprietor of the Excelsior Press, Felicani did the printing for the Community Church. Tom O'Connor kept the books for a rent-a-car agency in Wellesley about half a mile from where I lived. Both men welcomed me as a recruit. In our talks that evening we three went over the same ground, expounded the old dogma, demanded the secondary satisfaction of a posthumous pardon. Felicani was particularly indignant that twenty years after the execution of Sacco and Vanzetti, Governor Robert Bradford had refused to accept the Gutzon Borglum plaque offered to Massachusetts by a committee that included Eleanor Roosevelt. Borglum's bas-relief showed Sacco and Vanzetti in profile confronted by an arm holding a balance, the pan marked *Archaic Law* weighing down that marked *Justice.* Someday, Felicani predicted, that plaque would grace the State House grounds near the statue of another martyr, Anne Hutchinson. A rush of hand-clapping followed his prediction.*

Tom wanted to see the plaque included in a traveling Sacco-Vanzetti exhibit that would visit schools and colleges across New England. He appealed for support for his Vindication Committee. The day of vindication, that millennial event, he told his approving listeners, was not as far away as some people might think.

I have forgotten just what I said, but I remember I ripped into the prosecution, the off-bench and post-trial conduct of Judge Thayer, the equivocal ballistics evidence, Governor Fuller, and President Lowell. Particularly I had it in for Lowell. When I had finished, a woman in the back of the room asked with prim indignation, "Why aren't those people in jail?"

* Never cast in bronze, the plaque is now displayed in a corridor of the Boston Public Library.

5

The Road to Braintree

On beginning the book *Tragedy in Dedham*, I thought of myself as detached, impartial, ready to let the chips of evidence fall where they might. But I was more identified with Sacco and Vanzetti and their cause than I realized. Facts that reflected against them I tended to overlook. Finally there came a point, after I had written over three-quarters of my book, when the facts became too intrusive. If at the beginning I had really been as impartial as I thought I was, I should have written a different book. But could I have been impartial or merely developed another kind of partiality? Since then I have questioned whether it is possible for anyone writing history to be impartial, to dissolve his personal reactions in his material, in Ranke's celebrated phrase, to show how it really was.

Before writing anything I spent several days wandering about Braintree, talking with the police chief, the librarian, the editor of a Braintree paper, the head of the historical society, a local minister, and others, trying to capture the mood of the place, fixing its geography firmly in my mind. I had a vague impression of the town from my childhood, for before the new expressways had cut off the old turnpike, my father always drove through it on our summer trips to Cape Cod.

Braintree, ten miles south of Boston, is one of those former shoe-manufacturing towns on the old turnpike road, the first of a chain of such enclaves along the flat inland route to the Cape—Randolph, Stoughton, Holbrook, the Bridgewaters, with the shoe city of Brockton a few miles to the east. To drive through them is like driving through the same town over and over; the same Main Street, town hall, wooden Gothic church, drugstore, the flag over the post office, the Civil War monument topped by a soldier in forage cap and drooping granite mustache. Expressway traffic bypasses these towns and the shoe industry has long since migrated. Through its closeness to Boston, Braintree has expanded to a semi-suburb, losing much of its identity in the process.

Braintree in 1920 still managed to keep a small-town neighborliness. People on central Washington Street usually recognized one another even if they did not always speak. The faces of the Italian millworkers had come to seem familiar, though their names often did not. In that year Massachusetts automobile registrations soared to over a hundred thousand, and for the first time six-figure license plates appeared. Owners of vehicles in Braintree were still identifiable. The town drew its sustenance—some $200,000 a year—from its shoe factories: Rice & Hutchins beside the fence just behind the railroad crossing, Slater & Morrill in the hollow below, and Walker & Kneeland at the upper end of Washington Street. Slater & Morrill also had cutting rooms in the mansard-roofed Hampton House above their company offices. When the factory whistles blew at eight in the morning and five in the afternoon, a surge of workers followed. But the hours between, particularly the morning hours, were subdued, almost somnolent. Any stranger afoot on Washington Street, any out-of-town automobile, would be spotted at once.

The town remained a backwater, untroubled by the strikes and disorders marking the turbulent first years after the war. Its three-man police force had merely routine duties like keeping order at the polling places on voting days. Beyond these, Chief Jerry Gallivan was occupied mostly with petty, often juvenile incidents that rarely went as far as the district court. When Jerry was not at his home he could usually be found in front of his town-hall office, sitting on the steps with a quid of tobacco in his mouth, ready to pass the time of day with any man. There was little thought of a crime wave in Braintree. Yet the day before Christmas 1919, there had been a holdup attempt fourteen miles away in Bridgewater. On that cold and snowy morning the driver of a Ford truck, moving slowly because of the ice-encrusted roadbed, was carrying the payroll of the L. Q. White Shoe Company from the Bridgewater Trust Company to the L. Q. White main office. With him were a paymaster and a local constable. As they crossed the streetcar tracks, three men jumped out of a parked touring car and ran toward them. The lead man had a black mustache. He carried a shotgun, the other two pistols. When the driver failed to stop at their shout, the man with the shotgun knelt and fired. The other two fired their pistols. From his precarious seat on the payroll box, the constable fired back. No one was hit in the fusillade, but the driver lost control of his truck, which skidded across the car tracks and crashed into a telephone pole. Meanwhile, an oncoming streetcar had cut between the truck and the gunmen, who at this point lost their nerve and piled back into the car. The disappearing car was the last trace of the men. Witnesses said the touring car was a Buick and that the bandits looked foreign. A young doctor, John Murphy, in passing the wrecked truck saw a spent shotgun shell in the gutter, picked it up, and put it in his pocket.

Nobody in Braintree gave the fumbling Bridgewater attempt much thought, least of all Shelley Neal, the local agent of the American Express Company, a bouncy little man, long-nosed, short-tempered, proud of his official position. Each Thursday morning, wearing his American Express cap, he drove to the station with horse and wagon to meet the 9:18 train from Boston that brought some $30,000 in payroll money for the Slater & Morrill and Walker & Kneeland factories. He and his driver would take the metal box containing the money from the freight clerk, stow it in the wagon under the front seat, and start off for his office on the far side of the Hampton House, fifty yards down unpaved Railroad Avenue. It was all routine. Neal never thought to take any particular precautions. He carried a revolver mostly to impress his driver.

On that Thursday, April 15, it was 9:20 and the train still had not arrived. Neal checked the time with his Waltham railroad watch. As he put the watch back in his pocket he heard the engine whistle— two long echoing notes, a short, then a long—from the direction of Quincy. It always annoyed him when the train was late.

At 9:23 the train finally puffed in to the South Braintree station. Neal asked the freight clerk if he had stopped off with the engineer somewhere for a cup of coffee, and the clerk said, "Sure." By the time Neal and his driver had tucked the cashbox under the seat, it was almost half past nine. As the wagon joggled over the rutted road, Neal noticed half a dozen cars parked near the Hampton House. Usually he knew them all. But this morning there was one he did not know, a dark blue touring car almost in front of the Hampton main entrance. Its rear curtains were fastened in place, and as Neal drove past he caught a glimpse of a man hunched over in the front seat. Another man, haggard in appearance, stood under the portico leaning against a post. He wore an old army overcoat, and his face was pallid, sunken.

Once back at his desk Neal unlocked the metal box and took out two canvas money sacks, one for Walker & Kneeland, the other for Slater & Morrill. The Walker & Kneeland sack he placed in the safe, the other he tucked under his arm and started out for the Slater & Morrill office. From the gravel walk he could see the stranger still standing under the portico, his head lowered. Across the avenue was a small mud-streaked car Neal had not noticed earlier. As he neared it, the driver called out "All right!" to the man in the touring car. Just as Neal reached the portico, the stranger in the overcoat raised his head and the two stared briefly at one another. Neal couldn't help noticing the muddied whites of the other's eyes. The man kept his hands in his pockets, made no move.

Neal climbed the central staircase to the second floor, left the money at the Slater & Morrill office, and started down again. The pallid man was still leaning against the doorpost, but before Neal reached the vestibule, he had taken his hands from his pockets, crossed over to the touring car and climbed in. By the time Neal was outside, the car had driven away. The mud-streaked automobile had also disappeared.

During the course of the morning the touring car was seen cruising rather aimlessly through Braintree. Those who happened to notice recalled that there were five men in it, dark, probably Italian, except for the driver, who was "pale and sickly looking."[1] Later in the morning, two swarthy strangers, one wearing a felt hat, the other a cap, were seen walking along Washington Street, then standing for a time in front of Torrey's drugstore at the corner of Pearl Street. Just after noon a railroad detective saw them on a bench in the station, smoking cigarettes. At about three o'clock the same two were squatting on the pipe fence in front of the Rice & Hutchins factory. The touring car seen that morning had pulled up near the lower Slater & Morrill factory, and the sallow pinch-faced driver had raised the hood and was trying to adjust something in the motor with a screwdriver.

By three o'clock the Slater & Morrill bookkeeper had finished sorting out the payroll money—$15,776.51—and had placed it in some five hundred separate envelopes. These she packed in two steel cashboxes. She had scarcely finished when the paymaster, Frederick Parmenter, arrived with his guard, the twenty-eight-year-old Alessandro Berardelli. Berardelli was armed with a .38-caliber Harrington & Richardson revolver. Parmenter, a solid man in his forties with a thin mustache and a ready smile, kidded a bit with the girls in the office. Then he started off with his guard, each carrying a cashbox. Along the way he stopped a couple of times to chat, waved to the one-legged gate tender as he crossed the railroad tracks, stopped again just beyond the tracks to ask Jimmy Bostock, a Slater & Morrill repairman, to fix a pulley in the lower mill.

The two men who had been squatting on the fence were now standing by a telephone pole. Parmenter, his guard a few steps behind him, sauntered past in his heavy flat-footed walk. The man in the felt hat seemed to know Berardelli, for he said something to him, reached as if to put his hand on his shoulder. Suddenly shots rang out. Bostock saw it all in a confused sequence: the felt-hatted man, with a pistol in his hand; Berardelli begging for his life, then, after the shots, sinking down to a crouch, his hand groping for his revolver; Parmenter spinning round to receive a shot in the chest.

The paymaster dropped his box and staggered across the road. Again the gunman fired at him. This bullet pierced his abdomen, perforating the vena cava, the body's largest vein—a mortal wound. Parmenter collapsed in the gutter. The second gunman, a blunt, dark automatic in his hand, stepped over to Berardelli and fired several shots at the guard, who was on his hands and knees. Only one shot struck home, but this severed the great artery leading to the heart. Berardelli dropped convulsively, turned over, bubbles of blood oozing from his mouth. The gunman bent down to the dying guard and took his revolver. Peter McCullum, a shoe cutter, looking from one of the Rice & Hutchins lower windows, saw the sunlight flash on the nickel-plated barrel of "a white gun" in the man's left hand.[2] During the shooting the gunman's cap had fallen off. A third man with a shotgun now dashed out from where he had been hiding behind a brick pile near a construction site. The capless gunman and the man with the shotgun fired at Bostock. Both missed. Bostock turned and ran. The gunman fired in the air, and the touring car in the hollow started jerkily uphill, a fifth man beside the pallid driver in the front seat. As the car slowed down, the capless gunman fired several shots at workers gaping from the Rice & Hutchins windows, then he and the second gunman grabbed the money boxes and climbed into the backseat.*

* The many witnesses of the shootings, as might be expected, produced a confusion of accounts. It is at least indisputable that two men waylaid Berardelli and Parmenter, that the first man shot Parmenter and then Berardelli, and that Berardelli was killed by Bullet

The car, its oval rear window torn out and a shotgun protruding from the gap, reached the end of Pearl Street, swung abruptly left into Washington Street and disappeared. Dozens saw the two men sprawled in the roadway and the touring car as it moved erratically up Pearl Street, its engine misfiring. Hearing the shots, Louis Pelser, a shoe cutter in the Rice & Hutchins first-floor workroom, had peered out the window to see Berardelli in the gravel six feet below and the man with the pistol standing over him. The gunman raised his pistol arm and Pelser ducked under a table. When he peered out a second time, the touring car had just pulled up, giving him a close glimpse of the license plate. He wrote down the number on his cutting board: 49789.

After the gunmen had gone, Jimmy Bostock ran to the unconscious Berardelli and held him in his arms until he died. Then, almost at random, he gathered up four spent shells from the gravel. These he gave to the Slater & Morrill superintendent, Thomas Fraher. A worker from the lower factory picked up a dark cap lying near Berardelli's body and also gave it to Fraher.

Two days after the Braintree murder, the getaway car, a Buick, was discovered stripped of plates in the Manley Woods of Cochesett, an outlying section of West Bridgewater. On the front seat were a few coins and in the back a ragged brown overcoat. Beside the Buick were the tracks of a smaller car. The Buick was driven to the Brockton police station where Lieutenant Daniel Guerin dusted it in an unsuccessful attempt to obtain fingerprints. Although the maker's number had been chiseled off, the engine number was still intact, the number of a car stolen from Francis Murphy, a Natick shoe manufacturer.

That is how it really was on that afternoon in South Braintree so far as I could fit the jigsaw pieces together from the trial transcript, newspaper accounts, the reports of the Pinkerton Detective Agency, conversations with Shelley Neal and others in Braintree. The main facts were indisputable. Two men had been killed, two pistols and a shotgun fired, a payroll stolen. Five bandits were involved. The getaway car was a Buick. Was it the same car used four months earlier in the Bridgewater attempt? Was the "white gun" in the bandit's left hand Berardelli's nickel-plated revolver?

III. At the inquest several witnesses testified that as the Buick drew up, the two gunmen tossed the money boxes into the backseat. A third gunman jumped out of the still-moving car and shot at Berardelli, then struggling to his feet. Berardelli collapsed in the gravel. Whether the second or third gunman fired Bullet III remains inconsequential.

The botched Bridgewater attempt and the haphazardly successful South Braintree holdup were the work of rank if grimly determined amateurs, relentless of purpose but uncertain how to go about it. Herbert Ehrmann insisted dogmatically that the Braintree crime was carefully planned, the work of practiced criminals. What the evidence really shows is absence of planning. Whoever staged the crime was familiar with the town and the factories, knew that the payroll money arrived on the early morning train and that the schedule had recently been shifted from Friday to Thursday. Knowing this, professionals would have struck as the train pulled out of the station, pinioning Neal and his unarmed helper while they were hoisting the money box onto the wagon.

Or they could have seized Neal as he was carrying the cashbox with the two payrolls from the wagon to his office. Their last chance that morning would have been to waylay him on his way to the Slater & Morrill office. Something like that the bandits seemed to have had in mind, with the pallid driver as a lookout. When the man in the car across the street called out, that was their moment, but somehow in that moment they lost their nerve.

Nothing for them to do then but wait until midafternoon for Parmenter to appear with the Slater & Morrill payroll. So they drove about, until finally the driver stopped in the hollow on lower Pearl Street. While he tinkered with the motor, the others idled through the town. The two who had been loitering in the railroad station had moved on to wait for Parmenter at a pipe fence some fifty yards up from the Buick. It was a foolishly conspicuous place, just under the Rice & Hutchins windows, a crew of workmen digging a foundation across the street. Professional criminals would have confronted Parmenter and Berardelli with pistol and shotgun as the two came abreast of the Buick. Outnumbered, caught off guard, the two could have been easily overpowered. A simple holdup. No need to kill anyone unless, as was hinted, Berardelli recognized one of the bandits. Even the getaway was botched. Instead of heading the spluttering Buick up Pearl Street past factories and stores, the bandits should have driven off in the opposite direction, a sparse wooded road leading south to the Bridgewaters.

On the night of their arrest Sacco and Vanzetti had gone to West Bridgewater with two acquaintances, Boda and Orciani, to pick up an automobile left in a garage for repairs. Boda and Orciani; their names appear with brief inconsequence in the transcript along with a scant mention of one Coacci, who had already been deported as an anarchist. Who were these men? The district attorney suspected them of being the remaining three involved in the South Braintree killings. But there was no determining proof. How did Sacco and Vanzetti happen to get arrested in the first place?

That was the question I put to Tom O'Connor the first time I went to see him. "Somebody asked Thompson, their last court lawyer, that question," he said, "and all he could answer was 'Search me!' If you ask that question, you're on the right track."

Once I had begun my book, I used to drop in on Tom several times a week at the rent-a-car agency opposite the Wellesley Hills Post Office. I tried to arrive during his lunch hour. Generally I'd see him before he saw me, a gnomish figure hunched over his desk, munching a cheese or tuna-fish sandwich he had just taken from its wax-paper wrapping, a thermos jug of coffee next to his telephone and a book in front of him. If he caught sight of me through the window, he would wave for me to come in, then spend the rest of his lunch hour talking about the great case. "I have had a wife and a mistress in my life," he once told me. "My wife was my mother, my mistress was the Sacco-Vanzetti case." For that mistress he had sacrificed the house his mother left him, his savings and his own personal career.

He had grown up in an Irish enclave of Dorchester. His widowed mother had wanted him to be a priest, and he had led his class in parochial school, had been an altar boy, faithfully parroting the Latin words. At adolescence the revelation—that was what he called it— came to him that he no longer believed. "After that," he told me, "I kept seeing threads of gold running from all those shabby three-deckers to that brick church with its oversized rectory." He still remained the devoted son, living with his mother until her death. Then for a time he was a reporter for a small news service. But from the day he read John Nicholas Beffel's persuasive "Eels and the Electric Chair" in *The New Republic* of December 29, 1920, he found in the Sacco-Vanzetti case his life's purpose. He came to know more about it than anyone except possibly Felicani, who was party to the anarchist secrets.

Although I never saw his rented room in adjoining Newton, I imagined it brimming with books, pamphlets, newspaper clippings, folders, filing cabinets, and boxes full of documents. Whatever material I lacked he dug out for me, giving me much background information that I should otherwise scarcely have come to. As my work progressed, he would read each chapter, making corrections and suggesting additions. He saw my work-in-progress as the book he himself should have written but somehow could not. "You can dedicate it to me," he said one day. "That will be enough."

I had thought of Tom as a lifelong bachelor until one day Felicani mentioned that sometime in the twenties Tom had married a woman he had met through a personal advertisement in *The Nation*. The marriage lasted only a few weeks. Felicani did not know why, and Tom never mentioned it. Once Tom gave me a folder concerning one of the post-trial motions. Sandwiched among the pages were half a dozen pornographic photographs. It would have been embarrassing for him and for me if I had handed them back. So I said nothing and burned them.

One day I mentioned to him that a girl from Wellesley High School, a senior who said her name was Kathy, had asked me to help her in writing a paper on Sacco and Vanzetti. I had to tell her I was sorry but I did not have the time. When I mentioned this to Tom, he got quite excited. "Send her to me," he said. "Send her to me. We need the next generation!" With Tom's help Kathy finished her report, although I suspect it was mostly Tom's. It took the two of them several months. When Kathy had finished, Tom gave her a cartoon sketch he had made—he was quite good at drawing—showing him handing over a torch labeled *The Sacco-Vanzetti Case* to a girl labeled *Kathy*. Actually I had seen that sketch before Tom ever met Kathy, but then the girl had been labeled *Sylvia*. Tom had, I discovered, a stock of these sketches that he gave from time to time to susceptible young women, merely altering the face and the label.

In those years the chief activists of the Sacco-Vanzetti case were Tom, Felicani, Ehrmann, and Michael Angelo Musmanno, a justice of the Pennsylvania Supreme Court. All four had been active in the case while Sacco and Vanzetti were alive. All four had visited them in prison. Ehrmann in 1933 had elaborated his Morelli Gang theory in *The Untried Case*. Six years later Musmanno published his own Sacco-Vanzetti reminiscences, *After Twelve Years*. In the last hectic weeks of August 1927, he had dashed from one judge to the other seeking a writ of *certiorari* that would have stayed Sacco's and Vanzetti's executions, and he had repeatedly but vainly telephoned everyone from Supreme Court justices to President Coolidge.

Tom and Felicani kept in distant contact with Musmanno but

had little use for Ehrmann, who had no use at all for them. When I telephoned Ehrmann to ask if I might see him about a Sacco-Vanzetti book I was writing, he hesitated, said that anything he could tell me was in his own book, but finally invited me to his Brookline home the following Wednesday afternoon. Two Harvard undergraduates writing honors theses on the trial were already there when I arrived. I think Ehrmann lumped me with them. He was a tall man, with a leathery face so deeply fissured that it made his eyes bulge. Sitting by his blue-tiled fireplace, drinking rather raw domestic sherry, I sensed his impatience, as if he begrudged us his time. The undergraduates, at least, he regarded as worthy of encouragement. But why anyone like myself should presume to write another Sacco-Vanzetti book was beyond him. He had solved the case, and there was really nothing more to be said. After an hour, like a professor at the end of a lecture, he dismissed us.

Though Ehrmann did not make his career in the Sacco-Vanzetti case, he was greatly aided by it, for it gave him entrée to upper-class liberal circles in the city not readily open to a young Jewish out-of-state lawyer in the stratified Boston of his era. But if it helped his career, it made Musmanno's, for whom Ehrmann did not bother to conceal his contempt. "All he ever did," he told me on the second and last time I ever saw him, "was to carry somebody else's briefcase in the last five weeks."

Musmanno had come to Boston in the late spring of 1927, a flamboyant young man in a flowing brown poet's tie, bringing a petition on behalf of Sacco and Vanzetti from the Sons of Italy, of which he was the self-appointed representative. He had entered the case through the bedroom window of Mary Donovan, a hatchet-faced woman in her thirties who had given herself to the cause with fanatic devotion and who would pronounce the funeral oration over the two dead anarchists.

After the executions Musmanno returned to Pennsylvania as a recognized spokesman for his ethnic group, nicely balancing his defense of radicals with perfervid American patriotism and fundamentalist loyalty to the Catholic Church. As a Son of Italy he had defended Sacco and Vanzetti, not as anarchists—of which he maintained they were the most innocent variety—but as fellow Italians. His highly emotional oratory (in both English and Italian) appealed to the Italian ethnics then beginning to emerge in Pennsylvania as a political force. They saw him as a champion, in their bloc voting electing him first a judge of the court of common pleas, then later to the Pennsylvania Supreme Court.

Superficial, voluble, dramatic, carried along in the stream of his own words, he had a knack of getting on in the world. During his judgeship he had become a naval reserve commander, and in World War II he served for a time as General Mark Clark's naval aide. After the war he was one of the three judges of Military Tribunal II that would try the Luftwaffe's Field Marshal Erhard Milch at Nuremberg.

Brigadier General Telford Taylor, chief counsel for war crimes, had not wanted the theatrical Musmanno. He cabled the War Department that a commander's rank was inappropriate for the trial of a field marshal, whereupon to his chagrin the Pentagon sent on Musmanno raised to the rank of captain.

At Nuremberg Judge Musmanno insisted on wearing his naval uniform under his judicial robe, and when photographed would raise the sleeve enough for his four captain's stripes to show. He had brought with him a variety of uniforms. Not long after arriving he formed liaisons with several young women, former members of Hitler's staff who had been brought to Nuremberg for interrogation. The English historian David Irving in his book on Milch and the Luftwaffe noted that

> another of Hitler's secretaries who met him [Musmanno] described his passion for uniforms: he had multiple photographs taken with his arm round her outside the blitzed ruins of her home in Munich, changing into a different uniform for each shot.[3]

I had not heard of Musmanno until Tom O'Connor lent me *After Twelve Years,* warning me that it was not altogether accurate. I was still not prepared for the rhetorical exuberance, the skyrocket phrases shooting up and out of grammatical sight, the exhibitionist shifts into the historical present, the occasional lapses into the ludicrous. Musmanno, standing at what he called the "catafalque" of Sacco and Vanzetti—I presume he meant "bier"—sees the phantom figure of blindfolded Justice opposite him.

> She removes her blindfold . . . and then speaks. "Yes, Judge Thayer, the world saw what you did to those defendants; it saw what you did to those whose rights it was your sworn duty to protect. Would that I had listened while you cursed those you were to adjudge. Would that I had removed my blindfold when you set the scales."[4]

From newspaper accounts I gathered that when the Sacco-Vanzetti jury brought in its verdict shortly after sunset, it was a calm summer evening cooled by a slight breeze after a hot and cloudless day. That was not how Musmanno remembered it.

At 7:30 p.m. [according to his reconstruction] it was announced that the jury had agreed upon a verdict. Just about that time a storm broke. Rain pelted against the windows and fitful flashes of lightning threw grotesque shadows across the courtroom as the jurors filed in. Not one looked up. Attorney Moore, with his years of experience, interpreted this as a sign of a verdict which meant death. He drew a hand across his face in a gesture of despair. A cemetery stillness hushed every person in the courtroom. The only sound was the squeaking footsteps of the twelve somber men. The only movement was their measured paces to the jury box.[5]

And so on. As I gave the book back to Tom, I said: "Musmanno makes the heavens protest, and he wasn't even there. There wasn't any storm. It didn't rain a drop that night."

"Oh," said Tom, with a grimace. "He must have been reading Lear."

But how did it all begin? That was for me the persistent question.

"It began with that hick cop Stewart in Bridgewater," Tom said. "You've got to understand that to understand anything else. With his crazy Irish imagination he started it all. You know what he said right after they found the Buick? 'The men who did this job knew no God.' Every atheist a suspect! Without that hick cop weaving his fantasies there never would have been a Sacco-Vanzetti case."

6

The Road to Brockton

As police chief in rural Bridgewater, Michael Stewart did in fact give the initial impulse to the Sacco-Vanzetti affair, as Tom O'Connor reiterated. Yet, what to Tom seemed Stewart's wild Celtic fantasy appeared reasonable enough to me on looking through the record. Stewart had acted on a hunch, not irrationally. Police often act on hunches. It is part of their trade.

In the xenophobic atmosphere of wartime, Congress had passed the 1918 Immigration Act. Aimed chiefly at anarchists, the bugaboo of that period, it barred the entry and provided for the deportation of aliens advocating the forcible overthrow of the United States government. Shortly after the passage of the act, Stewart, at the request of the Immigration Service, picked up half a dozen local Italian anarchists. Taken before a federal judge, they were charged with violating the new act. So far as Stewart was concerned, that was the end of the matter. He supposed that those Italians had long since been shipped back to Italy. Such was not the case with at least one of them, Feruccio Coacci. After an anarchist friend had posted a thousand-dollar bond, he was released on bail, the judge making the release conditional on his marrying the woman he had been living with and supporting the two children she had borne him.

On coming to the United States, Coacci had first settled in Quincy, Massachusetts. There in 1915 he had taken up with an Italian peasant girl, Ersilia Buongarzone. Their two children were both delivered at the state almshouse in Tewksbury. In Quincy he made himself conspicuous through his anarchist dramatic society, Il Filodrammatica di Quincy, and through his collection of radical books available to all who wanted to read them.

Following President Wilson's 1917 war declaration, he left for Mexico with a group of East Boston anarchists. On coming back a year later, he worked for a time at the L. Q. White Shoe Company in Bridgewater. After his threatened deportation and his release on bail, he stayed on near Bridgewater. By the end of 1919 he was working in the Slater & Morrill factory in Braintree. In January 1920, he, with the pregnant Ersilia and their two children, moved into Puffer's Place, a ramshackle house rented by his friend Mike Boda on an obscure back road in Cochesett. Once the derelict two-story structure had been a small iron foundry. Clarence Puffer, a local handyman, had bought it and in a makeshift sort of way had converted it into a dwelling. Here and there in its mansard roof he had cut out gables that peered down over the scraggly dirt road. Except for the gables there was little to set it apart from the other shacks and squatter shanties scattered at longish intervals across the flat empty landscape.

The house, with its rotting front porch and a tumble-down shed in the rear, had been vacant for some time. Then in December 1919 Boda had rented it. No one paid much attention to the Italian newcomer, nor did he to anyone else. There were no near neighbors. Those down the road did notice the occasional automobile passing to and from Puffer's Place, particularly on weekends, for cars were no common sight on those back roads.

A short man with a sharp aquiline nose, a hairline mustache, and deep-set hazel eyes, Boda was a snappy dresser. His dark overcoat had a velvet collar, and he wore an amethyst stickpin in his tie and a green velour hat. If anyone had bothered to ask him, he would have said he was a salesman for a New York fruit-importing firm. Actually he had adopted the then novel trade of bootlegger. Shortly after moving to Puffer's Place he had bought himself a 1914 Overland. Some years earlier he had been living with his brother in an isolated Italian settlement on the outskirts of Needham, close to Wellesley, where the two of them had worked in a dry-cleaning shop. In 1917 he had gone with Coacci and the others to Mexico. Returning months later, he left Needham to take a job with the L. Q. White Company in Bridgewater. Before moving to Puffer's Place he had been living in Hyde Park with an anarchist comrade, Riccardo Orciani.

Wherever he worked, whatever he did, his avocation was anarchism. He belonged to Il Gruppo Autonomo di East Boston, known sometimes in English as the Libertarian Club. He had also helped set up the Mazzinian Educational Circle of Roxbury, an anarchist school for children. In 1916 he had been arrested during an antiwar riot in Boston's North End. It was his sole arrest. Usually he was cagey enough not to draw attention to himself and, unlike Coacci, he was not one of those marked down for deportation following the passage of the Immigration Act.

The police never caught up with Boda. On his return to Italy he made no effort to earn a living but took to thievery. After attempting to kill an army sergeant he was picked up by the police and exiled to the island of Lipari, where he was subsequently interviewed to no great effect by the eccentric Edward Holton James, a nephew of William and Henry James. Not long after that he was released by Mussolini to work as a police spy, mingling with and writing reports on Italian anarchist, Communist, and anti-Fascist groups in Switzerland and France.

Coacci liked to boast to his friends that he wanted to go back to Italy but was just waiting for the government to give him a free ride. He waited almost two years. Early in April 1920 he at last received notice to report to the East Boston Immigration Service on the fifteenth for deportation. He then quit his job at Slater & Morrill. On the fifteenth he failed to show up in East Boston. The next day he telephoned the immigration station to say his wife was sick and he needed a few extra days to look after her. Professionally suspicious, an Inspector Root of the Immigration Service telephoned Stewart to suggest that they both drop in on Coacci that evening. Since Stewart had another engagement, he assigned his night patrolman, Frank LeBaron, to go with Root.

When Root and LeBaron arrived at Puffer's Place, they found nothing wrong with Ersilia. Obviously Coacci had been lying. Nevertheless, the inspector offered to let him stay on an extra week. Coacci now insisted that he wanted to leave at once, that he had to get back to Italy to see his ailing father. Root, having private plans for the evening, reluctantly agreed to take him and told him to pack his bag. But before they left he suggested that Coacci leave some money behind for his wife and children. Coacci—who had $200 with him— said they did not need any. With his belongings tucked into a straw suitcase, he walked away quite jauntily. Ersilia stood in the doorway with the children, crying. On the eighteenth Coacci was put aboard a ship for Italy.

Even as Coacci was being hustled aboard ship, two horseback riders from Brockton came across the South Braintree Buick abandoned in the Manley Woods a mile or so from Puffer's Place. After the car had been taken to the Brockton police station, Stewart, with Inspector Albert Brouillard of the State Police, who had been sent down from Boston to work with him, went over to see it. Stewart now began to wonder vaguely whether Coacci might have had something to do with both the Bridgewater and Braintree crimes. Coacci was Italian, and the bandits were thought to be Italian. He had failed to show up in East Boston on the day of the Braintree murders, because of his wife's sickness, he said. Yet his wife had not been sick at all. He had been eager to be deported. Though he was now beyond reach, Stewart thought he should at least pay a visit to the Cochesett house.

That evening Stewart and Brouillard drove over to Puffer's Place. Boda, a man unknown to them, was there when they arrived. They told him they were from the Immigration Service and needed a photograph of Coacci. He let them in without hesitation and talked freely. Coacci, he said, was someone he did not like, his friends were "bad peoples." While ostensibly searching the house for photographs, Stewart came across a manufacturer's diagram of a Savage automatic pistol. Brouillard asked Boda if he owned a gun, and Boda showed them a .32-caliber automatic. When Brouillard picked it up and removed the clip, he noticed three cartridges in it. One of these, a Peters, he took out and placed in his pocket.

After poking through the house, Stewart and Brouillard examined the shed in the rear. Boda said he usually kept his Overland there but that it was now at the Elm Street Garage a mile down the road, being repaired. The shed, large enough for two cars, had a dirt floor. A burlap sack was hung across the window. On the righthand side two planks had been laid down for the Overland. The lefthand side, though partially raked over, showed the imprint of a tire much too large for an Overland but the right size for a Buick. Napoleon Ensher, a farmer living down the road from Puffer's Place, would later testify that, early in the spring, he had seen Boda driving past in a "large, dark" Buick, and Boda had nodded to him. Seventeen-year-old Paul MacDonald, who used to deliver milk to Puffer's Place and who remembered his customers warmly, told the defense lawyer William Callahan that he had twice seen Boda driving a Buick, information that Callahan and Moore kept to themselves.[1]

Stewart thanked Boda and said he might be back later to have a chat with him. Afterward, when the chief discovered that Boda had worked for the L. Q. White Company, he regretted he had not arrested him then and there, but at the time he had hesitated since West Bridgewater, as a separate township, was outside his jurisdiction and Boda himself had done nothing overt.

Two mornings later Stewart drove back to see Boda again. Boda was just eating breakfast when he caught a glimpse of the chief's car and ducked out of sight. Stewart pounded on the door, peered through the window at the dishes on the kitchen table, knocked again, and went away. The following evening he returned. This time the house was vacant, stripped of its furnishings. He then drove to the Elm Street Garage. Boda's Overland was still there. Warning the proprietor, Simon Johnson, that this was a serious matter, he told him that if anyone came for the Overland he must stall him along until he could call the police.

The trap was set, to be sprung on whoever might call for the Overland. For a week there was no sign. Then a long-distance call came in to Johnson's garage. It was Boda, who wanted to know if his Overland was ready. When Johnson told him it was, he said he would pick it up next day. He did not appear. Another week passed.

Three weeks had elapsed since the South Braintree murders, and the police were no further ahead in solving that crime than they were in identifying the criminals of the December holdup attempt in Bridgewater. All their clues had come to nothing. Yet there were certain clues that, if pursued just a little longer, might have led to Puffer's Place weeks or even months before Stewart confronted Boda there.

After the Bridgewater attempt, L. Q. White had offered a thousand-dollar reward for the apprehension of the bandits and had engaged the Pinkerton Detective Agency to conduct its own private investigation. Like all such agencies the Pinkertons had their underworld contacts. Since the bandits had been described as foreigners, probably Italians, Pinkerton agents spread out through Boston's Little Italy. On December 30, Pinkerton assistant superintendent H. J. Murray reported that he had had supper in Boston with an informant who told him that an

Italian mentioned yesterday had said that the men who were implicated in the Bridgewater holdup had occupied temporarily a shack in close proximity to Bridgewater and that the car that had been used was left there along with some overalls or disguise of a similar nature, used by one of the men implicated in the holdup; that these men were Italians, had deserted the car, returned to Quincy by trolley; that they are believed to be residing in the vicinity of Fore River Shipyard and are known to be anarchists.

Informant suggested that a thorough search of the country about Bridgewater be made, particularly the underbrush or any place with a shack or shed as that used by the Poles or Italians, be made.[2]

A Pinkerton agent, Henry Hellyer, spent some time with LeBaron searching for such a shack. "Officer LeBaron," he reported, "said that there was several places in Bridgewater where the car may have been secreted and took me round to several likely looking places, but he did not look into any of them."[3] After a week the Pinkerton investigations petered out. Following the Braintree murders, the Pinkertons came back into the case briefly, but found out little that local and state police had not already determined. Yet there was another possible, if tenuous, connection between the Bridgewater and Braintree crimes, for Hellyer noted in an April 19 report that Chief Gallivan had shown him a shell found near the abandoned Buick "for a Winchester shotgun. . . . Same as the one found on the scene of the Bridgewater attempted holdup last December."[4]

Johnson had begun to wonder if he would ever hear from Boda again. His small one-story house on North Elm Street near the railroad bridge was about a quarter of a mile from his garage. Finally, on the night of Wednesday, May 5, just after nine o'clock, there was a knock on his door. He had gone to bed. His wife Ruth answered, calling out from inside to ask who was there. A muffled voice said it was Mike Boda, come for his auto. Her husband whispered to her to go next door to the Bartletts, who had a telephone, and call the police. Ruth, on opening the door, was caught in the headlight beam of a motorcycle parked across the street. Boda stood about ten feet away in strangely shabby clothes. She could just make out a man in a checked mackinaw beyond him sitting on a motorcycle. As her eyes grew used to the light she saw two more men walking toward her from the railroad bridge. One wore a derby, the other a felt hat, and they were talking in what she thought was Italian.

Ruth Johnson was only twenty-one, and she was afraid. As she started out for the Bartletts' and moved from the headlight's glare into the shadows, she thought vague figures in the darkness were following her. When her husband finally appeared on the doorstep,

Boda shook hands with him, said he needed the Overland. He seemed nervous and impatient. Johnson asked if he had license plates. He said he did not but would take a chance without them. Johnson said he would take him to the garage as soon as his wife got back from the neighbor's, where she had gone to borrow milk.

Meanwhile, Ruth had got through to the police from the Bartletts'. As she walked back she could hear the strangers talking and caught the word *telephone*. Boda, increasingly uneasy, now told Johnson it was too late to get the Overland and that he would send someone with plates in the morning. He then climbed into the side-car of the motorcycle and was driven away. Although the taillight was out, Johnson managed to note the license-plate number. The other two strangers, the man in the derby and the man in the felt hat, walked up North Elm Street, following the Bridgewater-Brockton streetcar line. The Johnsons watched them until they disappeared. A mile or so beyond the Johnson house they passed a woman and asked her where the car stop was. She pointed it out to them. At 9:40 they got on the streetcar from Bridgewater.

On getting Ruth Johnson's message, Chief Stewart drove at once to the Johnsons' house. By the time he arrived, the strangers were already on the Brockton streetcar. How he knew they were on that car is not wholly clear, but he did know. From the Bartlett house he called the Brockton police and told them to pick up two foreigners on the Bridgewater trolley who had tried to steal an auto. At four minutes past ten, when the car arrived in Brockton, the police were waiting. Two officers boarded the car before it came to a stop and arrested the suspects, who were then taken to the station and searched. One had a drooping mustache. The other was clean-shaven but swarthy. They gave their names as Bartolomeo Vanzetti and Nicola Sacco. The clean-shaven Sacco had a .32-caliber Colt automatic tucked in his waistband, with eight cartridges in the clip and one in the barrel. He also had twenty-three loose cartridges in his pocket. Vanzetti was carrying a .38-caliber Harrington & Richardson revolver, its five chambers loaded. In his pocket he had four twelve-gauge shotgun shells and a penciled announcement prepared for printing that read:

> Proletarians, you have fought all the wars. You have worked for all the owners. You have wandered over all the countries. Have you harvested the fruits of your labors, the price of your victories? Does the past comfort you? Does the present smile on you? Does the future promise you

anything? Have you found a piece of land where you can live like a human being and die like a human being? On these questions, on this argument, and on this theme, the struggle for existence, Bartolomeo Vanzetti will speak. Hour—Day—Hall—Admission free. Freedom of discussion to all. Take the ladies with you.[5]

The two Italians were questioned, first by Chief Stewart, later by District Attorney Katzmann. Vanzetti said he was a fish peddler from Plymouth and for the last three days had been visiting Sacco in South Stoughton. On Sunday he had taken the train from Plymouth to Boston, had breakfast in a lunchroom on Hanover Street, then had gone to a moving picture. "I am sure I slept in Boston," he told an interrogator, "but I had a woman with me—that is why I did not want to tell you. A woman I met in Boston. I was not with her Monday night; I went to Stoughton Monday. I can't tell exactly what time I left the woman in Boston. I don't know where we stayed in Boston; she took me to a place. It is a woman I met that night; a woman who goes with everybody. I met her in Hanover Street. She asked me to come with her. I think she was an American she no speak Italian."[6]

Sacco and Vanzetti said that on Wednesday evening they had intended to see a friend of Vanzetti's in Bridgewater but, after reaching the town, decided it was too late and had taken the streetcar back. Vanzetti denied knowing anyone named Boda or Coacci. He had not seen a man on a motorcycle. He did not remember what he had been doing on April 15. He carried his revolver because he needed it for protection in his fish business. The shotgun shells were ones he had found in Sacco's kitchen cabinet and had put in his pocket intending to sell them.

Sacco said he was married and lived in South Stoughton, where he had worked for two years in the Three-K shoe factory. He had a young son. Two other children had died. He had never been in West Bridgewater before, nor had he seen a motorcycle there. Somewhere he had read about the Braintree murders in the *Boston Post* and remembered "there was bandits robbing money."

The district attorney had already learned that Sacco had not been at work on April 15 and became increasingly convinced that he had been involved in the South Braintree crime. Of Vanzetti he was not at first so sure. He brought over a number of persons from South Braintree who had witnessed the holdup. Some identified Sacco as one of the bandits. Some could not. At that time only one witness identified Vanzetti. However, other witnesses from Bridgewater picked Vanzetti as the man who held the shotgun in the abortive holdup there. Both men were indicted for the South Braintree crime, Vanzetti alone being indicted as one of the Bridgewater bandits.

The fourth man, who had sat on the motorcycle shining the headlight on the Johnson house and then had driven off with Boda, was traced by his license plate and picked up next day. He turned out to be Riccardo Orciani, a cocky aggressive man with a hairline mustache and sly features, a "real tough," according to Chief Stewart. Sacco and Vanzetti had been dismayed at their arrest. Orciani remained unconcerned. He refused to answer questions, and when he was brought face-to-face with Sacco and Vanzetti said he had never seen them before. Several witnesses had tentatively identified him as a South Braintree gunman, but he was able to produce a time card showing he had been working in a Norwood foundry on April 15. Although Katzmann assumed that someone else had punched the time clock, he decided there was not enough substantial evidence to place Orciani on trial. Nevertheless, the district attorney had formed his Braintree cast: Sacco, Vanzetti, Coacci, Boda, and Orciani.

7

The Anarchist Road

For all their evasive denials after their arrest, Sacco and Vanzetti were anarchists, members with Boda and Coacci of Il Gruppo Autonomo, which met regularly in East Boston's Naturalization Hall on Maverick Square. In that group Giovanni Gambera was the dominant figure, a man of wide-ranging mind, a lover of literature, close friend of the bookish Vanzetti. As an anarchist he insisted on anonymity—to protect his family, he said. The other comrades acceded. His circle of acquaintances was large. He had underworld, Mafia, and political connections, and was deft at disposing of illicit funds. All in all a man of mystery, a gray eminence under the black flag of anarchy.[1]

When Gambera first came to this country in 1908, he worked as a barber's assistant. Like so many Italians, he was familiar with masonry. Once he had saved a little money, he started a tile factory. At heart he remained an anarchist, flaunting his views in *Il Pungolo*. The last survivor of those directly concerned with Sacco and Vanzetti, in his old age he wrote a brief, somewhat reticent memoir of the case that had so occupied his young manhood.

The arrest of Sacco and Vanzetti cast an ominous shadow over Il Gruppo Autonomo. As Gambera noted:

> On the news of the arrest of Sacco and Vanzetti a special meeting of the members of the "Libertarian Club" in East Boston was held to discuss the arrest of the (2) two members of the Club, and how to help and defend them.
>
> After a discussion on the arrests and motive of said arrests, by an unanimously vote of all members, it was decided to nominate a committee to investigate. . . . The following members of the club were nominated and elected as follows:—

Prof. Felice Guadagni— Assistant editor of *La Gazzetta del Massachu-setts*, weekly paper.
Lucia Mancini— Relative of Nicola Sacco and friend of Bart Vanzetti.
Aldino Felicani— Linotyper and compositor of *La Notizia.* Dayly News Paper.
Giovanni G. Gambera— Collaborator and partly-owner of *Il Pungolo*, weekly Publication.
A collection from the present members was made to approximate two hundred dollars ($200.00) and the meeting was closed, after the unani-mous approoval to nominate Aldino Felicani as Treasurer of The Funds for "The Defence" of Sacco and Vanzetti.——
The four (4) nominated . . . decided immediately, that "Lucia Mancini" and "Aldino Felicani" should visit "Sacco," and "Guadagni" and "Gambera" should visit "Vanzetti,"—and inform them of the club meeting decision in regard to their legal defense, and fund raising for the expenses.[2]

Felicani would remain treasurer of the defense committee throughout its existence. He was then a militant, though when I came to know him in the fifties he told me he no longer believed in violence for political ends. He had left Italy in 1914 because of his antimilitarist activities as a journalist in Bologna. Arriving in the United States, he continued his career as printer, editor, and anar-chist, first in Cleveland, then in New York. In 1918 he came to Bos-ton. Vanzetti became his close friend, and shortly before Vanzetti's arrest the two of them were planning a new anarchist journal, *Cara Compagna.* Felicani's companion on that first visit to Sacco, Lucia Mancini, was a woman in her thirties, of striking appearance, with a hard, determined face. Initially she must have been looked at askance by the male comrades of the East Boston group—for Italians, even anarchists, tended to think that woman's place was in the home—but by the very force of her personality she had become one of the group's leading spirits. The first to be named, Guadagni, a graduate of the University of Naples, was proud of his education and, though an anarchist, relished his title of professor. Plump and volu-ble, he was almost as devoted to eating as he was to anarchism. Yet, in spite of his education, he subordinated himself to the self-educated ex-barber Gambera.

The four visitors found Sacco and Vanzetti very nervous, particu-larly Sacco. When the prisoners were told about the newly formed defense committee, they were "calmed and relieved."[3]

The East Boston anarchists were followers of Luigi Galleani. In the wake of mass immigration from Italy in the 1880s, anarchist groups had sprung up in cities across America. Theoretically anarchists recognized no leaders, merely guides and spokesmen, yet in practice anarchism produced its own preachers and prophets in such commanding figures as Merlino, Gori, and Malatesta, all of whom came from Italy to visit the United States. Francesco Merlino, who spoke Italian beautifully and English well, was the first to seek out his emigrant anarchist countrymen, arriving in America in 1892 and going on a speaking tour of the Italian communities. Three years later Pietro Gori, poet and playwright, spent a year in the United States traveling from city to city like an itinerant evangelist, accompanying himself on his mandolin as he sang revolutionary songs and preached the gospel of anarchism. Enrico Malatesta followed him, staying only a few months. But Galleani, who arrived in 1902, remained. Seven years earlier the Italian government had exiled him to the island of Pantelleria for his opposition to the Ethiopian war. Escaping to Egypt, he took his jailer's wife with him, by whom he later had five children. Not long after his arrival in the United States, he was arrested in the anarchist center of Paterson, New Jersey, and charged with inciting to riot. He fled to Canada. Then, under an alias, he slipped over the border to Barre, Vermont, another anarchist stronghold, where emigrant Carrara marble cutters had transplanted their politics as well as their skills to the Vermont granite quarries. In Barre he began his *Cronaca Sovversiva* (*Subversive Chronicle*), one of the most noted anarchist journals in the United States, particularly noted by the Department of Justice. Early in 1912 he moved to the shoe city of Lynn, Massachusetts, where he continued to publish his inflammatory paper until in 1918 it was finally suppressed by the government.*

Intense, learned, patriarchal, a magnetic speaker, he lectured at clubs and social studies groups, spoke at critical strike meetings. His lilting tenor voice captivated his audiences. He was first and last a revolutionary; for him there were to be no ameliorative gestures, no gradual process of reform. Rather there must be a cataclysmic last judgment of blood and fire. Only through revolution could the anarchist millennium be ushered in, that peaceable kingdom where the lion—by this time a grass-eating vegetarian—would lie down with the lamb. The anarchists' mission was not to send peace but a sword. Though they might die, theirs would be the liberating act of vio-

---

* For some years Boda worked on *Cronaca Sovversiva*, as did another anarchist of the East Boston group, Carlo Valdinoci.

lence. Echoing Tertullian, Galleani saw anarchism as "embodied in the martyrdom of its first heralds and sustained by the blood of its believers."[4] He spoke in almost mystical terms of Gaetano Bresci, chosen by lot from among the New Era anarchists of Paterson to go to Italy and assassinate King Umberto. François Ravachol, who had robbed and killed and bombed indiscriminately in Paris, he saw as an anarchist saint.

In their challenge to the social order, anarchists struck down kings, presidents, and beggars. Santa Ceserio killed President Sadi Carnot of France. Denjiro Kotoku tried to kill the mikado. Mateo Morral shot at King Alfonso of Spain. Luigi Luccheni stabbed the Empress Elizabeth of Austria through the heart as that harmless woman was strolling beside Lake Geneva. August Vaillant hurled a bomb into the French Chamber of Deputies. Attempts were made on the German kaiser, Bismarck, Czar Alexander, the shah of Persia. In 1892 Alexander Berkman, Emma Goldman's lover, wounded—though he failed to kill—the American arch-capitalist and steel magnate Henry Frick. Then in 1901 a half-mad half-anarchist, Leon Czolgosz, shot President McKinley during a reception at the Pan-American Exposition in Buffalo, New York. McKinley died eight days later. Such acts of terrorism—the propaganda of the deed as proclaimed by the Russian revolutionary Mikhail Bakunin—made anarchism a dreaded name.

It was a name particularly dreaded in the United States after Chicago's Haymarket Square Riot of 1886, when police attempted to break up an anarchist-sponsored protest meeting. The meeting was peaceable enough until the police—some 180 of them—arrived to disperse it. While their inspector and an anarchist speaker were engaged in an altercation, someone in the shadows threw a bomb that exploded among the police with a blinding flash. Seven policemen died then or in the riot that followed, with both sides exchanging revolver shots. More than fifty police were injured, and almost a dozen civilians killed.

In the wake of the bombing, seven well-known Chicago anarchists were arrested and tried for aiding and abetting the unknown bomber. They were found guilty and sentenced to death. Four were hanged, the others had their sentences commuted to life imprisonment. The four executed anarchists—later considered innocent even by conservative opinion—became martyrs of the cause, the date of their execution an anarchist holy day. But from that flash in Haymarket Square, anarchism—the image of a bearded madman with a smoking bomb in his hand—would remain an American bogey.

One of the first instructors in the use of explosives was the German Bakuninist Johann Most, who arrived in the United States in 1882. In his famous—or infamous, depending on how one regarded it—Pittsburgh anarchist manifesto of 1883, he called for the "destruction of the existing class rule by all means." As one practical means he published his *Science of Revolutionary Warfare*, a manual giving instructions on the use of dynamite and other explosives, the manufacture of bombs and fuses, and the use of poison. In 1906 Galleani offered an Italian version of Most's bomb manual, a forty-eight-page pamphlet, *La Salute è in Voi (Health Is Within You)*, "to eliminate the vulgar objection that subversives who continually preach individual and collective revolt to the oppressed, neglect to give them the means and weapons for it."[5] *La Salute è in Voi*, "an indispensable pamphlet for those comrades who love self-instruction," had been written by Galleani's friend Enore Mulinari, professor of chemistry at the Politecnico in Milan. Published in 1906, at twenty-five cents it was the most expensive pamphlet printed by *Cronaca Sovversiva*.

One bomb, the anarchist high priest Kropotkin proclaimed, made more propaganda than a thousand pamphlets. The year 1915 brought a spate of bombings to New York that included a number of churches. On the anniversary of the Haymarket executions a bomb went off in the Bronx courthouse. Then two young Italians of the Gruppo Gaetani Bresci were caught trying to plant explosives in St. Patrick's Cathedral. Galleani "deeply admired" such acts as portents, "ineffable, inexorable, like air and like destiny."[6]

The peasants and workers, the poor and the dispossessed, alienated from the land of their birth, had swarmed to America from Italy to find in the new world a life of similar rejection, of poverty and long hours and little hope. Scorned or disregarded by the native-born, locked in their slum enclaves, they remained apart. Anarchy offered many of them a cult's sustaining reassurance. Professor Paul Avrich, in his paper "Italian Anarchism in America," written for the 1979 Boston Public Library Conference, explained that

> the Italian anarchists were creating a kind of alternate society which differed sharply from the capitalist and statist society they deplored. They had their own clubs, their own beliefs, their own culture. . . . After ten or twelve hours in the factory or mine, they would come home, eat supper, then go to their anarchist club and begin to churn out their

pamphlets and newspapers on makeshift printing presses. . . . And in addition to newspapers and journals, a flood of books and pamphlets rolled off the presses, comprising an enormous alternative literature, the literature of anarchism.

Beyond their publishing ventures, the Italian anarchists engaged in a whole range of social activities. Life was hard for these working-class immigrants, but there were many moments of happiness and laughter. They had their orchestras and theater groups, their picnics and outings, their lectures and entertainments. Hardly a week went by that there was not some traditional social activity, but with a new radical twist. . . . Picnics were very important occasions, not merely to dance and drink wine and have fun, all of which was done, but also to collect money for the anarchist press. . . . New York and New Jersey anarchists made excursions up the Hudson in rented boats, and when they got up to Bear Mountain, or wherever they were going, they would have a picnic, and out would come the food and the mandolins, and then of course the collection.

Lectures were another frequent activity for the Italian anarchists, and especially the lectures of Galleani, whom they prized above all other speakers. The lectures were held in rented halls and in anarchist clubhouses—of the Gruppo Autonomo of East Boston, for example, or of the Gruppo Diritto all'Esistenza of Paterson or the Gruppo Gaetano Bresci of East Harlem, or perhaps of a Circolo di Studi Sociali, a "circle of social studies," hundreds of which existed throughout the country. How do we know about these groups? Look at any anarchist paper, and you will see them listed, with the weekly or monthly contributions of their members, 25 cents, fifty cents, a dollar, and it all added up. . . .

The Italian anarchists also had their dramatical societies, a particularly interesting aspect of the "counter-culture." . . . Amateur theater groups in the small towns and large cities put on hundreds of plays, some of them by Pietro Gori, such as *The First of May*. Another play that was frequently performed was called *The Martyrs of Chicago* and dealt with the Haymarket affair of the 1880's. . . .

Anarchist schools formed another part of their alternative culture, schools named after the Spanish educator and martyr Francisco Ferrer, who was shot in the trenches of Montjuich Fortress in October 1909. There were Italian and non-Italian Ferrer Schools in the United States, called Modern Schools, a name which suggests what they were aiming for—a school to match the modern, scientific age of the twentieth century, in contrast to the parochial schools, which the anarchists saw as drenched with the spirit of religious dogma and superstition, or the public schools, in which leaders and generals and presidents were glorified. . . .

Finally a word about celebrations, another example of how traditional modes of life were transmuted into radical occasions and expressions. Instead of celebrating Christmas or Easter or Thanksgiving, the three great holidays for the anarchists were the working-class day on May First, the anniversary of the Paris Commune on March 18th, and the anniversary of the Haymarket executions on November 11th. Every year, in every part of the country, hundreds of meetings were held to commemorate these occasions. In the same connection, one more point might be noted, namely baptisms. One reads of Emma Goldman, for example, making a coast-to-coast lecture in 1899 and stopping in Spring Valley, Illinois, among the Italian and French miners, who bring their babies to her so she can baptize them, not with the names of saints, but with the names of great rebels or of Zola's novel *Germinal,* which was so popular among the radicals of that period.[7]

There were, of course, anarchists and anarchists, of differing and sometimes contradictory views. Some, mostly of native stock, were in the older Godwin tradition: pacifists, with a distrust of all governments and a Rousseauistic confidence in liberated human nature. Thoreau might have considered himself that kind of anarchist. But the Italian anarchists for the most part divided into the Galleanisti and the anarcho-syndicalists. The Galleanisti were the fundamentalists, preaching violence, loathing all authority, with a quixotic vision of liberty and equality through destruction and chaos.

Though the Gruppo Autonomo anarchists remained theoretically Galleanisti, many were readers of Tresca's *Il Martello.* Indeed, the East Boston group was more a fellowship than an organization, without officers or dues-paying members. Doctrinaire differences were not as explicit as with the Marxists. Gambera and Felicani considered the unorthodox Tresca their close friend, turning to him for advice and help as a matter of course after the arrest of Sacco and Vanzetti.

Sacco had landed in East Boston in 1908 at the age of seventeen. Most immigrants arrived unkempt, in worn shoddy clothes. He, by contrast, looked almost dapper. A studio photograph taken at about this time shows him in a well-cut worsted suit, a colored handkerchief in his breast pocket. He is wearing a fashionably high collar, his low shoes glisten, and his hair is carefully parted in the middle. He would always be careful of his appearance. When he was arrested, he was wearing a derby, incongruous today, but at a time when workers still wore cloth caps, a mark of bourgeois respectability. During his trial he usually wore a bow tie, and his overcoat had a velvet collar.

He was born Ferdinando Sacco, one of seventeen children of a prosperous peasant family in Torremaggiore, a small town inland from the Adriatic spur of Italy's boot. At fourteen he left school to work in the fields. But he and his brother Sabino dreamed of America, the golden land. His father had a friend in Milford, Massachusetts, and when the two boys wrote him, he replied enthusiastically, urging them to come to the new world. After Sabino had finished his three years of compulsory military service, and before Ferdinando had answered his call-up, the brothers sailed for America.

Life in Milford, a life of odd jobs and casual subsistence, dissolved Sabino's fantasies of a golden America. At the end of the year he went back to Italy. His brother stayed on, living with an Italian family on Hayward Street and frequently visiting his cousin Nicola Sacco, with whom he had played as a boy and who had come to America before him. Freddie, they now called Ferdinando.

Milford, a wenlike town on the approaches to the hill country west of Boston, contained a number of shoe factories, their workers predominantly Italian immigrants. Oddly enough the town hall was the one structure to recall the old country to them. Constructed in the 1850s, yet somehow avoiding the Grant-Gothic revival, it had been built in a full-blown Renaissance style with pilasters and a frieze and a singularly imposing and ornate baroque bell tower topped by a gilded dome. Except for its wood, it could have been an Italian church. But to the newly arrived aliens the gray-granite bulk of the national guard armory, a fortress with round tower and machicolations then under construction almost opposite the town hall, echoed a more formidable assertion of authority.

Freddie Sacco's first job was as a waterboy and steamroller oiler for a road gang at $1.15 a day. After three months he was shifted to pick and shovel. Then for almost a year he knocked slag off pig iron at the Draper foundry in adjoining Hopedale. Three evenings a week he attended an English class—then compulsory for foreign workers—conducted by Mary DePasquale, a Milford elementary-school teacher who eked out her salary of $500 a year by giving night classes. The DePasquales were among the most respected and well-off families in Milford's Italian enclave, Mary's father, Antonio DePasquale, being the local undertaker. Most of the workers' houses were wedged together on mean streets, fronting the sidewalks with no intervening yard. But the DePasquales lived in a large square house on a large lot and possessed the only telephone in the Italian community, used freely by the others in any emergency. Mary, second-generation, bilingual, a graduate of Framingham State Teachers College, was looked on with awed respect by the Milford Italians. They formed the habit of turning to her in their problems and conflicts with local authorities. In her twenties, she became an informal social worker in spite of herself. Most of her other Italian pupils came to class in their work clothes, dirty and sweaty. Sacco always arrived washed and shaved and in a clean shirt.

Intent on being more than a pick wielder or a slag shoveler, Sacco in 1912 applied for a job at the Milford Shoe Company and was taken on as an apprentice in a three-month training course run by the plant superintendent, Michael Kelley. During that time he earned little or no money but by the end of the course he had made himself into a skilled edge trimmer. Soon he was earning $30 to $40 a week on piecework, high pay for that time and place.

Anarchist speakers like Galleani, Ettor, Giovanitti, and Tresca often came to lecture at Milford. It was at such meetings, before Sacco was out of his teens, that he became a born-again anarchist. This new faith he embraced with all a convert's zeal. He passed out pamphlets and leaflets and lecture announcements, he sent in his twenty-five-cent and fifty-cent contributions to *Cronaca Sovversiva* and *Il Proletario*, he collected money for "the propaganda." He lived his social life in the entertainments and picnics and dances that were a feature of the anarchist common cause. Sometimes he acted in plays. Religiously he attended the meetings of the Milford Circolo di Studi Sociali. From time to time his name appeared among the many in *Cronaca Sovversiva*'s "Picola Posta" ("Brief Notes") and on the back pages among the list of subscribers.

It was at a dance given for the benefit of a crippled accordion player that Sacco met Rosina Zambelli, a quietly pretty girl of sixteen with somewhat austere features and copper-red hair. She had just arrived in America from a convent school in Italy to stay with her parents. The two fell in love and eloped. Sacco was earning enough to support a wife. But the Zambellis were a pious family, and Rosina's father was furious that the daughter he had educated with such care should run off with a shoe worker, a radical, a *sovversivo*. "That man will end on the gallows!" he exploded in his bitterness— not so much a prophecy as a common Latin expression.

The Saccos' first home was in a small wooden tenement on Hayward Street. Rosina bent to her husband in her beliefs. Where she had been a Catholic, she was now an anarchist, accompanying him to meetings and entertainments. Together they acted in fundraising melodramas. Rosina became pregnant but the child died almost at birth. In 1913 their son Dante was born.

The Milford anarchists held a public meeting in August 1916 to aid the Mesabi Range Iron Workers of Minnesota in a strike that was led in part by Tresca. Since they had no permit, the police arrested three of the most conspicuous participants, among them Sacco. He was found guilty of disturbing the peace and sentenced to three months in jail, though the charge was dismissed by a superior court and he served no time at all. This was his only arrest until he was picked up by the Brockton police. That December his infant daughter Alba died. *Cronaca Sovversiva* noted in sympathy: "It was as if she did not value this wretched world of ours, dripping with blood and cowardice."

Sacco was a family man. Yet in spite of his affection for his wife and the fresh sorrow of his daughter's death, he remained foremost an anarchist. A few weeks after the United States declared war, Galleani gave the order: "Get out!" Sacco obeyed. At the end of May 1917, he left for Mexico with several dozen anarchist comrades, among them Mario Buda, who then took the name Mike Boda, and Carlo Valdinoci, now calling himself Pacco Carlucci. Sacco adopted his dead brother Nicola's name and his mother's maiden name of Mosmacotelli. It was on this hegira that he first met Vanzetti, who had grown a beard and called himself Bartolomeo Negrini, although his comrades in Mexico took to calling him Barbetta—Little Beard.

Vanzetti was three years older than Sacco, a northern Italian from a pious Catholic family. In his younger days he had defended his faith with his fists. Later, when his faith fell apart, he renewed it in anarchy. Itinerant, taking odd jobs as he went along, he moved aimlessly from place to place. Anarchism remained the fata morgana that drew him on beyond any thought of a fixed career. His reading was one-sided, mostly political, but for him books took the place of home and family. In his autobiographical pamphlet written in jail, *The Story of a Proletarian Life*, he recalled the scant free hours of his working years. "Ah, how many nights I sat over some volume by a flickering gas jet," he wrote, "far into the morning hours! Barely had I laid my head on my pillow when the whistle sounded and back I went to the factory or stone pits."[8]

In medieval times he might have been a wandering scholar,

trudging along the roads of Europe from one university to the other. Beyond his scholarly bent he was gifted, with the gift of words rather than of rational thought. Even his imperfectly acquired English broke through with astonishing force during the years of his imprisonment. I remember talking with Felicani about the power of Vanzetti's eloquence. "Yes," he said meditatively. "It was there. But where did it come from? Where did it come from?" And I recall the graceful movement of his shaping hands, as if he were describing a mystery.

As a child Vanzetti was one of the quiet ones who take to reading almost instinctively. He loved his studies "with a real passion," won the little prizes that his school offered, and might have ended as a teacher, or even a priest if he could have kept the faith. But when he was fourteen his practical-minded peasant father, having read that forty-two Turin lawyers had applied for a single job paying thirty-five lire a month, decided that education was a waste of time and apprenticed him to a pastry shop in Cuneo. There, as Vanzetti related in his autobiographical pamphlet, he worked for some twenty months in the kitchen from seven in the morning until ten at night. As soon as he could save enough money from his meager salary he moved on to Cavour, where for almost three years he worked in a bakery. Then he drifted from city to city as cook, baker's helper, dishwasher, caramel maker, always the rootless outsider, alien even in his own land. Finally, in 1907, he fell ill of pleurisy and his father brought him back to his native Villafalletto. With a curious choice of words for a professed atheist, he recalled:

> And so I returned after six years spent in the fetid atmosphere of bakeries and restaurant kitchens, with rarely a breath of God's air or a glimpse of His glorious world. Six years that might have been beautiful to a boy avid of learning and thirsty for a refreshing draught of the simple country life of his native village.[9]

Nursed by his mother, he spent one of the happiest periods of his life convalescing in those rural surroundings. Then his mother developed cancer and within three months she was dead. During her last weeks he nursed her, and she died in his arms. Her death left a void for him that no other woman would ever fill. Part of himself, so he wrote, was buried in her grave. From the emptiness of his old world he turned to the new. After wandering across France, he sailed from Le Havre to New York in the steerage of one of the great liners.

He came to that most impersonal of cities in a depression year, a stranger, jobless, with no knowledge of the language. "Where was I to go? What was I to do?" he wrote in his autobiographical pages. "There was the promised land. The elevated rattled by and did not answer. The automobiles and the trolleys sped by, heedless of me."[10]

Through fellow Italians he found a succession of jobs as dishwasher in fashionable restaurants. Seven days a week he worked, twelve hours one day, fourteen the next, for five or six dollars a week. The sculleries were usually windowless, and in their dampness and overwhelming heat steam rose like a cloud. Drops of water dripped from the grimed ceilings onto his head, his shoes grew sodden from the water of the overflowing sinks. Garbage littered the floors of the scullery and the kitchen beyond, where white-capped chefs bellowed at the waiters as they came and went through the swinging doors, the waiters showing their contempt for the wealthy diners by a ritual spitting in the soup.

After a year of such drudgery, Vanzetti quit. For some months he looked vainly for other work. Finally, with the last of his savings, he bought a boat ticket to Hartford, Connecticut. From Hartford he made his way across the southern New England countryside, knocking at doors to ask for work, sleeping in haylofts or abandoned sheds, passing from town to town, village to village, in all weathers, a scarecrow vagabond moving along the empty roads. He tried his hand at ditchdigging, farming, carpet beating, working with a road gang, ice cutting, whatever was offered him. In Springfield, Massachusetts, he worked briefly in the United States Arsenal, then found a job among Italians in a brick factory, but in a few months his restless spirit took him on to the stone pits of Meriden, Connecticut. When these proved too arduous he went back to New York and a brief job as an assistant pastry chef. Discharged soon afterward, jobless, homeless, he sometimes even slept in doorways. Abandoning New York for good, he went on the road again in New England. His next stay was in a barrack settlement of railroad workers near Springfield, Massachusetts. Then once more he drifted, taking jobs in factories here and there, working on a reservoir in Worcester, moving east across the state. In 1914 he reached Plymouth. Having some skill as a gardener, he worked at that for a while before joining a loading gang at the Plymouth Cordage Company, the largest rope yard in the world.

In Plymouth he boarded with an anarchist acquaintance, Vincenzo Brini. For four years he lived with the Brinis and their children—the closest he had come to finding a family since he left Villa-falletto. He was quiet, studious, kind to the children. Women played little role in his life. His fugitive sexual needs he satisfied on an occasional trip to Boston.

The Brini house was a stopover for passing anarchist leaders. Galleani, Tresca, Giovanitti came there, as did Malatesta himself on his visit to the United States. Whenever the anarchists gathered round the Brinis' kitchen table there would be evenings of turbulent talk until the early hours. The Brinis' son Beltrando recalled in later years how, lying in bed, he used to hear the echoing disputatious voices, the shouts and the laughter.[11]

Vanzetti's job at Cordage did not last long, and he resumed his odd-job routine. In 1916, the predominantly Italian Cordage workers went out on strike. Galleani, always with an eye for industrial conflict that might be fanned to insurrection, came on to agitate among the workers. Partisans later claimed that Vanzetti was one of the strike leaders. He was not. By 1916 he no longer worked for Cordage, though he did take charge of some of the money collected to help the strikers. He also wrote reports of the strike's progress under the name of Nespola for *Cronaca Sovversiva*. To the disgust of the anarchists, the Cordage workers rejected their strident militancy and after a month accepted a settlement with the owners. Vanzetti continued with his odd jobs and his anarchist activities of distributing leaflets, raising small amounts of money, and visiting the East Boston comrades of Il Gruppo Autonomo. There is one paradoxical and unexplained event in those scantily recorded years. On May 5, 1917, Vanzetti, the opponent of all government, took out his first papers for American citizenship.

Nineteen-seventeen, marking the entry of the United States into the war, was a year of both hope and discouragement for anarchists in America. Out of the turbulence of the March days in Petrograd, trickles of news, vibrant, distorted, reached overseas. Strikes spread in the Russian capital, mobs stormed the streets, workers and soldiers—even the whip-wielding Cossacks—for the first time fraternized. Then in mid-March the autocrat of autocrats, Nicholas II, abdicated. For radicals of all sorts the Russian conflagration glowed like a star in the East, leading to the revolution of their dreams.

In the light of these events in Petrograd, under this guiding star, Galleani had given the word, and the Gruppo Autonomo comrades fled to Mexico. At their trial Sacco and Vanzetti said that they had left the United States to avoid the draft.* Their real reason they dared not admit in court. That would not be revealed until 1953. In that year a book was published in Cesena, Italy, *Thirty Years of Anarchist Activity,* compiled by anarchists, some of whom had been comrades-in-exile of Sacco and Vanzetti. There, for the first time, the actual reasons for the Mexican flight are set down. Revolution in Russia, as the Gruppo Autonomo anarchists saw it, would soon be followed by revolution in Italy. Like the exiled Russians, they wanted to return to their native land, which, demoralized by years of corrupt government, by the war and the Italian defeat at Caporetto, seemed ripe for revolution. According to *Thirty Years,*

> several score Italian anarchists left the United States for Mexico. Some have suggested they did so out of cowardice. Nothing could be more false. The idea to go to Mexico arose in the minds of several comrades who were alarmed by the idea that, remaining in the United States, they would be forcibly restrained from leaving for Europe, where the revolution that had burst out in Russia that February promised to spread all over the continent.[12]

Leaving Massachusetts surreptitiously, Sacco and Vanzetti and their comrades made their way to Monterrey, that city in the foothills of Mexico's Sierra Madre Orientala. There, living in primitive adobe huts on the outskirts, among the rolling hills of the citrus country, they formed a cooperative society. It did not help them much. They lived in Mexico at a harsher subsistence level than they had known, a poverty even beyond that of Sicily. Sacco worked in a bakery, often taking his pay in loaves of bread that he brought back to the others. Week after week they waited in transit for the great revolutionary event overseas. But the war continued, and no revolution in Italy took place. Their small savings melted away even as their friends in America wrote telling of high wages in the wartime boom and how easy it was to avoid the draft. One by one the comrades began to slip back to the United States. Only a few kept to their original intentions. Sacco, missing his wife and child, was one of the first to return, though he was wary of going to Milford. Still under the name of Mosmacotelli, he lived for a time in the obscurity of a Cambridge slum while working for the New England Confectionery

---

* Aliens were not required to register for the draft and some of the East Boston anarchists must have been aware of this. Vanzetti, having taken out first papers, was, however, liable.

Company, making Necco Wafers. This he followed with a series of poorly paid jobs in Boston, East Boston, and as far north as Haverhill. His one better-paying job, in a Brockton shoe factory, he quit rather than buy a Liberty Bond. In October 1917 he got an unskilled job at Rice & Hutchins in South Braintree but gave it up after some months because it paid him only $13 a week.

Through acquaintances in Milford he learned that Michael Kelley, the factory superintendent who had taught him edge trimming, had started a small shoe factory just outside Stoughton on the Brockton Road, naming it the Three-K factory after himself and his sons George and Leon. In November 1918, a few days before the armistice, Sacco appeared at the Three-K factory to ask for a job. He had now resumed his original surname but kept the Nicola. At first Kelley could not remember him. Then he recalled the deft young Italian he had trained six years earlier, and he called in his son George. "If you want a good edge trimmer," he told George, "here's your man."

From then on Sacco worked as a piece hand at the Three-K factory, earning sometimes as much as $70 or $80 a week. Until he quit his job at the end of April 1920, he averaged $61 weekly; rarely did he earn less than $50. Michael Kelley owned a bungalow beside the factory, just beyond his own house. This he now rented to Sacco, who, living so close, was able to earn extra money as a part-time night watchman. In the spring Sacco planted a vegetable garden in an empty lot. His relations with the Kelley family were friendly, though Michael Kelley occasionally grew uneasy at his radical views.

Vanzetti shaved off his beard and left Mexico some weeks after Sacco. Again he drifted, with no particular goal, wandering from St. Louis, to Youngstown, Ohio, to Farrell, Pennsylvania, never staying more than a few weeks in any place. In the summer of 1918 he arrived back in Plymouth, and the Brinis found him a room on Cherry Street. For a year he worked at any odd jobs that came his way. Then, the following summer, he bought a pushcart and began to peddle fish in North Plymouth's Italian section. When he could get enough fish he was able to sell up to two hundred pounds a day, but sometimes the trawlers came back empty to Plymouth harbor. Then he would go to Boston to buy his fish, and when he did he would drop in on Felicani or take the one-cent ferry across the harbor to East Boston.

Through that first postwar year Sacco and Vanzetti went their routine ways, Sacco edging shoes, Vanzetti peddling fish. But in their meetings with the East Boston group they sensed the imminence of events in which anarchists were preparing to take their part. "Follow Russia's lead!" Emma Goldman exhorted a New York anticonscription rally in 1918. To radical militants, stirred by the Russian example, revolution seemed just round the corner. For if a few thousand Bolsheviks could seize power in such a vast country, revolution elsewhere could be much closer than anyone had dared hope. Before the momentous fact of the October Revolution, doctrinal differences blurred. Anarchists and Marxists drew together in that common cause. With Germany, Austria, Hungary, Italy, Bulgaria teetering on the edge of revolution, why should not the United States be next?

For America, 1919 was a year of turbulence and violence, of radical challenge and savage reaction. Never in one year had there been so many strikes—the great steel strike, the Seattle general strike, the packing-house strike, the coal strike, more workers involved in strikes than there would be in the next six years. Climax of that strike-riven year was the Boston police strike of September, when for two days the city was abandoned to the mob. Before the state guard finally took control, eight persons were dead, twenty-one wounded, thirty injured, and a third of a million dollars' worth of property destroyed or stolen.

To the eyes of nervous Americans, Boston loomed as a potential Petrograd. The *Wall Street Journal* predicted "Lenin and Trotsky on their way." Conservatives like United States Senator Henry Cabot Lodge feared the strike as the first step toward sovietizing the country. Radicals like the young Italian-born Louis Fraina saw in it the shimmering mirage of revolution. Fraina, who had been one of those instrumental in forming the nascent United States Communist party from the Socialist left wing, anticipated that the Boston crisis might create the decisive revolutionary situation the left wing had been waiting for ever since the October Revolution.* He saw himself as an American Lenin.[13]

Following the passage of the 1918 Immigration Law, the Department of Justice's Bureau of Investigation moved against aliens of the revolutionary left. The bureau, loosely organized by President Theodore Roosevelt's attorney general in 1908 and staffed with hangers-

---

* A left-wing manifesto called for the overthrow of capitalism, and the establishment of socialism through a proletarian dictatorship. After the break with the "Slowcialist" moderates, the left split into the English-speaking Communist Labor party and the Communist party made up of the semi-autonomous foreign-language groups.

on and friends of politicians, was far from the monolithic structure it would become as the Federal Bureau of Investigation. Its application of the new law was haphazard and capricious. Galleani, as the most conspicuous anarchist in America, was held for deportation. Tresca, editing his anarchist paper in New York, was not. Some of those seized were detained at immigration stations. Others, like Coacci, were brought into court and then released on bail. Boda and Orciani were not disturbed, nor were Gambera, Felicani, or Valdinoci. The Justice Department did have lists containing the names of several thousand subscribers to *Cronaca Sovversiva*, among them Sacco and Vanzetti, but the lists themselves remained buried in the inactive files, and in the bureaucratic reshufflings at the war's end many of these files became dispersed or lost. Even if the lists could have been consulted, it is scarcely likely that anyone would have connected Milford's Ferdinando Sacco—a common enough surname—with Nicola Sacco of Stoughton.* Yet fear hovered over the alien anarchists. Under this shadow the militants reacted with their own challenge. Since Most's day their response had been *La Salute è in Voi*.

Early in 1919, throughout the mill cities of New England, anarchist posters, appearing mysteriously overnight on walls, threatened:

GO AHEAD

The senile fossils ruling the United States see red! ... The storm is within and very soon will leap and crash and annihilate you in blood and fire. You have shown no pity on us! We will do likewise. *We will dynamite you!*

The threat was soon made good from coast to coast. On the first of March three Italian anarchists and an IWW organizer from Milford died when a bomb they were intending to plant at the American Woolen Company in Palmer, Massachusetts, went off prematurely.[14] At the end of April a small brown package was delivered to Seattle's mayor, Ole Hanson, who had put down that city's general strike. The package leaked an acid fluid, and an examination showed it to be a bomb. A similar package sent to former Georgia senator Thomas Hardwick exploded as his maid opened it and blew off both her hands. Hardwick's wife, standing nearby, was burned about the head and face. Thirty-six bomb packages, labeled *Sample-Novelty*, were

---

* In February 1920, a federal agent investigating radical activities did question George Kelley about Sacco, but nothing more came of this.

discovered in the mail addressed among others to the Ellis Island commissioner of immigration; the commissioner general of immigration; the chairman of the Senate Bolshevik Investigating Committee; Postmaster General Albert Burleson, who had earlier banned radical literature from the mails; Judge K. M. Landis, who under the provisions of the 1917 Espionage Act had sentenced Big Bill Haywood to twenty years in prison; the antilabor senator, William King; Attorney General A. Mitchell Palmer; Secretary of Labor William Wilson; Supreme Court Justice Oliver Wendell Holmes; John D. Rockefeller; and J. P. Morgan.

In mid-May Galleani was taken into custody.* Anarchists responded with a wave of bombings. On the night of June 2, explosions shook eight cities. A Pittsburgh judge who had presided over one of Tresca's trials had his house bombed, as did the chief inspector of the Bureau of Immigration. In New York a bomb killed a watchman on the steps of a federal judge's house. Bombs went off in Cleveland and Paterson, and in Philadelphia the rectory of Our Lady of Victory Church was demolished. Chief target of the bombers was Attorney General Palmer. Just as he was going to bed a terrific explosion blew off the front of his town house. Although he and his family were uninjured, the blast shattered windows on all sides, including those of the house directly across the street belonging to Assistant Secretary of the Navy Franklin Delano Roosevelt. Apparently the bomber, carrying a suitcase full of dynamite, had stumbled as he ran up the steps and set off the detonator, blowing himself to pieces. Parts of his body were scattered over the neighborhood, his head on a nearby roof, and several bloody fragments on the Roosevelt doorstep. According to Aram Bakshian, two small boys picked up a foot and the shoe containing it, which they carried home and kept in the refrigerator for several days until their mother discovered it.[15] Police combing through the debris found the remains of a cheap suitcase, two pistols, a derby, a sandal and the heel of a shoe, shreds of a pinstripe suit and a polka-dot bow tie, a laundry tag, and a piece of overcoat collar. Several dozen printed pink flyers entitled *Plain Words* littered the sidewalk and street. They read:

> The powers that be make no secret of their will to stop, here in America, the world-wide spread of revolution. . . .
> A time has come when the social question's solution can be delayed

* Galleani was deported to Genoa June 24, 1919, on the *Duca deghli Abruzzi*.

no longer; the class war is on and cannot cease but with a complete victory for the international proletariat. . . .

Do not say we are acting cowardly because we keep in hiding, do
not say it is abominable; it is war, class war, and you were the first to
wage it under cover of the powerful institutions you call order, in the
darkness of your laws, behind the guns of your boneheaded slaves. . . .

There will have to be bloodshed; we will not dodge; there will have
to be murder; we will kill because it is necessary; there will have to be
destruction; we will destroy to rid the world of your tyrannical institutions. We are ready to do anything and everything to suppress the capitalist class. . . .

Long live social revolution! Down with tyranny!

The Anarchist Fighters[16]

In the Roxbury section of Boston a bomb made of iron pipe
stuffed with dynamite and metal scraps demolished the house of a
Roxbury municipal court judge, A. H. Hayden. As with the other
bombings of that night, copies of *Plain Words* were strewn about the
area. A few weeks before, Judge Hayden had sentenced fourteen
members of the Lettish Workmen's Association to six to eighteen
months in jail following a May Day riot in which they had clashed
with the police.* Farther out in suburban Newtonville a bomb tore
off the side of a house belonging to State Representative Leland
Powers, who had sponsored an anti-anarchist bill in the Massachusetts legislature.

The *Plain Words* flyers, identical in color, paper, and printing,
obviously had a common source. There were no clues as to the source
of the explosives. Some of the bombs may well have been made in
Boston, for the East Boston anarchists had their own store of dynamite, though no one outside their circle was then aware of this and
the knowledge would not leak out until after Sacco and Vanzetti
were dead.

Shaken by his narrow escape, Attorney General Palmer saw "the
sharp tongues of the Revolution's head licking the altars of the
churches, leaping into the belfry of the school bell, crawling into the
sacred corners of American homes and seeking to replace marriage
vows with libertine laws."[17] Preparing a frontal assault on "foreign-
born subversives and agitators," he appointed William J. Flynn, for-

---

* The left-wing Letts had been denied a parade permit. Shouting "To hell with the police!" and led by Fraina, they had marched behind their red flag to confront the police. In
the swirling brawl that followed, a number of police and paraders were injured and a police
captain died of a heart attack.

mer head of the Secret Service and one of the country's most noted detectives, head of the expanded Bureau of Investigation, with all the government's crime-hunting agencies at his disposal.

Palmer was particularly concerned with identifying the man obliterated in the bombing of his house. But Flynn's agents had little more to go on than the bits and scraps of clothing picked up in the bomb debris. After some weeks of ferreting out leads they were able to trace the polka-dot tie to a New York manufacturer. Only a dozen ties of this pattern had been made, and three had gone to a small retailer who told agents he had sold just one. Other agents located the cobbler who had repaired the heel and an East Side tailor who recalled making an overcoat of material similar to the scrap found at the bombing site. All three remembered their customer. The composite picture that emerged from their descriptions and from subsidiary identifications was of Carlo Valdinoci, who had left Paterson for Washington the week before the bombings.* But beyond the dead Valdinoci there were no further clues.

On the strength of *Plain Words* Flynn took it for granted that anarchists had done the bombings. But the origin of the pink flyers remained hidden. The most that could be said was that the final *s* of *Plain Words* did not match the typeface of the other nine letters. Then in February 1920, Flynn received a tip from an informer, an ostensible direct-action anarchist who had once sold subscriptions to Malatesta's *Umanita Nuova* to, among others, Sacco, Vanzetti, Boda, and Orciani. He told Flynn that Roberto Elia, a printer at Canzani's printing shop in Brooklyn, had printed *Plain Words*.

Agents dispatched to the printing shop uncovered a stock of pink paper like that used for the flyers. Then, on going through the fonts, they came across the same deviant *s*. Elia and Canzani's typesetter, Andrea Salsedo, at first denied that they had had anything to do with the flyer or had even known of its existence. The color of the paper, they explained, was just a coincidence. But after being shown the distinctive *s* and threatened with a charge of murder, they broke down. Salsedo admitted that he had set the type for *Plain Words*, Elia that he had run off about seven hundred copies. Carlo Recchi, whom they named as one of the bombers, had furnished the manuscript and supervised the printing.†

Salsedo had come to the United States in 1902. In 1916 he went

---

* After Sacco's arrest, Valdinoci's sister Susie lived for a time with Rosina Sacco.
† Recchi escaped to Italy, as did several others named by Salsedo and Elia.

to Lynn, Massachusetts, to set type for *Cronaca Sovversiva.* Elia had arrived in New York in 1906. For a number of years he worked for an anarchist paper in Paterson, and at one time was associated with Galleani. Once the two anarchists had confessed, it was as if their inner resistance collapsed. They talked compulsively. Salsedo named the red Galleani group in Massachusetts as having been responsible for the 1919 bombings. In exchange for immunity and the promise of a free trip to Italy, both agreed to aid the government if they could be protected against their former comrades. With their own consent they were lodged on the fourteenth floor of the Department of Justice at 21 Park Row in Manhattan, where an office had been made over for them into a bedroom with twin beds. In no way were they restrained and twice a day they were allowed to see their lawyer, Narciso Donato. Donato told them that if he got them released they would be arrested under the New York State Anarchy Law, and advised them to remain where they were, with the understanding that "their whereabouts should remain unknown to all except their families, their attorney, and certain of their friends, and, further, that neither should be subject to interrogation or examination without the presence of their attorney."[18]

At first the two were interrogated at some length. Director Flynn came from Washington twice to talk with them. Elia, in a self-serving affidavit that he signed just before leaving America, admitted that he and Salsedo had been well treated and that after the first weeks of interrogation they were not questioned further. They had good meals. They were taken out for walks. They were even taken to the movies. But as winter gave way to spring, Salsedo became increasingly depressed. Whether conscience-stricken at having betrayed his comrades or fearful of anarchist vengeance, he could not sleep. "He would lie groaning and lamenting all the night," Elia wrote. "He complained continually of pains in his stomach and head. He was always nervous. He refused absolutely to eat. He showed clear signs of an unbalanced mind. . . ."[19] Early on the morning of May 2, while Elia still slept, Salsedo threw himself out of the window to his death.

For all the Justice Department's assurance of secrecy, word of Salsedo's and Elia's detention was soon out among the anarchists, and it was known more ominously that they had broken down and talked. How much had they told? How many secrets had they revealed? Who might be in peril because of them? These were questions anarchists asked each other.

In Boston, on Sunday, April 18, some twenty of the Gruppo Autonomo—among them Sacco, Vanzetti, Orciani, Boda, Felicani, and Gambera—met to discuss what should be done in the matter of Salsedo and Elia. Just what took place at that meeting has never been revealed. But there was much to be worried about. There was the dynamite. Obviously the group had been involved in the bombings at Judge Hayden's and Representative Powers'. There was Valdinoci's connection with the group. And there were the pink flyers brought to Boston from Canzani's print shop. The members voted to send Vanzetti to New York to see what he could find out.

Four days later he took the night boat. He stayed in New York for two days but could not learn very much. First he saw Tresca, who had no direct information. The details of Elia's and Salsedo's arrest he learned from Galleani's friend Luigi Quintiliano of the Italian Workers' Defense Committee. But as to what the two men in the Park Row bedroom had said and how long they would be held, he learned nothing.

Returning on May 1, Vanzetti told the East Boston group about his visit. Quintiliano had warned them to eliminate the evidence of "radical literature," and all agreed to follow his advice. As Robert D'Attilio explains in his illuminating article, "The Anarchist Dimension," radical literature "may have been an euphemism for *La Salute è in Voi* or explosives made under its guidance."[20]

Sacco and Vanzetti were not, as has been claimed by their liberal supporters, philosophical anarchists. They were militants of the Galleani school. David Wieck, professor of philosophy at Rensselaer Polytechnic Institute, himself an anarchist, made this clear at the 1979 conference in Boston, telling his audience bluntly that

> Sacco and Vanzetti were revolutionary anarchists: without this fact in the forefront the picture cannot be clear. . . . There has been much falsification of the history of Sacco and Vanzetti, for a variety of political and ideological reasons.[21]

"These men were genuine militant revolutionaries," Pernicone admitted at the same conference. "These were men who believed that, in order to transform society, to realize liberty and justice, capitalist society, as it existed in their time, had to be overthrown and overthrown violently."[22]

Though neither Sacco nor Vanzetti was more than a radical republican when they arrived in the United States in 1908, within a few months of each other, like many Italian immigrants they were drawn to anarchism. Listening to the eloquent and persuasive lay preachers like the charismatic Galleani, reading *Cronaca Sovversiva,* Giovanitti's *Il Proletario,* and anarchist pamphlets passed from hand to hand in mills and factories, they yielded their emotional consent with all the self-assertive allegiance of converts for whom truth does not exist beyond the boundaries of their faith. "Anarchism was the passion, the great idea of Sacco and Vanzetti," Professor Avrich wrote. "It was their obsession, their love, their chief interest on a day-to-day basis."[23]

From Charlestown State Prison, Vanzetti wrote three years after his arrest:

Oh friend, the anarchism is as beauty as a woman for me, perhaps even more, since it include all the rest and me and her. Calm, serene, honest, natural, vivil, muddy and celestial at once, austere, heroic, fearless, fatal, generous and implacable—all these and more—it is.[24]

In Sacco and Vanzetti a flame of paranoia flickered beneath the surface. Within their anarchist cult was the communion of belief. Outside were enemies, capable of any infamy. Who was not for them was against them. Shortly before his execution Vanzetti wrote "The Testament of Those about to Die," signed both by him and Sacco. It concluded: "Remember La Salute è in Voi!"[25]

8

The Road to Dedham

The day after their arrest Sacco and Vanzetti were taken to the Brockton police court and charged with carrying concealed weapons. Advised by a local lawyer, William Callahan, hastily appointed to represent them, they pleaded guilty. In a turmoil of indecision the members of the defense committee turned to a fixture of the Plymouth Italian community, Doviglio Govoni, a court interpreter. Like Angelina De Falco, Govoni drummed up legal business on the side. Following his advice the committee engaged two local lawyers, John Vahey for Vanzetti and James Graham for Sacco. Vahey, a former district judge, had considerable experience in criminal and labor cases and was something of a political power in the county.

Since Bridgewater is in Plymouth County, Vanzetti went on trial before Judge Webster Thayer in the Plymouth court on June 22, 1920, accused of being the shotgun-wielding bandit in the failed Bridgewater holdup. Graham assisted Vahey in the defense. The trial, lasting a week, aroused little interest. Boston papers gave it a few lines in their back pages, and even the Plymouth weekly *Old Colony Memorial* mentioned it only perfunctorily.

Vanzetti's trial dealt chiefly with identification. Both sides agreed to exclude any mention of his political views. Five witnesses testified to his having been the man with the shotgun, and Vahey was unable to shake them, although there was a certain ambivalence in their recollections of the length of the gunman's mustache. In rebuttal the defense produced twenty-one witnesses to testify to Vanzetti's presence in Plymouth on December 24. Eleven witnesses said he had sold them eels on that day. Admittedly Vanzetti had sold eels—a traditional Christmas Eve dish among Italians—but this might well have been on the twenty-second or twenty-third since it was customary for Italians to salt their eels a day or two in advance. Most of these witnesses, Vanzetti's friends and neighbors, had to speak through an interpreter, and District Attorney Katzmann was able to undermine their credibility by demonstrating how uncertain they were about dates other than December 24.

"This cross-examination taken alone," Professor Morgan wrote a quarter of a century later, "tends strongly to show that a group of Italians had framed an alibi for Vanzetti."[1] Chief defense witness was the thirteen-year-old Beltrando Brini, who told how he had gone the rounds with Vanzetti on the morning of the twenty-fourth to help deliver eels. But under the district attorney's questioning, the boy admitted he had rehearsed his story six or seven times with his parents and with Vahey.

In a forceful summing-up, Vahey did his best to dispute the reliability of the prosecution's witnesses. Vanzetti declined to take the stand in his own defense, although his refusal left many questions unanswered. Why had he lied on the night of his arrest? Why was he armed? Why were those four shotgun shells—similar to the shell picked up in Bridgewater—in his pocket?* Why was he unwilling to explain what he had been doing on December 24? Vahey and Graham conferred with him at length on whether he should testify. To keep silent and let the jurors decide between the eyewitnesses and the alibi witnesses, Vahey warned him, would make him suspect in their eyes, however the judge might instruct them.

In 1958, replying to a letter from Montgomery, Graham wrote:

> There were only three people who ever knew whether Vanzetti's failure to take the stand in the Bridgewater trial was on the advice of counsel or his own decision. They were Mr. Vanzetti, Mr. John P. Vahey and myself. We spent considerable time with him at the Plymouth County Jail as the case was drawing to a close when it had to be decided whether he would take the stand or not. . . . He was carefully and thoroughly advised as to the evidence that had gone in as to what inference the jury might draw if he failed to take the stand despite what the judge might tell them in his charge. . . . Toward the very end of the discussion Mr. Vahey said to Vanzetti, in substance, "I can advise you as to what the District Attorney may inquire about and the effect of your

---

* Three of the shotgun shells in Vanzetti's pocket were Peters, the fourth a Winchester. The spent shotgun shell picked up in the Bridgewater gutter was a Winchester.

failure to take the stand, but you are the one who has to make the decision as to whether you will testify or not."[2]

After further discussion Vanzetti said, "I don't think I can improve on the alibi which has been established. I had better not take the stand."

In his charge, Judge Thayer advised the jury:

> You must stand between the parties . . . with fairness, with impartiality, and say what is the fact and what is the truth. Because the witnesses are Italians no inference should be drawn against them. People are supposed to be honest, to be truthful, to be innocent.[3]

Both Katzmann and Vahey expressed themselves content with the judge's remarks. After five hours of deliberation the jury returned with a verdict of guilty. Even Morgan considered the Plymouth trial fair. "This evidence by eyewitnesses, standing alone," he wrote, "was quite as satisfactory as is usual in cases of this sort, and was sufficient of itself to justify a verdict of guilty."[4] A recent book on Sacco and Vanzetti, a sophisticated plea for their innocence, admits that "Judge Thayer's conduct of the trial would strike almost any reader of the transcript as perfectly fair, and even Vanzetti, writing immediately after the trial, did not object to it."[5]

Six years after the trial, Vanzetti, the once obscure radical, had emerged as an international figure, accepting himself in his dilemma as a martyr to the bright cause of anarchy. In two short articles that he then wrote in the Charlestown prison, he described the Plymouth trial as a "legal lynching" by judge and prosecutor. The state witnesses were rabble, perjurers, and a Bridgewater newsboy who identified him "a mental defective whose lack of shame and consciousness proved him to be feeble minded." Vahey, he claimed, had betrayed him, and over $70,000 had been spent to purchase his conviction.[6]

In Morgan's measured opinion, Vanzetti's statements both of the Plymouth and Dedham trials were not sustained by the printed word. "He [Vanzetti] attributes low motives to witnesses against him and virtue to all who favored him. His readiness to ascribe corruption to all who did not support him seriously impairs the value of all his assertions about the Plymouth trial."[7]

Early in 1961 David Felix interviewed Arthur Nickerson, the last surviving Plymouth juror. Nickerson and his fellow jurors had been chiefly concerned with the matter of identification. The radical issue was never mentioned. "I didn't know anything about all that until

afterward," he told Felix. "To me it was a trial about a holdup. . . .
All of us looked on the man there as a poor devil. It didn't make any
difference what he was. The thing was—what did he do? If there was
anything else I would have hollered."[8]

Even when I had come to accept Sacco's guilt, I remained convinced that Vanzetti was innocent, though I considered his Plymouth
trial fair.* The witnesses who believed they had seen him on that
snowy morning wielding a shotgun must have seen someone who—
unfortunately for Vanzetti—looked like him. I could not go along
with revisionists like Montgomery and Felix who held that Vanzetti
was guilty. He did, nevertheless, know who the guilty were, and
so—however innocent—must be considered an accessory after the
fact. Ultimate proof of this is in a memoir of Gambera's. When he
and Guadagni visited Vanzetti the day after his arrest,

Vanzetti told us as follows:—

"BELIEVE ME," I was not a part "or had any knowledge of the "So.
BRAINTREE robbery and murders," and not "much knowledge" of the
Bridgewater attempt of Hold Up."[9]

When I showed Gambera's memoir to Phil McNiff, he remarked
that "not much knowledge" might just as well have been "knew
everything." "Yes," I said. "Whether he knew a little or a lot, he
knew." Once, while I was still on good terms with Felicani, I asked
him: "Do you suppose, under certain circumstances, Sacco or Vanzetti could have killed?" "Sacco could," he said, "but Vanzetti could
not." Then, as if he had given something away, he added quickly,
"But of course Sacco never did."

The Plymouth verdict left the East Boston anarchists stunned,
uncertain in the face of the coming Dedham trial. To them Sacco
and Vanzetti were merely comrades in trouble. But for Moore they
were symbols. Even before his arrival he sensed that their case would
be his great case, the culmination of his career. Indeed, it was to be
his creation and his triumph—and in the end his defeat.

Where Vahey, at the Plymouth trial, had carefully avoided any
mention of radicalism, Moore planned to make radicalism the touch-
stone of Sacco's and Vanzetti's defense in Dedham. That their trial
would be unfair and the judge biased, he took for granted. This was

* In his preface to *The Legacy of Sacco and Vanzetti,* Morgan wrote: "Our system does
not guarantee either the conviction of the guilty or the acquittal of the innocent. Certain
safeguards are erected which make it much more difficult to convict the innocent than to
acquit the guilty, but all that our system guarantees is a fair trial."

class war, as he had seen it in the West with the IWW. When he sent out word that a frame-up was in the offing, he knew that his radical friends from coast to coast would respond.

Moore combined in his legal self the attributes of recruiter, publicity agent, promoter, and fund raiser. He said so himself. From a makeshift office in Boston's Olympian Building near Scollay Square, he sent out a constant stream of letters and appeals. Buoyantly confident, abounding in energy and enthusiasm, he vitalized the case, gathering round him a core of young assistants with a sense of mission. Next to the single window of that crowded room, interrupted by indeterminate comings and goings, a blonde Lithuanian stenographer, Wilhelmina Breed, pounded away at a secondhand typewriter. Though her charm was somewhat diminished by a cast in one eye, Moore, for all that he had only recently married, predictably fell in love with her. According to a friend, he was always engaging pretty secretaries, cooling off on the wife he had, and taking up with the secretary.[10]

Two young left-wing journalists, Art Shields and John Nicholas Beffel, sat in opposite corners behind the blonde secretary, chain-smoking and grinding out propaganda leaflets, too passionate in their belief to be overly troubled by facts. Shields's tendentious pamphlet, *Are They Doomed?*, was the first full-length presentation of the Sacco-Vanzetti case. Beffel's *New Republic* article, "Eels and the Electric Chair," was the first mention of Sacco and Vanzetti in a national publication, the first direct appeal to intellectuals. According to Beffel, Sacco and Vanzetti, after their arrest, had been taken from shoe city to city and placed on display for identification. Mob temper, he wrote, was high, and they were hooted and jeered. All this, though telling enough as propaganda, bore little relation to fact. Vanzetti's lawyers, Beffel wrote even more imaginatively, "would not let him take the stand [at Plymouth] in his own defense unless he would agree to conceal that he had radical beliefs about the economic conflict. He refused to make that pledge . . . and his attorneys kept him from testifying."[11]

Shields and Beffel were joined by Frank Lopez, a Spanish anarchist Moore had saved from deportation, who now took charge of propaganda for Spain, South America, Mexico, and Cuba, where the anarchist movement was strongest. At his workroom on nearby Battery Street, Felicani launched appeals to Italians and Italian-Americans.

Though as anarchists Sacco and Vanzetti neither sympathized

nor cooperated with the organized labor movement, Moore fashioned them into archetypical figures of the workingman. Vociferously he reiterated that Sacco and Vanzetti were victims of a conspiracy, that they would not and could not get a fair trial in the prejudiced atmosphere of Massachusetts. One of his former assistants, the twenty-two-year-old Eugene Lyons, stopped off at the Olympian office on his way to Italy, where he hoped to take part in a second October Revolution. In 1919 he had been working for Moore in Tulsa, Oklahoma, in the successful defense of the IWW organizer "Big Bill" Krieger on a trumped-up charge of dynamiting the house of a Standard Oil official.* On learning now that Lyons was headed overseas, Moore instructed him to hunt up certain witnesses and evidence and urged him to arouse all Italy to the significance of the Sacco-Vanzetti case.

In the strikes and tumult of that year, Italy was not to be aroused by an impending murder trial in provincial Massachusetts, but Lyons did manage to get a few articles into the Socialist paper *Avanti!*, which Mussolini had once edited, and to persuade the deputy representing Sacco's native village to bring up the Sacco-Vanzetti affair in the Chamber of Deputies, "the first jet of foreign protest in what was eventually to become a pounding international flood."[12]

Once Lyons returned from Italy, minus his revolution, he went to Boston to become publicity director of the Sacco-Vanzetti Defense Committee, supporting himself meanwhile by hack newspaper work for a local tabloid. "It was," he recalled, "a motley and colorful and rather high-pitched company that gathered around the defense at this stage. Some were moved by an undiluted urge to save the two men, others were interested solely in the propagandist value of the case, still others got an emotional kick out of the battle."[13]

During his Boston years Moore kept open house at 3 Rollins Place, a cul-de-sac on the less proper side of Beacon Hill. That small four-story brick building, with its side entrance and whimsical false front, became a rallying place for Sacco-Vanzetti adherents, prospective witnesses, wobbly roughnecks Moore had saved from jail, fiery Latin anarchists and impassioned free-thinkers, free-versifiers, emancipated young women, undefinable enthusiasts, doctrinaire liberals, restrained academics, and dogmatic revolutionaries. The shabby house echoed Greenwich Village, with nights of talk, sudden com-

---

* Krieger, in spite of his appellation a stocky man, with "dead-fish" eyes, later joined the Communist party and became Whittaker Chambers's party sponsor.

panionship, bootleg drinking, pairings and unpairings, casual love
and flaring affections. Edna St. Vincent Millay's candle burned
brightly at both ends there, her verses reflected in its light.*

> And if I loved you Wednesday,
> Well, what is that to you?
> I do not love you Thursday—
> So much is true.[14]

Felicani, a Puritan in his anarchism, referred to the house as "the
harem." A decade later Lyons remembered its tense bohemian quality, shadowed always by the impending fate of the two anarchists. "If
anyone could record that house," he wrote, "its people, its compli-
cated cross-currents of conflicting political philosophies, the erotic
overtones characteristic of nervous strain, what an incredible novel it
would make."[15]

Originally the trial had been scheduled for March 1921, but after
Moore requested more time for preparing his defense, it was postponed until May. In those months he was able to reach the Boston
beyond East Boston by interesting the New England Civil Liberties
Committee in the case, although its secretary, John Codman, was at
first hesitant, having recently served on a jury in Dedham where he
had been impressed by District Attorney Katzmann's "ability and
fairness." But Moore persisted and finally, in mid-February, Codman's committee issued a circular letter declaring that the evidence
against Sacco and Vanzetti was "unsubstantial," the real reason for
their prosecution being that they were "foreigners and are active and
influential radicals." Later Moore persuaded Codman to go so far as
to say that "there is something more than a possibility that Sacco and
Vanzetti will not be given a really fair and impartial trial." Through
the committee a number of women of dogmatic goodwill were enrolled, functioning in the reformist tradition of Henry James's *The
Bostonians* as genteel nonconformists within the Back Bay circle of
conformity. By means of these formidably assured ladies Moore was
able to reach out to the power centers of Boston, where many a State
Street lawyer or broker would find himself aiding the defense committee at the urgings of a maiden aunt or social-worker niece.

Bluebloods and bluestockings, many of these women had been fa-

---

* Edna St. Vincent Millay came to Boston to take part in the 1927 picketing of the State
House. Her "Justice Denied in Massachusetts" is the only enduring poem in the ragbag of
Sacco-Vanzetti versifications.

miliar callers at Julia Ward Howe's town house, Green Peace, and
had heard her recite "The Battle Hymn of the Republic" in her
reedy ancient voice. Mrs. Howe—dead only a decade—was their last
link with the shining days of abolitionism and its heroic female figures: Lucy Stone, the Grimké sisters, Lucretia Mott, Lydia Maria
Child. For them nothing had since measured up to that great purpose, not opposition to the war with Spain, not woman suffrage, not
pacifism, not progressivism, not the Anti-Vivisection League, not the
League of Nations. In the William Lloyd Garrison tradition, they
were in earnest, they would not equivocate, they would not retreat,
they would be heard. They lacked only a cause.

Then, with the arrest of Sacco and Vanzetti, the shining days appeared again. Months before the trial a phalanx of female supporters
formed: Alice Stone Blackwell, daughter of the pioneer women's
rights crusader Lucy Stone, and herself editor of *The Woman's Journal;* Jessica Henderson, head of the antivivisectionists and so ardent a
suffragette that she was once jailed during a parade in honor of President Wilson for picketing on Boston Common because the woman-
suffrage amendment had not yet been passed; a Harvard professor's
wife, Cerise Carmen Jack; Virginia MacMechan, a Bostonian from
rural Sharon; Louise Rantoul of the Federated Churches of Greater
Boston, a grand-niece of Harvard's President Lowell; Elizabeth
Glendower Evans of a score of committees. Herbert Ehrmann dedicated his *Case That Will Not Die* to an even dozen of "Those Gallant
Women Who Faithfully Tended the Flickering Flame of New
England Idealism from 1920 to 1927." Many more would be drawn
into the momentum of the case. When Katherine Anne Porter came
to Boston as a protester in August 1927, she noticed "those strangely
innocent women enlisted in their altar societies, their card clubs,
their literary round tables, their music circles, and their various
charities in the campaign to save Sacco and Vanzetti. On their
rounds they came now and then to the office of my [Communist]
outfit in their smart thin frocks, stylish hats, and their indefinable air
of eager sweetness and light, bringing money they had collected in
the endless wittily devious ways of women's organizations."[16] To the
tough-minded Communists they were known as "sob sisters."

During Miss Porter's week in Boston, Mrs. Henderson invited her
to lunch.

> I did not then know she was a vegetarian [Miss Porter wrote] and when
> she asked me what I would like, I asked for broiled lamb chops. She

shuddered a little, the pupils of her eyes dilated, and she gave me a little lecture on cruelty to animals, just the same.

"I could not eat any food that had the taint of suffering and death in it; imagine my dear! Eating blood?"

I retracted at once, in painful embarrassment, and ate a savory lunch of scrambled eggs and spinach with her, and things went on very nicely. Still, I could not avoid seeing her very handsome leather handbag, her suede shoes and belt, and a light summer fur of some species I was unable to identify lying across her shoulders. My mind would wander from our topic while, bewildered once more by the confusions in human feelings, above all my own, I gazed into the glass eyes of the small, unknown, peak-faced animal."[17]

In that Boston of the eighties James had described so mordantly, he had modeled his fictional Miss Birdseye on the transcendentalist reformer Elizabeth Peabody. Miss Birdseye "belonged to any and every league that had been founded for almost any purpose whatever. . . . She was in love only with causes, and she languished only for emancipations. But they had been the happiest days, for when causes were embodied in foreigners . . . they were certainly more appealing."[18]

Miss Birdseye had a descendant in Elizabeth Glendower Evans, the prototype of Upton Sinclair's Cornelia Thornwell, elderly heroine of his Sacco-Vanzetti novel, *Boston*. But Sinclair, in his naïve partisanship, revealed secrets he was unaware of in describing Cornelia's compulsive attendance at "anarchist or socialist or atheist or pacifist or pro-German meetings."[19]

Mrs. Evans was old enough to remember the Civil War. As a girl, abolitionist slogans still ringing in her ears, she had wanted to become a missionary. A poorer cousin of the Boston Gardiners, at twenty-six she married a wealthy Pennsylvania lawyer, Glendower Evans. Four years later he died, leaving her his fortune intact. Like a homing pigeon she returned to Boston and Cambridge. In the nineties she enrolled as a special student at Radcliffe, at the time Gertrude Stein was there, studying philosophy under Royce and Muensterberg.

Her interests were varied but nicely philanthropic. One of the leaders of the League for Democratic Action, she helped found the New England Civil Liberties Committee and the Community Church. Although never herself a jobholder, she at one point joined the Women's Trade Union League, becoming in 1912 a delegate to the Boston Central Labor Union. When the textile workers of the Amoskeag Mills, of which she was a stockholder, went out on strike, she supported them. Nor were her dividends imperiled by her support of the 1912 and 1919 Lawrence strikes. Though she joined the picket lines, she did not divest.

She was a militant champion of woman suffrage and the minimum-wage law. She was a trustee of the Massachusetts State Training School, a member of the Women's City Club. She was one of the peacemakers who in 1915 went with Jane Addams to the International Conference of Women at the Hague. In Boston's 1919 Red raids, she posted bond for sundry alien radicals held on Deer Island. In 1920 she supported the Socialist candidate for president, Eugene Debs, and once stood on a soapbox on Boston Common in pouring rain to speak for him. Her charities and causes were extended enough to require a secretary. If she had to be on a desert island, she once said, her preferred reading would be Emerson's essays. Like Saki's heroine of "The Byzantine Omelette," she had the comfortable if unadmitted feeling that the system, with all its inequalities and iniquities, would probably outlast her.

Among the women who for seven years gave their time and a share of their income to the Sacco-Vanzetti defense, Mrs. Evans was preeminent. Primarily through her, liberal upper-class Boston entered the case. Initially her women friends predominated, although she was able to enlist her civil rights associates and such like-minded men as John F. Moors of the brokerage firm of Moors & Cabot, endower of Radcliffe and patron of liberal causes. Later, through her long chain of acquaintances, she would reach out to, among others, Samuel Eliot Morison and H. L. Mencken. She was the link between her amorphous group and the defense committee.

Beyond Boston the press and the general public remained indifferent to the case. But below the surface a groundswell was rising. Moore's message that Sacco and Vanzetti were victims of a conspiracy, that their trial would not and could not be fair in the prejudiced atmosphere of Massachusetts, spread in ever-widening circles. In the months before the trial his charges of a frame-up and unfairness evoked a rising clamor, particularly overseas. In Paris, Communists early made the case their own, while in the Latin countries aroused anarchists threatened to destroy the Massachusetts persecutors of their innocent comrades. In 1921, as winter gave way to spring, threats to the court, the judge, and the prosecution arrived daily. By the time the trial opened at the end of May, Judge Thayer was receiving over seven hundred hostile letters a week, many of them death threats.

Needing a local lawyer both in and out of court, Moore had brought in Jerry McAnarney from Quincy, one of three lawyer brothers. The McAnarneys were second-generation Irish Americans sprung from the proletarian matrix, preserving their ethnic and religious loyalties as they moved upward, but in their mobility turned political heretics. For the McAnarneys had become Republicans. John, the urbane eldest brother, was president of the Norfolk County Bar Association, whereas the middle brother, Thomas, had been appointed a district judge by Governor Coolidge. Though Thomas took only a minor part in the defense, he did advise his brother and at times appeared in court. Another shadowy figure assisting in the defense was William Callahan, Sacco's and Vanzetti's Brockton lawyer.

Jerry, capable but irascible, tended to trip over his syntax when he got excited. As convinced as Moore that Sacco and Vanzetti were innocent, unlike Moore he never lost the confidence of the doomed anarchists. Nevertheless he was and would remain Fred Katzmann's friend. Moore trusted his subordinates as subordinates, but his was to be the "laboring oar." Jerry might help, but this case belonged to him.

In response to the growing threats, the courthouse at the trial's opening was fortified as if it were under siege. Deputies and police guarded the corridors and doorways, examining each entrant for weapons. Outside the austere granite building, troopers of the newly organized State Constabulary, bandoliers over their shoulders, patrolled the area on horseback or rode up and down adjacent streets on motorcycles with sidecars. In their olive-drab uniforms they looked like veterans of the American Expeditionary Force—as most of them were.

And nothing happened. No pickets demonstrated. No protesting crowds formed. No arrests were made. After those first martial days the troopers withdrew, deputies resumed their routine duties. By the end of the week half the courtroom's seats were empty, and as the six-and-a-half-week trial continued, fewer than a third remained occupied. Not until the last days would the courtroom fill up again. Though attendance had thinned out, Mrs. Evans continued to appear regularly with her friends, as self-contained as if she were at Friday Afternoon Symphony, taking voluminous notes, every now and then nodding encouragingly to the two prisoners behind the lattice.

Each morning the jurors filed in solemnly one by one. Each

morning Sacco and Vanzetti were led to the metal-latticed enclosure, their handcuffs removed. Each morning Sheriff Capen, thumping with his staff, opened court with "Hear ye! Hear ye!," tapering off to "God Save the Commonwealth of Massachusetts." Through the languid days of burgeoning summer, witness succeeded witness, the voices droning on like the hum of bees, interrupted by the sharper-pitched lawyers' voices or the slight nasal voice of Judge Thayer.

Seven prosecution witnesses identified Sacco as one of the bandits; four identified Vanzetti. The defense produced a dozen witnesses to deny that either Sacco or Vanzetti had been in South Braintree on the day of the crime. Five witnesses claimed that Vanzetti was peddling fish in Plymouth on that day, while seven other witnesses—all but one Italian—said that Sacco had been with them in Boston. In the jurors' minds prosecution and defense witnesses roughly canceled each other out. What did not cancel out for the defendants was the evidence of the guns and the bullets. "You can't depend on the witnesses . . . ," juror Seward Parker told Edward Simmons of the *New Bedford Standard-Times* in an interview three decades later, "but the bullets, there was no way of getting around that evidence."[20]

Vanzetti, when questioned after his arrest about his revolver, told the district attorney he had bought it four or five years earlier at a store on Hanover Street. He had paid $18 for it. At the same time he had bought a sealed box of cartridges, most of which he had shot off on the beach at Plymouth. There were only six left in the spring of 1920 and these he had loaded in the revolver a few days before his arrest.

In the months before his trial Vanzetti had learned that his Harrington & Richardson was a cheap revolver worth only four or five dollars, that it had *five* and not *six* chambers, and that the bullets in them were of two different brands—three U.S. and two Remingtons—and could not have come from the same box. Under Katzmann's questioning he had to admit he had lied, even though his lies had had nothing to do with protecting his friends. According to his amended story, a few months before his arrest he had bought his revolver from a friend, Luigi Falzini, and had paid five dollars for it. The revolver was loaded when he bought it, and he had never fired it. That was why he did not know whether it had five or six chambers.

Falzini, appearing on the witness stand, said he had sold his revolver to Vanzetti early in 1920. Three months before, he had bought it from Orciani. It was loaded then and he had never used it. For several weeks Orciani acted as Moore's chauffeur. But although he was in and out of the courthouse daily, he declined to appear as a corroborating witness.

It was the prosecution's contention that Vanzetti's Harrington & Richardson was the same revolver that had been taken from the guard Berardelli, as he lay dying in the gravel. Vanzetti's story failed to disprove this. He could give no reason for having said he had bought his revolver long ago on Hanover Street. The sealed box of cartridges had unsealed itself. When he learned that a .38-caliber Harrington & Richardson had only five chambers, the best he could do was to claim he had not owned his revolver long enough to know, had never fired it. His story could scarcely have impressed the jury.

Nor could Sacco's. After the Brockton police had found the Colt and the thirty-two cartridges on his person, he explained that he carried the Colt for protection on his job as night watchman in a shoe factory. The cartridges were left over from a sealed box he had bought on Hanover Street two years earlier at the time he bought his Colt. He had intended to fire them off in the woods that afternoon, had tucked the Colt into his belt and forgotten about it.*

Like Vanzetti, Sacco was then unaware that his cartridges were of different brands and could not have come from the same box. There were in fact sixteen Peters, three Remingtons, seven U.S., and six Winchesters of a type no longer manufactured. At the trial he shifted to saying he had bought his cartridges during the war and because of wartime shortages the storekeeper had filled an already opened box with whatever cartridges he had on hand. His Colt he had really bought in Milford.

Under the district attorney's grinding cross-examination, he could give no adequate reason for his lies. None of his friends, he admitted, would have been injured if he had told the truth about the gun and the cartridges. Pressed as to why he had originally said he had bought a "brand-new" box, wavering under the barrage of questions all he could reply was "I don't see the way I could answer."[21]

The four spent shells that Jimmy Bostock had picked up near Berardelli's body and handed to Fraher, the plant superintendent,

* During tests held in 1961 in the State Police Ballistics Laboratory, I received permission to tuck Sacco's revolver into my belt. With its bulk pressing against my side, I could not take a step without being aware of it.

were all .32-caliber and also of different makes—one Remington, two Peters, and an obsolete Winchester that would henceforth be referred to as Shell W. When Captain William Proctor of the State Police arrived in Braintree later that afternoon, Fraher handed the shells over to him. Following the arrest of Sacco and Vanzetti, Proctor also received the pistols and cartridges taken from them.

Dr. George Magrath, the medical examiner who performed the autopsy on Berardelli, had removed four bullets from his body. Using a surgical needle, he scratched a Roman numeral on the base of each as he extracted it. Bullet III, the mortal bullet, bent somewhat out of shape from having struck the guard's hip-bone, turned out to be an obsolete Winchester, its W trademark still visible. From the scorings on Bullet III and Shell W it was apparent that they had been fired in a Colt automatic such as Sacco was carrying. Bullets I, II, and III and the two bullets taken from the paymaster's body had been fired from a Savage or, according to later experts, a .38-caliber Harrington & Richardson.*

At the start of the trial Katzmann proposed to Moore that they both agree not to claim that any particular bullet came from any particular weapon. Moore was at first willing but soon developed second thoughts. For if Sacco was innocent, Bullet III and Shell W could not have come from his Colt. This Moore hoped to be able to prove by tests made with Sacco's weapon. He and Assistant District Attorney Williams then made arrangements for a joint test-firing. Williams, who would prepare and present most of the prosecution's ballistics evidence, had felt obliged to engage Captain Proctor as one of his experts because of Proctor's official position. But on the advice of Dr. Magrath he brought in Charles Van Amburgh, a technician with the Remington Arms Company, as a second and more competent expert.

Proctor and Van Amburgh conducted the tests for the prosecution, with James Burns of the U.S. Cartridge Company factory in Lowell acting for the defense. A fourth defense expert, J. Henry Fitzgerald from the Colt Company, was not present. The tests were held on the grounds of the Lowell factory.

Burns was unable to locate any obsolete Winchester cartridges, although he and his assistants scoured towns for thirty miles between Lowell and Dedham. The older type Winchester bullets had a concave base and a knurled cannelure—a groove with raised millings

---

* Certain Spanish-type automatics produce ejector marks similar to those made by a Savage. It is at least possible that one of the bandits used a Stehr rather than a Savage or a Harrington & Richardson.

around the bullet's circumference. The newer Winchesters were flat-based and smooth. Burns used U.S. cartridges as substitutes because he considered them more like the obsolete Winchesters. Van Amburgh used Peters and the newer Winchesters. With Proctor looking on, Burns fired eight shots into a box of oiled sawdust. Van Amburgh fired six shots, three Peters and three Winchesters. The bullets and shells were then retrieved.

Ballistics evidence at the trial was based chiefly on caliper measurements of Bullet III and the Lowell test bullets, since the comparison microscope—the one sure means of determining whether a given bullet has been fired from a given weapon—had not yet been invented. Before testifying, Proctor told Williams that he believed Bullet III had been fired from a .32-caliber Colt. Whether it had been fired from Sacco's Colt he could not say. It might have been; it was—to use the conventional legal term—"consistent" with being fired from it. That was the most he could say in court.

On the stand Proctor demonstrated his lack of expertise by being unable to strip Sacco's pistol. When asked if he had had much to do with Colts, he replied, "Not much." He had no opinion as to whether Bullets I, II, III and the two taken from the paymaster's body had been fired from the same weapon, though later he contradicted himself and said he thought they might have been. Finally Williams put the direct question to him: "Have you an opinion as to whether Bullet 3 was fired from the Colt automatic that is in evidence?" Falling back on legal phraseology, Proctor replied: "My opinion is that it is consistent with being fired from that pistol."[22] That conventional legal phrase, passing almost unnoticed at the time, would haunt the case for years to come.

Van Amburgh, more capable and assured on the stand than Proctor, pointed out to the jury a number of markings on Bullet III much like those on the Lowell test bullets. Using a microscope he indicated parallel scorings, in particular "one streak along each bullet fired in Sacco's gun" that also appeared on Bullet III. Yet even he would go no further than to say he was "inclined to believe that it was fired, No. 3 bullet was fired from this Colt automatic pistol."[23]

The two defense experts were more positive. Both said that in their opinion Bullet III had not been fired from Sacco's Colt, although they failed otherwise to agree. Burns denied that pitting marks in a barrel could be of any value in the identification of a bullet. Fitzgerald held that they were crucial, but insisted that the markings on Bullet III differed from the markings on the test bullets.

Katzmann and Williams had been reluctant to use Proctor. As Williams explained to David Felix in 1962, "We felt we had to put Proctor on to identify the exhibits because he was head of the State Police. He knew very little about bullets and he used the word 'consistent' because he wasn't competent to testify to more than that—he wasn't saying that this particular bullet came from this particular—Sacco's—pistol. He hadn't made the actual tests—didn't know how."[24]

However the jurors might evaluate the opinions of the ballistics experts, they had before their eyes the similarity between Sacco's six obsolete Winchester cartridges and the obsolete Winchester Bullet III and Shell W. All the jurors interviewed by Simmons agreed that this was the most telling piece of prosecution evidence. Almost as damaging to Sacco and Vanzetti were their efforts to account for their actions on the night of their arrest. Why had they lied at their first interrogation? Why had they gone to Bridgewater to meet Boda and Orciani? What were they planning to do with the automobile? Where were they headed and what for? Facing these questions would involve them in a tangle of contradictions.

Both admitted that they had lied when they were first questioned, because, they said, in the government's countrywide drive against Reds they feared for their own safety and that of their friends. First to testify, Vanzetti explained that they needed the Overland to collect radical books and pamphlets "from the houses and homes . . . three, five or six people have plenty of literature, and we went, we intend to take that out and put that in proper place."[25] Half a dozen possessors of such incriminating literature lived in Bridgewater. He planned to visit them that night but had to admit he did not know their names or addresses. Boxed in by the district attorney's cross-questioning, he wavered, amended his story, now said they had planned to collect material in other towns, in Brockton, Plymouth, Everett, Salem, and Haverhill.

Brockton is four miles northwest of West Bridgewater, Plymouth eighteen miles to the east, Everett twenty-nine miles north, Salem fourteen miles northeast of Everett, Haverhill almost on the New Hampshire border twenty-one miles northwest of Salem. To travel to such non-sequent cities haphazardly in the darkness along unfamiliar roads, looking for houses without addresses and persons unknown, was an impossible journey. What Vanzetti demonstrated was his ignorance of Massachusetts geography. Caught in the web of his own illogic, worn down by the district attorney's relentless interrogation, he wilted. When Katzmann finally asked him: "Was it your intention not to take any literature on the night of May 5th?" Vanzetti hesitated, then replied, "No."[26]

Struggling to extricate himself, Vanzetti now said he had come to Bridgewater to see a friend, Pappi, and urge him "to tell the Italians to come on Sunday to the meeting." He and Pappi had worked together in the Cordage plant, but he had not seen him since, although he knew he lived in Bridgewater. He did not know his address or even his real name, for Pappi was a nickname. After seeing Pappi, he intended to go on to Plymouth to find a safe storage place for the as yet uncollected radical literature. Again he could furnish neither a name nor an address.

Vanzetti's revised story made even less sense than his first. There was indeed a Vittorio Papa of *East* Bridgewater whom he had known, but he had not seen or heard from him in six years. After returning from New York on Sunday he had talked with friends in Boston, idled away the rest of the day, had gone to a moving picture, and had spent the night with a woman he had picked up on Hanover Street. Where was the urgency? Untroubled by the news of Salsedo's death, he had gone to Sacco's house, where he stayed until they left Wednesday night for Bridgewater. Yet, as the district attorney brought out, in those three days neither Sacco nor Vanzetti had made any attempt to dispose of Sacco's collection of anarchist books and papers. Instead Vanzetti was preparing an announcement of a public meeting to express his political views. Where was the fear? The penciled announcement in Vanzetti's pocket had left blanks for time and place. How, Katzmann asked, could he have instructed Pappi—if he had found him—to get his Italian friends to go to an undesignated and unscheduled meeting? Vanzetti did not know. Again he tried to fall back on his story of collecting literature. It was a hopeless effort.

Sacco, having listened to the more verbally nimble Vanzetti ensnare himself, proceeded cautiously. He explained that at an anarchist meeting in Boston, "we decided to get those books and papers, because in New York there was somebody said they were trying to arrest all the Socialists and the Radicals and we were afraid to get all the people arrested."[27] They wanted the Overland to pick up those books and papers. Boda and Vanzetti were to take the automobile to see Pappi in West Bridgewater—although Sacco did not know what street. Then they were to drive to Plymouth. He and Orciani were going to Brockton on the motorcycle to see about getting Vanzetti's meeting announcement printed, and there they would warn friends to get rid of their radical books, circulars, and papers.

Sacco admitted that in spite of warnings from New York he had done nothing to get rid of the radical material in his own house. Although he was leaving with his family in three days to take a ship back to Italy for good, he said he feared deportation. They were going to collect books that night—if they had time.

Pappi's name had first come up after Sacco's arrest, when he had said he had been going to Bridgewater to see him. Under the district attorney's barrage of questions, he now admitted this was not so. "Did you have any intention of seeing Pappi that night?" Katzmann finally asked him. Sacco lamely admitted that he did not.

As one reads the record, their alibi is self-contradictory. So it must have seemed to the jury. Sacco and Vanzetti were out to collect papers. They were not out to collect papers. They were going to see Pappi. They were not going to see Pappi. They were afraid. They showed no signs of being afraid. The district attorney had a simpler explanation. Sacco and Vanzetti and their two comrades had gone to West Bridgewater that night because they wanted the car for another robbery. The explanation was direct. It was plausible.

Defending Sacco and Vanzetti before the Lowell Commission six years later, Thomas McAnarney said he had "spent considerable time with these two men as to what they were doing at this Johnson house this night, and they persisted in telling me they were intending to get an automobile to gather up this socialistic and communistic literature." When Lowell asked if the radical purposes of the prisoners did not account for their conduct, would there be any question of their innocence, he replied: "There wouldn't be any defense in my mind. No explanation."[28]

There was an explanation, however, one that Sacco and Vanzetti did not dare use. If they had told the truth, it would have been worse for them in the eyes of the jury than their poorly contrived fiction. For they had wanted Boda's Overland on that May night to collect dynamite from comrades who had hidden it.

Several months after their execution, Moore told Upton Sinclair that "Sacco and Vanzetti admitted to him that they were hiding dynamite on the night of their arrest and that was the real reason they told lies and stuck to them."[29] It was an awkward revelation for Sinclair, then engaged in writing *Boston* and passionately convinced of Sacco's and Vanzetti's innocence. Honest enough to feel that the unwelcome fact must be dealt with, he compromised by attributing Moore's statement to his fictional Henry Cabot Winters, the conservative lawyer son-in-law of Cornelia Thornwell. "I know that those fellows were up to some devilment the night they were arrested," Winters told his disbelieving mother-in-law. "They told a tangle of lies to the police. . . . I am told that their own lawyers knew they were hiding dynamite—the men have admitted it."[30] Dynamite had been used before by the East Boston anarchists. Dynamite would be used again. Some time after the executions a bomb would demolish much of Judge Thayer's house, injuring his wife. The executioner's house would also be bombed.

Several days before Sacco took the stand it was nosed about among the reporters that he was memorizing a speech written for him by Moore. It was the opportunity Moore had been planning and working for, to transform the matter-of-fact murder trial into a manifesto, a challenge to the bourgeois social order. Sacco, in his defiance, would talk beyond the court and the jury to a world outside that had already begun to listen.

After the frustrations he had suffered in trying to explain what he was doing in Bridgewater on the night of May 5, he bided his time. That time did not come until the following day when Katzmann asked what he had meant when he said he loved a free country. Then, in a searing moment of release, Sacco's words tumbled out in angry confusion, half-remembered phrases from Moore mixed with his own dogmatic thoughts. Staring at the district attorney, he began:

I teach over here men who is with me. . . . I could see the best men, intelligent, education, they been arrested and sent to prison and died in prison for years and years without getting them out, and Debs, one of the great men in his country, he is in prison, still away in prison because he is a Socialist. He wanted the laboring class to have better conditions and better living, more education, give a push his son if he would have a chance some day, but they put him in prison. Why? Because the capitalist class they don't want our child to go to high school or to college or Harvard College. There would not be no chance, there would not be no—they don't want the working class educationed; they want the working class to be a low all the times, be underfoot and not up with the head. So sometimes, you see, the Rockefellers, Morgans, they give fifty,—mean they give five hundred thousand dollars to Harvard Col-

lege. . . . I want to ask him who is going to Harvard College. What benefit the working class they will get by those millions dollars they give by
Rockefeller, D. Rockefellers. They won't get, the poor class, they won't
have no chance to go to Harvard College. . . . I like men to get everything that nature will give best. . . . So that is why I love people who
labor and work and see better conditions every day develop, makes no
more war. We no want fight by the gun, and we don't want to destroy
young men. The mother has been suffering for building the young man.
Some day need a little more bread, so when the time the mother get
some bread or profit out of that boy, the Rockefellers, Morgans, and
some of the peoples, high class, they send to war. Why? What is war?
The war is not shoots like Abraham Lincoln's and Abe Jefferson, to fight
for the free country, for the better education, to give a chance to any
other peoples. . . . They are war for business, million dollars come on
the side. I want to destroy those guns . . . that is why I my idea I love
Socialists. That is why I like people who want education and living,
building, who is good, just as much as they could. That is all.[31]*

As Sacco spilled out his words Mrs. Evans would break off her
notetaking to nod her approval. Only at the very close of the trial, a
week later, when the lawyers made their summations and the judge
his charge to the jury, was the courtroom full. Neither Moore nor
McAnarney took any exception to Thayer's charge. At three on the
afternoon of July 14 the jury finally went out.

The jurors could have brought in a verdict that same afternoon
but decided it would look better if they waited until after their evening meal. What went on in the jury room we know chiefly through
the unpublished memoirs of the youngest juror, John Dever, a
twenty-seven-year-old clothing salesman. As a poor Irish-Catholic
boy, Dever had grown up in Barre, Vermont, playing with the children of the quarry workers, too familiar with Italians to have any
prejudice against them. After his discharge from the army in 1919,
until he was called to jury duty, he lived in a lodging house on upper
Beacon Street.† When from the jury box he first saw Sacco and Van-

---

* There was irony in Sacco's mention of Harvard, for Katzmann, class of 1896, as a poor
boy had worked his way through college by tending furnaces and—since he had a fine tenor
voice—singing at churches and funerals. Wanting to be a lawyer, he lacked the money to
go to the Harvard Law School, though the tuition was only $125 a year. Instead he studied
law nights at Boston University while working days as a meter-reader for the Edison Company. There is a further irony in that John D. Rockefeller, Jr., was one of those who in 1928
funded the publication of the six volumes of the Sacco-Vanzetti trial transcript.

† Mistaking his name for Old Yankee and his address for fashionable, Sinclair in *Boston*
portrayed Dever as a proper Bostonian. Dever died in 1956, leaving behind him several
thousand unsorted pages of what he called "Memoirs of the Sacco-Vanzetti Case." These
are now in the Sacco-Vanzetti Collection of the Boston Public Library.

zetti, he was struck by their clean-cut appearance and hoped there would not be sufficient evidence to find them guilty "beyond a reasonable doubt."

According to Dever, by the time the jurors had filed out of the courtroom they had made up their minds that Sacco and Vanzetti were guilty. Dever suggested that before talking they ought first to take an informal ballot. He and another juror voted for acquittal, not because they had any doubts but merely to open up a discussion. For several hours the twelve jurors discussed the various aspects of the case, particularly the guns and the bullets, but there was no difference of opinion, no dispute. They took no second ballot. All were convinced of the defendants' guilt.

Just after sunset the jury brought in its verdict. Sacco and Vanzetti stood up as the clerk of court intoned the eighteenth-century legal formula:

> Mr. Foreman, look upon the prisoner. Prisoner, look upon the Foreman. What say you, Mr. Foreman, is the prisoner at the bar guilty or not guilty?

Twice the clerk intoned. Twice the foreman replied, "Guilty." Suddenly Sacco's voice rang out through the courtroom: *"Sono innocente!"* "I am innocent!"—a cry that would echo far beyond the granite building and provincial Dedham.

But the last word went to Fred Moore. After court had adjourned, he walked alone down High Street to Gilbert's Lunch in Dedham Square. Lieutenant Daniel Guerin of the Brockton police, who had testified briefly on a technicality, was already at the counter drinking a cup of coffee. With the professional aplomb of one lawman to another, he nodded condolingly to the lawyer and said, "Tough luck, Mr. Moore."

"What could you expect," Moore answered him, "with the case I had?"*

* Guerin, who testified about examining the Buick when it was brought to the police station, told me about Moore's remark when I talked with him in 1960. He also explained that he had dusted off the car for possible fingerprints but the surface had been too smudged for him to get any impressions. Fred J. Cooke, in an article, "The Missing Fingerprints," that appeared in *The Nation*, December 22, 1962, tried to make out that the prosecution had secreted fingerprint evidence that would have exonerated Sacco and Vanzetti. There was no such evidence.

9

The Road to Charlestown

At the time when I was having difficulty getting permission for new tests on the Sacco-Vanzetti guns and bullets, I turned to Judge Reuben Lurie for help. "Such tests," I told him, "might at last prove them innocent." As a state superior court justice, he declined to intervene. "I am not so much concerned with Sacco's and Vanzetti's guilt or innocence," he said. "What really concerns me is whether they had a fair trial." Peripherally connected with the defense in the last months of the case, he obviously thought they had not. I was more concerned with proving them innocent. But however one regarded it, those were the two primary questions on which the whole structure of the Sacco-Vanzetti case was based. Were they guilty? Was the trial fair?

Were they guilty? Even while still believing them innocent, I was troubled by inconsistencies. Many points that I might have considered while writing my book, I skipped over. Shelley Neal in my one interview with him had told me that an Italian he knew in South Braintree had seen and recognized Sacco at the scene of the shootings but refused to make this public out of fear and ethnic loyalty. Convinced at that time of Sacco's innocence, I brushed the remark aside, neglecting to write down the name Neal gave. Before I could ask again, Neal was dead. Years later a Henry Rapp, who owned a small fireworks factory in Hanover a few miles from Braintree, told me that one of his Italian workmen had known Sacco and spotted him among the South Braintree bandits. Rapp said the man had since died but he refused to give me his name for fear that it might still affect the man's family.

These were hearsay matters, but perhaps little indicators, if one could bring oneself to listen to them, as I at the time could not. There was the matter of the cap picked up near Berardelli's body that the prosecution claimed was Sacco's. A week before the trial, George Kelley, the son of the owner of the shoe factory where Sacco worked, had been shown the cap and asked if he could identify it. Kelley was friendly with Sacco, and had even visited him in jail. He did not want to give any opinion. When pressed, he refused. Sacco might be a friend, but anarchists were anarchists. "I have an opinion about the cap," he admitted finally, "but I don't want to get a bomb up my ass!"[1] During the trial Stewart salvaged several hairs from the cap as well as several from a comb Sacco was using. He handed them to the medical examiner, Dr. George Magrath, who put them on a slide and examined them through a microscope. They were, he said, identical. Magrath thought that such evidence should prove conclusive as far as the cap was concerned, but Katzmann decided against presenting it lest the defense and the newspapers ridicule him for attempting to hang the defendants by a hair.[2]

On the day of the crime Sacco had admittedly been absent from work. He claimed he had gone to Boston on that day to apply for a passport at the Italian consulate. Earlier in April he had been to the consulate and was told to come back with two photographs. He returned with an oversize family photograph. As a rule several hundred people came each day to the consulate, and a week after Sacco's arrest the consulate clerk, Giuseppe Adrower, could no longer remember him. Although he had returned to Rome, he did recall the oversize photograph, as he stated in a deposition.

Sacco had had a passport before, and he knew what size photo was required. Bringing the oversize photograph seems more a deliberate act to establish his presence. Adrower set down the date as April 15, but it is most unlikely that he could recall the specific day, especially since he was vague in recalling other dates.

Sacco testified that after visiting the consulate he had gone to Boston's North End and had lunch at Boni's Restaurant. The seven witnesses who said that they had seen him there on April 15 provided what Musmanno referred to as "Sacco's ironclad alibi." Thirty years after the trial, the iron-clad alibi was to turn paper-thin with the admission of a former Boston anarchist, Anthony Ramuglia, that he had been coached to perjure himself for Sacco. At the request of his comrades of the East Boston anarchist group, he had agreed to testify that he had seen Sacco at Boni's Restaurant in Boston on April 15,

1920. Only when he was about to appear in court did he suddenly re-member that he had been in jail on that day. On learning this, the anarchists picked another comrade whose perjury would be less li-able to discovery.

Was the trial fair? "If these defendants got a fair trial," Edmund Morgan wrote, "neither they nor their friends have any complaint against the Commonwealth of Massachusetts. Whether they were actually guilty no one but the perpetrators of the crime can know. Whether they got a fair trial or not can only be a matter of opinion."[3] Sacco-Vanzetti partisans have always held that in the anti-Red hys-teria of the time, no foreigner, no radical, could have had a fair trial in a Massachusetts court. They point to the Department of Justice's sweeping round-up of alien radicals in December 1919, the heavily guarded courthouse at the beginning of the Sacco-Vanzetti trial, the presumed bias of a nativist jury against radicals, the constant fear under which Sacco and Vanzetti and their friends lived—a fear more than sufficient to account for the lies they told at their arrest.

When on the last day of May 1921, the Dedham trial opened, U.S. Attorney General A. Mitchell Palmer's Red raids had been over for a year and a half, and the attorney general left as a rather ridicu-lous figure after his ominously erroneous prediction of a "slaughter of high officials" on May Day, 1920. A year later, with President Hard-ing in the White House restoring "normalcy" and Harry Daugherty replacing Palmer, the Red scare—despite the Palmer excesses, basi-cally a reaction to the 1919 wave of bombings—had vanished from the public's brief memory, no longer a matter of interest or concern. Even at the time of the Braintree holdup there was little or none of the claimed atmosphere of terror and repression. As Robert Murray, in his even-handed study *Red Scare*, points out: "After January 1920 the anti-Red hysteria subsided almost as quickly as it had developed. . . . By the fall of 1920 the Great Red Scare was dying. Hysteria as such, had all but disappeared before the spring had passed."[4] Nor had it been that prevalent in the smaller Massachusetts towns. Coacci, out on bail for two years and debonairly telephoning the Im-migration Service, scarcely gives the impression of a man sick with fear of the authorities. Orciani, as Moore's chauffeur during the Dedham trial, remains cockily self-assured. Vanzetti himself seems less than anxious as he pencils his notice for a public meeting. Where is the hunted alien waiting for the fateful knock on the door, cower-ing in terror of arbitrary arrest and police brutality?

That a Yankee jury in Dedham would react with unfailing and unreasonable harshness to a radical alien defendant was disproved a year before Sacco's and Vanzetti's trial, in the very courtroom in which they were convicted and with the same judge presiding. In April 1920, a Lett immigrant, Sergei Zagroff, appeared before Judge Thayer charged with advocating anarchy and the overthrow of the government by violence. Zagroff had been picked up in a radical club the walls of which were hung with pictures of the new Bolshevik leaders. He freely and volubly admitted that he was an anarchist and opposed to the American form of government—a deportable offense. Nevertheless the jury found him not guilty. Judge Thayer, taking the strictly legal point of view that to advocate the overthrow of the government by violence was a violation of the Criminal Anarchy Statute, upbraided the jurors. Whereupon the practical-minded foreman stood up and replied that the jurors had freed Zagroff because they "understood the definition of 'advocating anarchy,' as given by the court, to be the act of a person who actually used force in bringing about his aims and not just the advocacy of those aims when he talked on the subject."[5]

As to the fairness of the Sacco-Vanzetti trial, it has been generally overlooked that this issue was not raised for almost six years. Not until March 1927, when Frankfurter's *Case of Sacco and Vanzetti* appeared, was the charge openly made. Commenting on Frankfurter's assertions, Supreme Court Justice Oliver Wendell Holmes wrote to his friend Harold Laski:

> My prejudices were all with Felix's book. But after all, it's simply showing, if it was right, that the case was tried in a hostile atmosphere. I doubt if anyone would say there was no evidence warranting a conviction.[6]

Only in August did the last defense lawyers—Arthur D. Hill, Elias Field, and Michael Angelo Musmanno—formally petition the Massachusetts and then the United States Supreme Court to reverse the judgment of the Dedham court on the grounds that Judge Thayer "was so prejudiced and biassed . . . that he was at all times incapable and incompetent to act as a judge in said cause and said subsequent proceedings."[7]

Whatever later animadversions on the trial, those who were actually present during those six and a half weeks may be assumed best able to judge its fairness or unfairness: the jurors and the court officers; the reporters; the defense lawyers. In 1950 the *New Bedford Standard-Times* feature writer, Edward Simmons, interviewed John Dever and six other surviving jurors as to their feelings about the trial then and at present. "It is nonsense," Dever told Simmons, "to say we were prejudiced against Sacco and Vanzetti because they were Italian anarchists." The verdict, he said, resulted from a study of all the hard evidence. "Various pieces fitted into the chains of evidence, which to my mind, not having a weak link, were pretty strong." Dever admitted, "I was a defendant's man all the way through the trial. I don't mean I was determined to vote for their innocence regardless, but I was going to find them not guilty until the facts proved otherwise to my definite satisfaction."[8]

None of the jurors had changed their opinions about the trial. "The outstanding thing about the trial was the judge," juror George Gerard told Simmons. "The fairest judge I ever saw or heard of." Juror Frank Marden also praised Judge Thayer's fairness. "I have never had a bit of reason to think the trial was anything but fair," he said. "I don't think we jurors thought of the defendants in any way except as two persons accused of murder." Juror John Ganley thought Thayer was "absolutely fearless and absolutely on the level. He was trying to do his job thoroughly and not leaning either way." The last juror chosen, Seward Parker, asked: "Why should we want to pick up two Reds and try to convict them for murder? We did not know if they were Reds and we did not care. To my mind, and I really think this, the judge tried to help the defendants. He was square with us, too. . . . I had no difficulty in my own mind arriving at the verdict. . . . If I remember anything with absolute clarity, it was the judge's fairness." In 1961 David Felix interviewed one of the last surviving jurors, Harry King, a welfare agent living near Boston. "I know there was a lot of talk about it afterward, radicalism and all that," King told Felix. "The jury didn't mention it when we discussed the evidence. . . . I'm a church member. I was a deacon then. I wouldn't make a decision on a man's life unless I was sure I was doing right. . . . Well, I have no regrets about the decision—only that I was picked to make it."[9]

That these jurors were of predominantly Yankee stock lay in the ethnic composition of Norfolk County. The flatlands Italians were mostly aliens who had brought with them a well-founded distrust of all governments. Once here, they showed no eagerness to become citizens and carefully avoided being listed in the census or any other public record. Not until the New Deal arrived, with its cornucopia of welfare projects, were they persuaded to emerge and identify themselves. There would have been no question of their serving on a Dedham jury in 1921. They were not eligible.

Never before in the county's history had so many veniremen been rounded up for a single trial. Moore was determined to reject all jurors of professional middle-class background. It took four days and 650 prospective jurors to complete the jury as compared with seventy-five to one hundred in an ordinary murder trial. Sheriff's deputies had to scour the county to bring in candidates, sometimes picking them off the street or at a sporting event or once even at a wedding reception. Those finally selected were small-town people: a real-estate agent, a shoe worker, a photographer, a farmer, a machinist, a grocer, a mason, a factory storekeeper, a clothing salesman. "Did you know this jury is probably the most expensive the Commonwealth ever got?" Moore asked a reporter rhetorically.

Simmons also interviewed Edwin Hauser, one of the two official court stenographers at the trial.

> You can't put it too strongly [Hauser said], my belief in the justice of the verdict and guilt of the men and fairness of the trial.
>
> Of course, I've seen a lot of murder trials, and other trials in 40-odd years and I think I'm in a position to be a pretty good judge. At the time of the trial there was not a single person I ran across in the courtroom who thought they were innocent. With one exception, a newspaperman. . . . There was no question about Thayer's fairness. There was no question about his courage either. . . .

Radicalism, Hauser felt, played no part in the verdict:

> We, the other stenographer and I, heard every word said, we heard every consultation between judge and counsel and prosecution. There was not a single word relating to that trial involving the court that we did not hear. And in my mind there was no question that Sacco and Vanzetti were guilty as charged.

That the working press generally considered the trial unfair was an impression subsequently created and sponsored by the voluble and eccentric *Boston Globe* reporter Frank Sibley. Sibley, a gaunt six-foot-four figure who wore a Windsor tie and a Latin Quarter hat, became such a Sacco-Vanzetti partisan that his paper had to take him off the trial. His colleague, Lucien Thayer, who had attended every session, considered the trial fair. "I know Frank didn't think so," he told me in an interview forty years later, "but Frank was a romantic. It's hard to attend a murder trial without developing feelings for or against the defendants, and Frank was a defendants' man. I thought it was a proper trial and a proper verdict. I still think so." After listening sympathetically to Moore during the trial, a woman reporter on the *Boston Herald* wrote that "those of us who knew Judge Thayer in the Bessie May Sheels case in Lawrence, two years ago, know that friends of liberals and radicals ... can rest perfectly secure in the fact that every right of the defendant is being protected. ... So alert is he in administering justice to the fullest degree that he protects the defendant when the defense is slow to move and hesitant to act."[10] Another reporter, Dorothy Wayman, who covered every day of the trial, interviewed both prisoners and talked at length with the lawyers on both sides, could find nothing to take exception to either in the trial or in the conduct of the judge.

Even a *Nation* editor who had attended several court sessions took a relatively moderate view of the proceedings, although he did fall back on "a reasonable doubt." The case of Sacco and Vanzetti, Arthur Warner wrote in September 1921, before intellectual attitudes had hardened, was no Mooney case*

> with powerful interests set out to get rid of a prominent labor leader, deliberately fabricating a case against him and resorting to bribery and perjury to convict him for a capital crime. Nothing of the sort happened to Nicola Sacco and Bartolomeo Vanzetti. ... Neither man was a prominent labor leader. Both were too alien and too extreme for the established American labor movement. ... Nobody pretends that these two insignificant Italians were "framed up" as Mooney was.

Warner thought that the ballistics experts canceled each other out and that the evidence of the witnesses on both sides was "not worth a hill of beans." Judge Thayer's old-fashioned rhetoric he considered "sophomoric and bombastic ... but it does not appear to be one-sided except with regard to emphasis placed on consciousness of guilt."[11]

The death threats and violent letters that Thayer constantly received were unnerving, and there is no doubt that he talked compul-

---

* Tom Mooney, an aggressive union leader, was one of those convicted of bombing a San Francisco Preparedness Day parade in 1916. Sentenced to death by hanging, he had his sentence commuted to life imprisonment. His trial, with perjured witnesses and false evidence, was afterward shown to be so patently a frame-up that the jurors who found him guilty and the judge who sentenced him publicly repudiated their position. Mooney's case became a liberal cause, but not until 1939 was he at last pardoned.

sively about the case outside the courtroom. But nothing he said off the bench affected his conduct on the bench. Most of what he is accused of having said took place in the years after the trial. In private conversation he may or may not have referred to "anarchist bastards," though the accusation comes at third-hand. Robert Riordan, who had covered the trial for the *Brockton Enterprise,* told Felix he was inclined to believe that Thayer had said all they claimed he had said—off the bench—"but he was a different man on the bench. . . . It was a fair trial conducted by a fair judge. . . . It was a trial by the book."[12]

During the trial Moore and Judge Thayer were often at odds. The prim New Englander took offense at the western lawyer's casual manners, his appearing in court in his stocking-feet on a hot day, his taking noon catnaps on the grass in front of the courthouse with a newspaper over his face. But the transcript shows that the judge ruled twice as often in favor of the defense as he did for the prosecution. At the trial's end, after the jury had gone out, Moore told Thayer that no matter what the jury might decide, no one could say that the defendants had not had a fair trial. It was not a remark that a former general counsel for the IWW would feel constrained to make out of politeness.

Jerry McAnarney never lost the confidence of the defendants and the defense committee, as Moore later did. Yet in his closing arguments at the trial's end he told Thayer:

> I want to say to you one of the pleasant things that occurs in this case . . . was the patience of the Court and the District Attorney. . . . Mr. Katzmann . . . has been, as he always has been, a perfect gentleman. . . . I want to say on behalf of these men—I say it to those men and their friends, that they have had every patience, every consideration. I want them to know that we have done—that everything has been done as Massachusetts takes pride in doing, granting to any man, however lowly his station, the fullest rights to our Massachusetts common laws.[13]

At the Lowell Committee hearings six years later, Sibley accused Thayer of being "anything but dignified, especially when the counsel for the defense were presenting their case, he would sit forward in his chair with an air of prejudice, and scorn."[14] Sibley did not like the judge's look. That was the most he could say.

Among the spectators at the trial's opening was the established Boston lawyer William Thompson, friend of Frankfurter, a Harvard man of broad if local horizons, contemptuous of the provincial Thayer. Thompson would succeed Moore as counsel for Sacco and Vanzetti and in the end embrace their cause with uncritical fervor. It was he who, years after the trial, first made a formal issue of Judge Thayer's prejudice. Appearing before the Lowell Committee, he gave his impressions of that trial's first morning:

> Katzmann would say something and Moore would object to it. He was jumping up all the time. He would make objection after objection. Judge Thayer would sit there and look at Moore with the fiercest expression on his face, moving his head a little. Moore would say "I object to that" and Judge Thayer . . . would sit back and say "Objection overruled." It wasn't what he said, it was his manner of saying it. It looked perfectly straight on the record; he was too clever to do otherwise. I sat there for a while and I told John McAnarney, "Your goose is cooked. You will never in this world get these men acquitted. The judge is going to convict these two men and see that nothing gets in the record; he is going to keep his records straight and you have no chance."[15]

Even by Thompson's admission it seems an insubstantial sort of bias that leaves no trace of itself in the record, that consists merely of nods of the head and tones of voice. Yet Thompson's fervor for his clients and his dislike of Thayer distorted his recollections. For he was in the courtroom only when Thayer was examining prospective jurors. There could have been no question of Moore's jumping up and objecting or even opening his mouth, since in a Massachusetts court it is the trial judge who in the examination of the jurors asks *all* the questions, including those suggested by counsel. As a more accurate indication of Judge Thayer's attitude, in mid-June he told the State Police officer who was acting as his trial bodyguard that he thought the prosecution had a weak case and he did not think Sacco and Vanzetti would be convicted on the evidence thus far presented.[16]

Moore, in his various motions for a new trial, never raised the question of Thayer's prejudice. When the issue belatedly flared up, he and McAnarney remained stubbornly silent. Perhaps the whole question of fairness was best summed up by Justice Holmes, to whom everything had been presented that the defense could produce from the record and elsewhere relevant to Judge Thayer's conduct. "I doubt," he wrote to Laski in 1930, "if those two suffered anything more from the conduct of the judge than would be a matter of course in England."[17]

In the full Platonic sense the Sacco-Vanzetti trial was not an ideal trial, with a judge above the passions and prejudices of this world, a prosecution and a defense intent solely on bringing out the truth, a jury of disinterested yet highly intelligent men who had nevertheless never heard of the crime or the defendants, witnesses with total re-call impelled only by a sense of civic duty, experts who were really experts. Such trials are not granted to ordinary fallible mortals. No trial has ever been ideal. Yet carefully examined, the Sacco-Vanzetti trial—in spite of the tenaciously held myth—is seen to be reasonably fair, relatively free from bias and prejudice.

The trial had aroused no general interest outside eastern Massa-chusetts. The *New York Times* gave a few lines to the guilty verdict on one of its back pages. Several liberal journals took up discussion of the case, as did the foreign-language press. But papers like the *New York World* and the *Chicago Tribune* disregarded it completely. Ini-tial support came from the needle-trade unions of New York, Phila-delphia, and Chicago, whose members—predominantly Jewish and Italian—identified themselves instinctively with the two convicted radicals.

September and October 1921 saw protests in the foreign work-ing-class districts of several American cities. At a meeting in New York's Central Opera House on November 25, the Communist Fred Biedenkapp explained that "the aim of the Department of Justice was to get a hold of Sacco and Vanzetti. How to get a hold of them? First get them and then find out what we will do with them. And so it came to pass on May 5th, Sacco and Vanzetti were arrested on a streetcar by the Chief of Police, a Captain Proctor of the Constabu-lary of Massachusetts and charged with being radicals and dangerous characters."[18] Later Biedenkapp embroidered the myth to a Harvard audience, telling them that Sacco and Vanzetti "could be found wherever a labor trouble arose, championing the cause of the work-ers. In this way they acquired the reputation of 'Agitators' and gained the hostility of the police."[19]

But it was outside the United States that the extended mass agi-tation sprang up. Demonstrations took place that autumn in France and Italy, with lesser demonstrations in Switzerland, Belgium, Spain, Portugal, Scandinavia, and South America. A bomb exploded in the American embassy in Paris. Another was intercepted in the Lisbon consulate. Reds in Brest stoned the consulate there. American con-suls in Mexico were threatened with death if Sacco and Vanzetti were executed. In Rome thousands of workers marched on the American embassy demanding justice for their compatriots.

Some of this agitation was anarchist-inspired, some actually spontaneous, but most of it was directed by Communist leaders in Paris. For all their tenacity, the anarchists were no longer a mass organization, and so far as European developments were concerned, the East German historian Johannes Zelt is correct in claiming that "from the beginning the Communists stood at the head of the Sacco-Vanzetti campaign." Early in September the French Communist Party's Committee for Action had drawn up a resolution declaring that "only direct and clearly revolutionary action can save the Italian liberators Sacco and Vanzetti from the death penalty to which they have been condemned."

In October President Harding received a protest telegram signed by Anatole France, Romain Rolland, and Henri Barbusse. Anatole France, in one of the last statements before his death, cabled *The Nation*:

> Listen to the appeal of an old man of the old world. . . . Do not let this most iniquitous sentence be carried out. The death of Sacco and Vanzetti will make martyrs of them and cover you with shame. . . . Save Sacco and Vanzetti. Save them for your honor, for the honor of your children, and for the generations yet unborn.

Rank-and-file demonstrators had scarcely heard of Sacco and Vanzetti when they received orders to take to the streets. Sometimes their banners even inscribed the names as "Sachi and Banzet." Although European protesters included men of goodwill of all beliefs and persuasions, control of the movement remained in Paris in the hands of the Communist International, and later the subsidiary Red Aid, founded by the Cheka chief, Dzerzhinski.

When, contrary to European procedure, the guilty verdict was not quickly followed by sentencing and execution but by a long sequence of appeals and postponements, agitation faded away. In the fourth volume of the 1921 *New York Times* index the Sacco-Vanzetti case makes its first large-scale appearance. Over half a page in that October-December index is given to tabulating foreign demonstrations and protests against the verdict. But even as Moore succeeded in getting successive postponements through his inventive motions for a new trial, interest dwindled. For almost five years the case remained dormant, the concern chiefly of members of the defense committee and their sympathizers. Those were the years Lyons called the period of "Early Darkness," in contrast to the 1927 period of "Belated Chic." In 1922 there were only a few lines on Sacco and Vanzetti in the four volumes of the *Times* index. By 1925 the index references were negligible. So little outside interest endured that Sacco's name was even misspelled as "Sacca."

Moore continued working indefatigably to keep the case and his clients alive. Always pressed for funds, he wrote countless dunning letters, cajoled his radical friends and associates, appealed unabashedly to prominent strangers, cultivated sympathetic elderly women. "The one hope for these boys," he wrote to a friend, "now rests in the hope that we may be able to unearth new facts. This means endless investigations. It means that every clue as to the real bandits must be followed up expertly and carefully. As you know this means money."[20] In the next two years Moore filed five supplementary motions for a new trial. One, over the alleged prejudicial remarks of a deceased juror, was negligible. Two motions concerned witnesses whom he had browbeaten to change their stories, although once out of range of his overweening presence they changed back again. He was relentless. No scruples stood in his way. According to Lyons, "Moore had no conscience once he decided his client was innocent. He would stop at nothing, frame evidence, suborn witnesses, have his people work on witnesses who had seen the wrong things—I pity anyone he went after."[21]

One of the defense witnesses, Frank Burke, a Brockton glassblower, had testified that at the time of the shooting he had been standing at the corner of Railroad Avenue and had seen the getaway car move slowly up the hill toward the Rice & Hutchins factory, where two men piled into the backseat, one climbing over into the front seat next to the driver. The car passed within ten feet of Burke, the man in front snapping a pistol at him and shouting: "Get out of the way, you son of a bitch!" That man was not Sacco, Burke had said emphatically. Though no one was then aware of it, before the trial Burke had for some time been working for Moore.

After the trial Burke produced an itinerant peddler, Roy Gould, who said he had been near the South Braintree railroad crossing when the shooting began and that the gunman in the front seat of the getaway car had fired at him. A bullet had gone through his overcoat. The gunman was not Sacco nor was Vanzetti in the car. In May 1922, Moore presented an affidavit from Gould as "new and independent testimony" in his second motion for a new trial.

It so happened that Burke and Gould were old friends, and it seemed a curious coincidence that both should have been by chance in Braintree on the holdup day without spotting one another. It seemed even more curious that Burke and Gould were both members of the IWW, though an old friend of Moore recalled "a number of roughneck Wobblies whom Moore had saved from jail or the noose at various times and who hung around like faithful dogs in the hope of serving him."[22] Some decades later I had a telephone call from a woman who said she was Gould's niece. "I read your book," she said, "and I just wanted to tell you that my uncle was a rogue. After he said a bullet passed through his overcoat, he burned the coat in the incinerator in his back yard. I saw him do it."

Moore had no compunction about falsifying evidence. One of his trial witnesses, James Hayes, a Stoughton mason—Moore referred to him privately as "a Communist who doesn't believe Sacco was guilty"—testified that on April 15, returning from Boston, he had seen Sacco on the afternoon train. Sacco, recalled to the stand, said he was sitting in the coach near Hayes and remembered his face. After Moore had returned to California he admitted to Upton Sinclair that Hayes's story was a fabrication.[23]

Moore's fifth motion would have the most lasting effect, the motion on which Frankfurter based much of his book's argument. It was also the motion that persuaded Governor Dukakis to issue his 1977 proclamation. Its basis was an affidavit from Captain Proctor, who now declared that—by arrangement with the prosecution—he had been willfully misleading in his trial testimony, that he had really had no evidence to convince him that the mortal bullet taken from the dead guard's body had come from Sacco's Colt.

Through his labor connections Moore had been able to gather in the support of union locals from coast to coast. Thanks to accommodating union secretaries the defense committee's letterhead bristled with the names of endorsing unions, endorsements of which the members themselves were scarcely if at all aware. "Moore did a good job," Felicani told Felix. "He penetrated the labor movement when we were completely out, when nobody would listen to us. I say this, he was sincere."[24]

The driblets of money that came to the defense committee from various Italian workmen's groups and labor organizations added up to thousands of dollars. But Moore spent money almost as fast as it came in. It slipped through his fingers like sand. Employing friends as aides and investigators, he scoured the country for clues, ranging as

far north as Maine and upper New York State, as far south as the federal penitentiary in Georgia. Trail after trail he traced to its dead
end.

After a suicide attempt by Sacco in the spring of 1923 and his
diagnosis as suffering from psychosis of a paranoid character, Moore
had him committed to the Bridgewater State Hospital for the Criminally Insane, where he would stay for five months. Sacco never
forgave him for signing the commitment papers. He had long re-
sented Moore's bohemian way of life, the Rollins Place "harem,"
Moore's casual use of defense funds for entertainments and theater
evenings and even for an eye operation for his blonde stenographer.
Yet Moore had kept his clients alive for three years. He had brought
them visitors, arranged for their English lessons, encouraged them in
every way, despite Sacco's latent hostility. The reward for his efforts
had been the sullen suspicions of the anarchist militants. Short of
funds and hampered by the doctrinal disaffection of the defense
committee, in April 1923—with the support of Mrs. Evans, John
Codman, Alice Stone Blackwell, and Norman Thomas—he had organized an independent New Trial League. Sacco's reaction was savage. He wanted no more of Moore. "I can see how clever and cynic
you are," he wrote Moore in stammering anger,

> because after all my protest, after I have been chase you and all yours
> philanthropist freinds, you are still continue the infamous speculation
> on the shoulder of Sacco-Vanzetti case. So this morning before these
> things going any more long, I thought to send you these few line to ad-
> vise you and all your philanthropist friends of the "New Trial League
> Committee" not to print any more these letters with my picture and
> name on, and to be sure to take my name out if they should print any
> more of these little pamphlets, because you and yours philanthropist
> has been use if from last three years like an instrument of infamous
> speculation. It is after all my protest you and all your legione of friends
> still play the infame game. . . . Mr.—Moore—! I am telling you that you
> are goin to stop this dirty game! You heare me?
>
> Maney time you have been deluder and abuse on weakness of my
> comrades good faith, but I want you to stop no and if you please get out
> of my case, because you know that you are the obstacle of the case. . . .
> but my—dear Mr. Moore! I see that you are still in my case and you are
> still continued to play your famous gam. Of course it is pretty hard to
> refuse a such sweet pay that as been come to you right long—in—this
> big—game. It is no true what I said? . . . Another word, if this was not
> the truth you would quit this job for long time. . . . I know that you are

the one that brings in always in these mud in Sacco-Vanzetti case. Otherwise how could I believe you when you been deluder me maney times with your false promise? Well—! anyhow, wherever you do if you do not intent to get out of my case, remember this, that per September I want my case finish. But remember that we are right near September now and I don't see anything and any move yet. So tell me please, why you waiting now for? Do you wait till I hang myself. That's what you wish? Lett me tal you right now don't be illuse yourself because I would not be surprise if somebody will find you some morning hang on lamppost.

Your implacable enemy now and forever,
Nick Sacco[25]

How hurt Moore was he showed only indirectly in the courtesy of his reply:

Dear Mr. Sacco
Enclosed you will find a copy of my withdrawal as your counsel, filed today.
I wish you every possible success in your battle for justice.

Following his withdrawal, Mrs. Evans in an open letter to the friends of the New Trial League wrote that "had it not been for Mr. Moore's devotion to the case, Sacco and Vanzetti would undoubtedly have been under the sod years ago."[26] Frankfurter in his memoirs described Moore as a "blatherskite," but others closer to him respected his efforts. Vanzetti never turned against him.

In November 1924 Moore left Boston for California driving an old Dodge touring car, his sole permanent acquisition from the case, alone, in a frayed suit and cracked boots, with three hundred borrowed dollars in his pocket. Stacked in the rear seat were several dozen packages of little tin signs for attaching to rear number plates that read: IF YOU CAN READ THIS YOU'RE TOO D—N CLOSE. By selling these at filling stations and garages he hoped to cover his expenses on the way. He was filled with a sense of failure as he left. In October Judge Thayer had denied all five supplementary motions. Moore had failed as a lawyer, as an organizer, even as a money-changer. Added to his sense of failure was his lost belief in his clients' innocence. He had spent much time following the trail of a criminal group he had come to believe was involved in the South Braintree crime. "But," Eugene Lyons wrote, "when he got near the end of the trail the Italian anarchist members of the Defense Committee called him in and ordered him to 'lay off.' They wouldn't say why, but the inference is that they feared his line of investigation."[27] Coda, head of the committee, warned him that if he continued that line he, Coda, would personally kill him.

Moore gave four years of his life to the Sacco-Vanzetti case. It was his creation, his great gesture, his great cause. He would never again plead an important case. In 1932 he died of cancer.

10

The Road from Charlestown

ACCO-VANZETTI partisans have tried to make out that
Moore's remarks to Upton Sinclair were those of an embittered man, his mind poisoned by his dismissal from the case. But
Moore's doubts developed long before he left the defense, and he had
imparted them to Mrs. Evans and Roger Baldwin of the American
Civil Liberties Union, among others. After I learned about this I
wrote to Baldwin. He replied that it was true, but when I asked if I
might quote him he refused.

Two weeks after Moore left, Thompson took over as chief counsel. Increasingly indignant at what he considered the persecution of
two innocent radicals, he would go far beyond Moore in his attacks
on the prosecution. As an associate remarked of his casework, "He always got emotionally involved and he always believed the other fellow was a crook."[1] His immediate concern was with technical legal
maneuverings, appeals to higher courts—nothing to make newspaper headlines. Those were the doldrum years. For all the efforts of
the defense committee, for all the occasional labor-union endorsements, locally and internationally the case sank out of sight.

Meanwhile, the good ladies of Boston warmed to the satisfaction
of having at last found a cause worthy of their city's abolitionist past.
"We propose to stand by Sacco and Vanzetti," Mrs. Evans wrote, "as
a second stands by a duellist. . . . We propose to see that every ethic
of justice is observed. If it is not, we can multiply our voices a mil-
lion-fold to spread the news across the land." Over the years she and
her friends would serve as surrogate aunts for the prisoners, visiting
them regularly, bringing them books, fruit, and flowers, writing to
and receiving letters from them. Sacco and Vanzetti became their
tame anarchists, gentle utopians abjuring violence, proletarian Bron-

son Alcotts, "dreamers of the brotherhood of man, who hoped to find it in America"—an anonymous person wrote on slips inserted in the magazines of the Boston Athenaeum's reading room on the day of the two men's execution.

At his arrest Sacco could speak a little English, though he could not write it. Each week Cerise Jack came to the Dedham jail to give him lessons. He was not bookish, and he learned slowly. Not for a year did he venture on his first English letter. Most of his scant, though often moving, correspondence was with Mrs. Jack and with Mrs. Evans, whom he came to regard as a maternal figure. "Since the day that I have meet you, you been occupied in my heart my mother her place," he once wrote her.[2] Yet there were times when, in his doctrinaire anarchism, he turned against these noblesse oblige women with their easy lives and mannered ways. At one point he refused to see any more of Mrs. Jack and her "philanthropist friends." It was left to Vanzetti to write her apologetically that he hoped "Nick will feel much better, and retake his good attitude toward you and those who deserve so well it."[3]

Vanzetti was more pliant, dazzled by his prolonged exposure to these upper-class women. His English teacher, a Mrs. Virginia Mac-Mechan, drove in regularly from her Sharon estate. An eager learner, whimsical in his use of an unfamiliar language, he was even at the beginning strangely susceptible to its cadences. "Our friend tells me that my English is not perfect," he wrote Mrs. Evans in the spring of 1922. "I am still laughing for such a pious euphension. Why do no say horrible?"[4] During his imprisonment his fibrous talent for using an alien tongue grew astonishingly. "I have brought my pebble to the altar of freedom and life," he wrote Mrs. Evans.[5] His letters are threaded with such fresh-minted phrases interspersed among his memories of the outside world—the windy beaches of Cape Cod that he loved, stars glimpsed briefly on a winter night, summer mornings in Italy in his father's garden. He was not a logical thinker but on occasion his thoughts struck deep. The year before his death he wrote:

> I am sure of nothing, I know nothing. When I think of a thing and try to understand it, I see that in the time, in the space, and in the matter that thing is, both before and after, related to so many other things that I, following its relations, both backward and forward, see it dissappear in the ocean of the unknown . . . and myself lost in it.[6]

The rigid creed of anarchism remained the bedrock of the two men's thoughts, echoing their paranoia when it emerged, although in the published letters—as selected by Gardner Jackson and Marion Frankfurter—the more violent passages have been excised and alterations made in spelling, grammar, and, in some cases, meaning.* Vanzetti saw the liberation of life "through a terrific lavacrus of blood."[7] "We did not come to be vanquished but to win," he wrote Alice Stone Blackwell, "to destroy a world of crimes and miseries and to rebuild with its freed atoms a new world."[8] It was a world for which it was necessary that "100 enemies fail to each of us."[9] Though the women who rallied to Sacco and Vanzetti preferred to disregard the fact, the two anarchists were on a path of blood, never repudiating the anarchist tradition of violent overthrow. It was not a fact, as Professor Wieck pointed out at the Boston Public Library conference, that liberal sympathizers in the case have felt comfortable with.[10]

At the Dedham jail, where he still remained awaiting sentence, Sacco was not allowed to work. Vanzetti, serving the sentence in Charlestown prison for his conviction in the Bridgewater holdup, was assigned to the shop making the state's automobile license plates. During the day he painted plates, but he had a free hour before breakfast, another at noon, and the hours remaining between his 4:10 evening meal and the 8:55 lights-out. From these free hours he wrung each precious minute with letters in Italian and English, expanding his means of expression in articles and poems to be published in *L'Adunata dei Refrattari*, writing a brief autobiography, *The Story of a Proletarian Life*, and *Events and Victims*—an account since lost of his experiences in the Springfield Arsenal—translating Proudhon's *The War and the Peace*, denouncing the two trials, always writing. Night after night engrossed in his work, it was as if paradoxically he had found in his prison years the fulfillment of his years of wandering. "Today I have written, written and written all the time," he wrote to Mary Donovan on a free April Sunday of his last year. "Now it is late and I am tired."[11]

The doldrum years ended on November 16, 1925, when a trusty in the Dedham jail, Edward Miller, came to Deputy Jail Master Oliver Curtis to ask if another convict, Celestino Madeiros, under

---

* On July 3, 1927, Sacco wrote Mrs. Evans of his buried life "where none we can see in that four sad wall and a lap of sky that disepere under the wing of a tattefly." Jackson changed "in that" to "but," "disepere" to "disappear," and "tattefly" to "bird." In 1961 I spent part of an afternoon with Jackson and the elder Arthur Schlesinger, and asked him then why he had made these various changes. In some embarrassment he said he had merely wanted to clear up a few solecisms. "Gardner," said Schlesinger, "you have violated the first law of an historian. You have tampered with the text!"

sentence of death for murder, might borrow a pamphlet containing the financial report of the Sacco-Vanzetti Defense Committee that the deputy happened to have. Curtis handed it to him. The report showed that almost $300,000 had been raised. Half an hour later Miller returned the pamphlet with a note addressed to "News Editor Boston American Paper Boston Mass," that read:

> Dear Editor
>   I hear by confess to being in the shoe company crime at south Braintree on April 15 1920 and that Sacco and Vanzetti was not there
> (Signed) Celestino F. Madeiros

Curtis put the note aside.

Two days later Madeiros handed Miller a similar note to pass to Sacco. A petty hoodlum, epileptic and dull-witted, given to sudden violence, Madeiros possessed the animal cunning that often substitutes for intelligence. As a child he had been brought from the Azores to New Bedford and had grown up in the slum streets of the city's Portuguese section. Even before he left school he had been arrested over a dozen times. His life after that can be traced in police-blotter entries. In 1920, one step ahead of the New Bedford police, he moved to Providence, where he settled in a seedy rooming house known as Zack's Hotel with a red-haired girl he had picked up somewhere along the way. From there, sporting a naval officer's discarded uniform, he took to soliciting funds for a nonexistent organization called the American Rescue League, supposedly to aid the children of servicemen. After several profitable months working the streets of Pawtucket, Taunton, Fall River, New Bedford, and other nearby cities, he was arrested by the Providence police and charged with larceny and impersonating a naval officer. While out on bail he was again arrested, this time for breaking and entering, and was sentenced to six months in the house of correction. After his release he took up with a circus girl, following the circus across the country through Texas and as far as Mexico, then north to Tacoma. By early 1924 he was back east, working as a bouncer and carpenter at the Bluebird Inn, a roadhouse and dance hall of dubious repute in Seekonk, four miles from Providence. He owned two revolvers, and one of his amusements was to lie in bed with a plump little Italian hostess named Tessie and shoot flies off the ceiling. Finally, after a gunfight with the Bluebird's owner, he left.

A few months later he went to live with a small-time criminal,

Jimmy Weeks, in a shack on Oak Street, Randolph, only three and a half miles from Braintree, the same street the bandits' getaway car had taken four years earlier. While there he grew familiar with the Randolph area and picked up a certain amount of gossip about the Sacco-Vanzetti case. Running short of money, he decided to hold up the First National Bank in Wrentham, some dozen miles away. With Weeks as an accomplice, he worked out the details over a few drinks in an Andrews Square speakeasy in South Boston.

On November 1 he and Weeks, joined now by two drifters, Alfred Bedard and Harry Goldenberg, drove to Wrentham in a stolen Hudson touring car. In the course of the holdup Madeiros wantonly shot down and killed the eighty-year-old bank cashier. He, Weeks, and Bedard were soon arrested and all three confessed. Goldenberg had disappeared and was never found. Weeks and Bedard were allowed to plead guilty to second-degree murder. They received life sentences. The lawyer for Madeiros, Dedham's Francis Squires, while admitting his client's guilt, tried to argue that he was insane. The jury, unimpressed, took less than an hour to find him guilty. Ordinarily he would have been executed within a month or two. But the judge, a bearded three-hundred-pound eccentric, had long wondered what would happen if in his charge to the jury he should omit the conventional phrase that a man is to be considered innocent until proven guilty, and in Madeiros's case he did omit it. He soon found out, for on Squires's appeal the state supreme court ordered a new trial. It was while this appeal was pending that Madeiros wrote his two notes.

As soon as Thompson learned of Madeiros's confession, he hurried to Dedham to talk with him. In a rambling, at times incoherent account, Madeiros said he had been one of the five South Braintree bandits. The other four were Italians, freight-car thieves whom he had met in a Providence bar several nights before the holdup. One was called Mike, another Bill. He did not know the names of the rest. While he talked, Thompson jotted down notes on the back of an envelope. As Madeiros told it, the four had picked him up at his Providence rooming house in a Hudson touring car at four in the morning of April 15. They had first driven forty-five miles to Boston and from there back to Providence, "just spending time."[12] Then they started out again for Boston, arriving about noon and spending more time in a South Boston speakeasy. Finally they drove to Andrews Square before going on to Randolph.

In the Randolph Woods they switched to an open Buick brought there by a sixth man. The Buick was the car they used in the holdup. During the robbery Madeiros sat in the backseat "scared to death,"[13] a Colt .38 in his lap—to hold the crowd back—though he did not use it. He could not see much because of the flapping side-curtains, but he did see the payroll money, which was tossed into the car in a black bag. They then drove to the Randolph Woods, retrieved the Hudson, and left the Buick with a man to drive it away.

The four had arranged to meet Madeiros the next night in a Providence saloon, but they never showed up. Later he went looking for them unsuccessfully in cabarets in New York and Chicago.

Though Madeiros was willing to talk to Thompson, he was not willing to sign an affidavit until after his second trial. When that took place—in May 1926—the jury quickly returned a guilty verdict. Madeiros then agreed to the affidavit that he and Thompson worked out. Some of its details varied from his informal first confession but the substance remained the same: the two trips from Providence to Boston; his sitting passively in the backseat of the Buick during the holdup; the payroll money in a black bag; the gang switching cars in the Randolph Woods. But now he stated that on the second Boston trip they had driven to Andrews Square to get information at a saloon there about the payroll shipment. Then they had spent some time in a South Braintree speakeasy two or three miles from the place of the crime. As a postscript Madeiros added that he knew the names of the other four but refused to tell who they were.

That Madeiros's story was a fabrication should have been clear to anyone with even a superficial knowledge of the South Braintree crime. According to his schedule, the bandits could not have arrived in South Braintree until shortly before Parmenter and his guard started down Pearl Street with the payroll boxes. Parmenter had set out at quarter past three. Yet Neal, the South Braintree express agent, had spotted the Buick and two of the bandits at half-past nine in the morning, an hour when, according to Madeiros, he and his companions were making their first run to Boston. Just after ten o'clock Harry Dolbeare, a piano tuner, on walking down Washington Street had seen the Buick career past with five men in it. At eleven-thirty Lola Hassam, looking for work, had noticed the Buick parked in front of the lower factory, a dark thickset man tinkering with the motor. She asked him the factory's name and he told her. William Tracy saw two of the bandits near Torrey's drugstore at noon and an hour later William Heron, a railroad detective, saw the two sitting on a bench in the station, the same men who would shortly shoot down the paymaster and his guard. Obviously all five bandits had been in Braintree since early morning.

The Hudson, the rendezvous in the Randolph Woods, and the Andrews Square speakeasy derived from Madeiros's part in the Wrentham holdup. But any credibility he might remotely have had was destroyed at the outset by his statement that the payroll money was in a black bag. His claim that the four other bandits had gone back on their promise to share the loot with him and that he had subsequently searched for them in New York and Chicago cabarets was merely ridiculous.

Why should a man under sentence of death have made such a contrived confession? What did this awkward fraudulence gain Madeiros? In fact, it gained him two years of life, for his execution was repeatedly postponed because of the possible need for his testimony in Sacco-Vanzetti appeals. His first conviction had been overturned. There might be some way to overturn the second, particularly if he had the resources of the Sacco-Vanzetti Defense Committee behind him. In any condemned man's mind the Micawberish hope always lingers that something may turn up. Reading the committee's financial report had made this hope tangible to Madeiros. An organization that had already raised over a quarter of a million dollars might be of some help to him. He had nothing to lose.

If, before making his confession, he had bothered to inform himself of the details of what had really happened in South Braintree on that April afternoon, he could have avoided his more obvious gaffes, could have arranged his story to let himself and his four companions arrive in Braintree at nine in the morning, could have had the payroll money in two metal boxes rather than in an imaginary black bag. He could have familiarized himself with the town's topography, conspicuous features like the large water tower near the railroad crossing. But even then his story would have fallen apart with his account of switching cars.

After the holdup the getaway Buick had turned left from Pearl Street into Washington Street, backtracked down and across several side streets, and then headed south, a route that led through Randolph to North Stoughton, Brockton Heights, and West Bridgewater to the Matfield railroad crossing. A mile and a half beyond Braintree the car with its five passengers passed Walter Desmond, a tobacco salesman. The time was 3:12. Eight minutes later it was sighted in Randolph by Albert Farmer and his wife. At 3:30 John Lloyd and Wilson Dorr, working in a sandpit three miles farther on, noticed the car because of its speed. Francis Clark and Elmer Pool, driving a bakery wagon in Stoughton, a mile beyond the sandpit, were forced over as the car passed them. Clark noticed that the rear window was out. When the car neared Brockton Heights at 3:45, it was going so fast and churning up so much dust that it alarmed sixteen-year-old Julia Kelliher on her way home from school. She tried to make out the license number but could not catch the initial figure. The other four, 9789, she scratched in the sand with a stick.

Flashing past Clark and Pool, the Buick had taken less than ten minutes to cover the six miles to Brockton. But the getaway car took half an hour to go the six additional miles to the Matfield crossing. Nowhere along the road until then would there have been time to switch cars and change license plates. Nor would professional criminals in any case have been so stupid as to reuse the telltale plates. The numbers that Julia Kelliher had scratched in the dust were the ones that Louis Pelser had written on his cutting board as the murder car passed under his factory window. He and Julia had seen the same car. Any transfer of cars took place beyond Brockton Heights.

Between the Heights and Matfield the escape route ran through West Bridgewater only two miles from Puffer's Place, close to where the Buick had been abandoned a hundred yards from the road on a bypath so overgrown with shrubbery that no stranger would be aware of it. Police noticed tire tracks of a smaller second car on the ground. Here, during that unaccounted gap of over twenty minutes, the switch must have taken place. Once again Madeiros's makeshift confession collapses.

For Thompson, nevertheless, his talk with Madeiros presented the solution that the Sacco-Vanzetti case had lacked. But not until after Madeiros's second conviction did he feel free to act. He then filed a motion for a new trial based on the confession. Accompanied by Frankfurter to the Dedham courthouse, he argued with passion and eloquence before an impassive Judge Thayer.

Five months later, on October 22, 1926, Thayer ruled against him. A judge, Thayer concluded, "before setting aside verdicts of a jury on newly discovered evidence, must be satisfied of the probable truthfulness of such evidence."[14] Madeiros's confession he regarded as "unreliable, untrustworthy and untrue."[15] Consequently he was obliged to deny the motion.

To those unaware of the shallow fabric and gross inconsistencies of Madeiros's confession, Judge Thayer's denial seemed a narrowly arbitrary act. So it seemed to F. Lauriston Bullard, chief editorial writer of the *Boston Herald*, Beacon Hill–Back Bay's morning breakfast paper. Coached by Frankfurter, Bullard wrote an extended piece on October 26 expressing doubts that had "solidified into convictions" about the conduct of the Sacco-Vanzetti case and asking for a new trial on the basis of new evidence.

Bullard's editorial—which won a Pulitzer Prize—marked new stirrings in the Sacco-Vanzetti affair. The case was beginning to emerge from its long period of dormancy and move beyond the restricted circle of urban liberals and alien radicals. That May the Massachusetts Supreme Court had rejected Thompson's appeal from Judge Thayer's denial of the first five supplementary motions for a new trial. Overseas his decision was like the tolling of a bell. In the next fifteen months the case would become a passionate issue, a battle cry in all corners of the world. Millions of men in dozens of countries, most of them with only a hazy and erroneous notion of the facts, would identify themselves with the condemned Italians. Anticipating the Supreme Court's adverse decision, the Red Aid's Central European headquarters in Berlin began to flood Europe with Sacco-Vanzetti propaganda and plans for a united front of artists, writers, actors, scholars, and teachers.

The anarchists had never ceased their sporadic and individualistic action, but international anarchy—persisting mostly in the Latin countries—no longer rivaled Marxism as a world movement, as it had in Bakunin's day. The Sacco-Vanzetti case contained, among many other things, the last gesture of international anarchism. Yet the anarchists by themselves could have accomplished little. It was the executive committee of the Communist International, with its tight organization and intricate networks, that was able to stir the streets. By the end of 1926 the groundwork had been laid for the worldwide agitation to come.

In 1925 the American branch of the International Red Aid had been set up in Chicago as the International Labor Defense. For the Communists the Sacco-Vanzetti case was an issue ripe for manipulation. By exploiting it, the party hoped to confirm its pose as the champion of the oppressed and for the first time develop into an American mass movement. After his expulsion from the party, James Cannon, the International Labor Defense's executive secretary, admitted to James Burnham* in the course of a convivial evening that he considered Sacco guilty.[16] But to the Communists, guilt or innocence was immaterial. What mattered was the inflammability of the cause.

Latecomers though the Communists might be, they took the attitude that it was they who had organized the significant protest movement. In America, as abroad, they were able to bring about sensational results. The International Labor Defense poured out posters and buttons and press releases, organized meetings all across the United States, and collected large sums for what Cannon called "the protection" of Sacco and Vanzetti. Almost none of the money collected worldwide by the Red Aid ever reached the defense committee.† Outraged by Communist tactics the committee warned in its *Official Bulletin*: "We are absolutely opposed to the collection of funds and the use of this cause to further special political or economic interests." Through the quiescent years the committee had kept both the case and the defendants alive. Now, as the tempo rose, so did the committee's activity. The headquarters on Boston's Hanover Street became a small publishing house. Tables and typewriters and filing cabinets were wedged in by bales of pamphlets that served as seats for volunteer workers and visitors.

The vague murmurs of 1926 increased to angrily distinct voices that grew to a roar in the spring of 1927 after Frankfurter's "The Case of Sacco and Vanzetti" appeared in the *Atlantic Monthly* and shortly afterward as a 118-page book. Since the early stages of the case Frankfurter had been moving deftly behind the scenes. Now he stepped forward into the spotlight. Thompson had accused Thayer of prejudice only in denying the Madeiros motion, but Frankfurter, in searing language, for the first time accused the judge of prejudice and bias during the trial itself. "Outside the courtroom the Red hysteria was rampant," he wrote; "it was allowed to dominate within."[17] Deliberately, according to Frankfurter, the judge had excited the emotions of jurors still in the grip of war fever. Yet Frankfurter's only objection to the judge's charge was the generality that it "directs the

---

* A former Communist, author of *The Managerial Revolution*.

† Felicani told me that of the half-million dollars collected by the ILD only $6,000 was turned over to the defense committee.

emotions only too clearly."[18] Nor did he bring out any specific fact about the judge's other actions during the six and a half weeks of the trial. Accepting Madeiros's story as a fact, he characterized "with deep regret" Thayer's rejection of the Madeiros motion as a "farrago of misquotations, misrepresentations, suppressions and mutilations,"[19] of which, however, he gave no examples. In addition, he accused the government of conspiring against Sacco and Vanzetti, and the prosecution of falsifying ballistics evidence.

Frankfurter's *tour de force* was quoted, reprinted, paraphrased, dispatched in translations overseas. That a respected professor of law at America's most prestigious university should have written such a denunciation of Massachusetts justice gave the case a vast and receptive national and international audience. "Your name will be ranked with Voltaire," a lawyer enthusiast wrote him.[20] That most liberal of Supreme Court justices, William Douglas, recalled that the book "had been our bible."[21] H. G. Wells, after reading it, became so indignant that he proposed the word *Thayerism* to describe "the self-righteous unrighteousness of established people." Millions read his angry statement in the *London Sunday Express* for June 5, 1927:

> I do not see how any clear-headed man, after reading the professor's summary, can have any other conviction than that Sacco and Vanzetti are as innocent of the Braintree murder, for which they are now awaiting death, as Julius Caesar, or—a better name in this connection—Karl Marx.

In the United States such leaders of enlightened public opinion as Walter Lippmann and Heywood Broun took up the cause in a series of impassioned articles. Those who considered themselves the intelligentsia responded with uncritical mass emotionalism, accepting the innocence of Sacco and Vanzetti and the infamy of the trial as a matter of faith. Even to examine this dogma with an open mind was considered intellectually contemptible, an earlier equivalent of supporting Senator Joseph McCarthy or joining the John Birch Society. For if Felix Frankfurter, Walter Lippmann, John Dewey, Norman Thomas, Jane Addams, Robert La Follette, Sherwood Eddy, H. L. Mencken, John Dos Passos, and hundreds of others of equal note in the literary and academic worlds were so volubly convinced of the two men's innocence, how could any cultivated man think otherwise?

Frankfurter's essay and the sentencing to death of the two men a month later set off the conclusive stage of the case with volcanic suddenness and intensity. Moore had indeed achieved the success he had dreamed of, for in the next four months the names of Sacco and Vanzetti echoed round the globe. President Coolidge was bombarded with messages from Europe under the mistaken assumption that he could overrule state court verdicts. A plethora of letters and telegrams arrived daily for Governor Fuller from such notables as Rabbi Stephen Wise; novelist Gertrude Atherton; biographer Ida Tarbell; Harvard professor of philosophy William Ernest Hocking; the Harvard Law School's dean, Roscoe Pound; historians Arthur Schlesinger and Samuel Eliot Morison; Woodrow Wilson's son-in-law Francis Sayre.

Fuller had started out in life as a bicycle mechanic in lower-middle-class Malden, Massachusetts; with the advent of the auto he became the head of the Packard agency for New England when Packard was the Rolls-Royce of America. Yet for all his money—and he was one of the richest men in the state—he remained a parvenu in his Beacon Street mansion, in awe of the old Boston ascendancy. When Episcopalian bishop William Appleton Lawrence suggested to him that he name a committee to reexamine the controversial case, the suggestion was in the nature of a command.

During the last third of a century Bishop Lawrence's voice had become the ethical voice of established Boston. With his stocky figure and glowing face, the bishop looked a cherubic Puritan. Descended from the founders of the Bay Colony, he had concluded the reconciliation of upper-class Boston with Episcopalianism that had begun with his predecessor, Phillips Brooks, who had even preached before Queen Victoria. The bishop had already been stirred to doubt about the Sacco-Vanzetti verdict after reading Professor Frankfurter's book, and when he was approached by Thompson in regard to the case, he knew at once what his duty was, noting in his diary:

> Sent to Governor a letter saying that in the Sacco-Vanzetti sentence thousands of citizens felt that they had not had a fair trial and asking the Governor to call leading and trusted men to his advice.[22]

The bishop's second cousin, Harvard President Lowell, on reading Frankfurter's book, had also taken pen in hand to write the governor that men like himself with no sympathy for anarchists were troubled by charges that the Sacco-Vanzetti trial had been unfair and the verdict unwarranted by the evidence.

Fuller's response to the bishop's letter was to appoint a three-man advisory committee while at the same time making his own investigation. For the governor, no man could be more trusted than President Lowell, his first choice for the committee. Its other members were a retired probate judge and local novelist, Robert Grant, and President Samuel Stratton of the Massachusetts Institute of Technology. The committee was to review all aspects of the case and decide whether the trial had been fair and whether the defendants were indeed guilty beyond a reasonable doubt. After two months of investigation the committee gave the governor its report. Sacco, the members found, was guilty beyond a reasonable doubt. "On the whole," the committee concluded, "we are of the opinion that Vanzetti was also guilty beyond a reasonable doubt."[23] The phrase "on the whole" would arouse much controversy later.

A week after the committee report was made public, Governor Fuller, having completed his own investigation, refused to consider granting clemency. On August 8 Massachusetts Supreme Court Justice Sanderson, after listening to Thompson's testimony that the rights of the defendants had been violated by Judge Thayer's prejudice, denied an application for a writ of error and stay of execution. Nothing now stood between Sacco and Vanzetti and the electric chair. For all the frenetic activity of their partisans in those August weeks—hasty appeals to the state and federal supreme courts, the delaying paraphernalia of *certiorari* and *habeas corpus*—the advisory committee's report, with Governor Fuller's decision, had made the executions all but inevitable. Desperately the defense committee issued a call for "the leaders of American letters, science, art, education and social reform" to come to Boston. "Come by train and boat, come on foot or in your car! Come to Boston! Let all the roads of the nation converge on Beacon Hill!" Sympathizers swarmed to the city in those August weeks—the dedicated, the troubled, the bohemian, the self-seeking and the selfless, the lovers of justice and the strikers of poses, activated by Frankfurter with cultist devotion. Men and women wearing black armbands and carrying placards denouncing the imminent executions began picketing the State House. Academic conformity, which can be even more rigid than middle-class conformity, belatedly took up the Sacco-Vanzetti cause, in part with sincere deliberateness but more often as an avant-garde gesture. The 381 protesting petitioners from Mount Holyoke, the 326 from Bryn Mawr, the 203 from Wellesley, the faculty and 650 students from the University of California, the 36 Amherst faculty members, the hundreds of names from so many other well-known American colleges and universities were making a reflex response to an appeal to themselves as an elite. Members of assorted law faculties that included Yale, Columbia, Cornell, and the Universities of Kansas, Indiana, Ohio, Illinois, Minnesota, Missouri, Alabama, and Texas appealed to Governor Fuller for commutation on grounds of reasonable doubt. Three members of the defense committee brought a petition to the Massachusetts State House containing 474,842 names from all countries and two weeks later forwarded 153,000 additional names collected by the Swiss Union of Workers.

Within Massachusetts the general public reacted to such outside criticism with xenophobic hostility. The speaker of the Massachusetts House of Representatives received prolonged applause at a banquet when he said that the Commonwealth's answer to outsiders was "mind your own business." The reaction of the little streets was even more savage. In the working-class districts of South Boston and Charlestown and Brighton and Ashmont, feeling against Sacco and Vanzetti combined with social jealousy of the better-known colleges and universities, resentment at the aggressive self-righteousness of intellectuals, suspicion of academic attainments as being tainted with subversion. If the wiser-than-thou professors from Harvard and Yale were taking it on themselves to demand that Sacco and Vanzetti should be freed—then so much the worse for Sacco and Vanzetti! When in the spring Granville Hicks, then teaching English at Smith College, tried to organize a local protest meeting for Sacco and Vanzetti, the townspeople broke it up. As Hicks admitted, it was not just the rich and powerful who were against the two anarchists. "It was also the doctors, the lawyers, the shopkeepers, the farmers, the workers. It was practically all my neighbors in Northampton except for the other members of the college faculty. The battle was between the intellectuals and everybody else."[24]

The battle reached its climax in those heat-hung August days before the executions. Police patrolled the Boston streets with rifles. Buses arrived from New York draped with red streamers, those inside singing "The Red Flag" as they neared their destination. Protesters held gigantic meetings on the Common. Picketing of the State House developed into a ritual, almost a minuet, as picketers wearing black armbands trudged up and down chanting slogans and carrying placards lettered JUSTICE IS CRUCIFIED, JUSTICE IS DEAD. A police lieutenant would give them seven minutes to disperse, and when they did not, they were led by police officers down Beacon Hill to the Joy Street Station, where they were locked up briefly in the rank, smoke-filled detention room, singing "Solidarity Forever" before being released on bail. For a time bail was supplied by Edward Holton James, the wealthy eccentric nephew of Henry and William James. His pockets stuffed with money, accompanied by a plump Portuguese fancy boy, James bailed away until his funds gave out. His place was taken by Zara du Pont—aunt to most of the du Pont dynasty and one of Ehrmann's dedicated dozen—wielding a well-filled purse and a brass ear-trumpet.

Once released the pickets went back up the hill to the State House. Katherine Anne Porter, arriving in Boston with a small Communist group, spent several days alternately picketing and getting arrested.

> On the picket line [she wrote half a century later] I took a good look at the crowd moving slowly forward. I wouldn't have expected to see some of them on the same street, much less the same picket line and in the same jail. I knew very few people in that first picket line, but I remember Lola Ridge, John Dos Passos, Paxton Hibben, Michael Gold, Helen O'Lochlain Crowe (once Jim Larkin's mistress), James Rorty, Edna St. Vincent Millay, Willie Gropper, Grace Lumpkin. . . .
>
> We were as miscellaneous, improbable, almost unassorted a gathering of people to one place in one cause as ever happened in this country. I say almost because among the pickets I did not see anyone identifiably a workingman, or "proletarian," as our Marxist "dialectitians" insisted on calling everybody who worked for his living in a factory, or as they said "sweatshop," or "slave mill," or "salt mine." It is true that these were workdays and maybe all the workingmen were at their jobs. . . . There were plenty of people of the working class there, but they had risen in the world and had become professional paid proletarians, recruits to the intelligentsia, dabbling in ideas as editors, lawyers, agitators, writers who dressed and behaved and looked quite a lot like the bourgeoisie they were out to annihilate.[25]

Day after day she would be led off to the station by the same mild little blond officer, "Irish, very patient, very damned bored with the whole incomprehensible show."[26] Each day he would start off by asking her what she had been doing since the day before.

Her group was headed by Rosa Baron,

> a dry, fanatical little woman who wore thick-lensed spectacles over her blue, accusing eyes—a born whip hand, who talked an almost impene-

trable jargon of party dogma. . . . This demonstration had been agitated for and prepared for many years by the Communists. They had not originated the protests, I believe, but had joined in and tried to take over, as their policy was, and is. Their presence created the same confusion, beclouding the issue and discrediting the cause as it has always done and as they intended it to do. . . . They were well organized to promote disorder and to prevent any question ever being settled—but I had not yet discovered this; I remarked to our Communist leader that even then, at that late time, I still hoped the lives of Sacco and Vanzetti might be saved and that they would be granted another trial. "Saved," she said, ringing a change on her favorite answer to political illiteracy, "who wants them saved? What earthly good would they do us alive?"

I was another of those bourgeois liberals who got in the way of serious business, yet we were needed, by the thousands if possible, for this great agitation must be made to appear to be a spontaneous uprising of the American people, and for practical reasons, the more non-Communists, the better. They were all sentimental bleeders, easily impressed.[27]

After his sentencing in April, Sacco had been taken from the Dedham County Jail to Charlestown State Prison, where Vanzetti had been confined since being sentenced for the earlier Bridgewater holdup. For the first time in six years the two men were brought together, under the shadow of the electric chair.

In the last hectic August week Isaac Don Levine—to the fury of Mary Donovan—came from New York to set up a Citizens National Committee for Sacco-Vanzetti at the Hotel Bellevue, next to the State House. Centrally located, the committee headquarters at the Bellevue's Parlor D, rather than the defense committee's Hanover Street headquarters, became the focus of defense activity. Most of the protesting personages, from Ida Tarbell and Edna St. Vincent Millay to Oswald Garrison Villard and John Dewey, gravitated to Parlor D. At this point the Massachusetts attorney general gave secret permission to the State Police to monitor Parlor D "using a dictograph or other device." All that survives is a fragment of anonymous conversation recorded at 1:30 on the morning of Tuesday, August 22:

"Come in."
"Hello. Well it looks as if they will die tomorrow."
"Yes, but you know they are guilty and that we have put up one grand and glorious fight for them even though we didn't have a chance."

"Do you really think they are guilty?"

"Yes, I do."[28]

On Wednesday, Boston became a beleaguered city, the center of world attention. From the state prison pressroom, Western Union and Postal Telegraph had installed eighteen wires, four for direct communication overseas. Charlestown's Prison Point Bridge was closed and the slum streets about the prison roped off for a mile and patrolled by mounted troops with tear gas and gas masks. Machine guns were set up on the prison walls and catwalks. As the twilight faded, searchlights probed the darkness above the gray tenements. Three hundred patrolmen surrounded the prison, supported by fifty state troopers, seventy mounted police, twenty motorcycle officers, and seventy-five Boston & Maine railroad police. In Charlestown's City Square a crowd of several thousand milled about beyond the barriers. Hundreds stood in Boston's newspaper row looking up at the bulletin boards. Local radio stations announced they would not shut down at ten but stay on the air until after midnight, the time set for the executions. Yet except for the ineffectual attempt of a small group of militants to break through the Charlestown barricades, the city remained passive. The turbulence that occurred lay far beyond Boston.

Earlier in the month protest bombs had gone off in the New York subway, in Philadelphia, at the house of Baltimore's mayor, and in a number of cities overseas. In Uruguay a statue of Washington was demolished. One of the Dedham trial jurors living in Milton had his house dynamited. On the execution day itself there were more protests in the big cities. Guards with riot guns patrolled the Capitol in Washington. In New York the Communist Sacco-Vanzetti Emergency Committee called for a general strike. Philadelphia police used clubs to break up a turbulent Sacco-Vanzetti meeting. Violence broke out in European capitals as mobs converged on United States embassies.

At midnight Boston was so hushed that a church clock striking the execution hour echoed clearly over the city. Madeiros, waiting in the death house with the other two, was the first to go, led by two guards to the electric chair, shuffling, almost inanimate, sunk in a saurian torpor. He sat like an automaton, saying nothing as the electrodes were fastened to his legs and arms, the headpiece adjusted, and a black mask placed over his face. At a nod from the warden, the executioner pulled the switch.

Sacco and Vanzetti sustained their role to the end with dignity, courage, and loyalty to their faith, fortified by the cold solace of martyrdom. They had become more than themselves, symbols, and never more so than in this last hour. Their names, as they were so well aware, echoed round the globe, their fate was a world concern. Sacco, who preceded Vanzetti, walked to the electric chair and sat down unaided but looked about wildly as a guard began to adjust the straps. Then, controlling himself, in the iron tradition of his belief he called out loudly in Italian: "Long live anarchy!" More quietly, he added in English: "Farewell my wife and child and all my friends." As the mask covered his eyes and the executioner's hand felt for the switch, in that last second he moved beyond anarchy, friends, wife, children, to that deepest and most elemental part of himself. "Mamà!" he called out just before his voice was extinguished.

When the guards came for Vanzetti, he knew that the other two were already dead. He entered the death chamber, his head erect, his step firm. Just inside the door he paused and said with great precision: "I wish to say to you that I am innocent. I have never done a crime, some sins, but never any crime. I thank you for everything you have done for me. I am innocent of all crime, not only this one, but of all, all. I am an innocent man." He shook hands with the warden, the deputy warden, the prison doctor, and two of the guards, then sat down in the chair. After his eyes had been covered and the guard was adjusting the contact pad to his bare leg, he spoke again. "I now wish to forgive some people for what they are doing to me," he said quietly. The warden's eyes were full of tears as he gave the signal to the executioner.

After the news flashed from Charlestown that Sacco and Vanzetti had at last been executed, the reverberations were international. Demonstrations in American cities were duplicated and in many cases exceeded all over Europe. In Paris the Communist daily *L'Humanité* printed an extra sheet on which was splashed the single black word *"Assassinés!"* Crowds surged down the boulevard Sebastopol, ripping up lampposts and tossing them through plate-glass windows. Protective tanks ringed the American embassy, and sixty policemen were injured when a mob tried to set up barricades there. Five thousand militants roamed the streets of Geneva the evening before the executions, overturning American cars, sacking shops selling American goods, gutting theaters showing American films. One of the greatest demonstrations in the history of the Weimar Republic took place in Berlin; there were tumultuous demonstrations in Bremen and Wilhelmshaven and Hamburg, and a two-hour torchlight parade in Stuttgart. During that turbulent week half-a-dozen German demonstrators were killed. No one was killed in England, but on the night of the executions a crowd gathered before Buckingham Palace and sang "The Red Flag." Flags few at half-staff on London's Labour party building, as they did throughout the Soviet Union. Not only in Europe but in Shanghai, Tokyo, Calcutta, Mexico City, Buenos Aires, the names Sacco and Vanzetti had become familiar syllables, with the image fixed of two dissenters from the American way of life being done to death for their dissent. Mass demonstrations took place from Moscow to Melbourne.

To overseas intellectuals, disillusioned by the collapse of Wilsonian idealism, the Sacco-Vanzetti case was one more devastating example from postwar America, to be set beside Prohibition, Chicago gangsters, the white-sheeted Ku Klux Klan, and the Tennessee monkey trial. The fate of the two men was what one might expect from the heartless materialism of the transatlantic republic that had won a war with its money and the blood of others and now wanted the money back.

For three turbulent days the bodies of Sacco and Vanzetti lay on view at Langone's funeral parlor on Hanover Street before being taken the four and a half miles to the Forest Hills Crematory. Sunday, the day of the funeral, turned chill and windy with fog drifting in from the harbor. By the time the funeral procession started at two o'clock, a drizzling rain had begun to fall. The air smelt of bladder wrack and the coming autumn.

Some eight thousand militants accompanied Langone's two massive Cunningham hearses over the police-prescribed route. Those just ahead of the hearses carried large floral displays of red roses and scarlet carnations. Soon finding these too heavy, they tore them apart, scattering the flowers in the street. Many of the marchers wore scarlet armbands with black lettering:

REMEMBER

JUSTICE CRUCIFIED

August 27, 1927

The procession moved down Tremont Street in the rain, then straggled through the lodging-house district of the South End to Washington Street and under the el structure to Forest Hills. Now and again marchers clashed with the police, jeered and catcalled, and a few even threw stones. The rain pelted down now. More and more marchers dropped out. Only a few hundred reached the crematory, where several thousand sympathizers who had come by car or on the el were waiting outside on the soggy grass.

The chapel was too small for any but relatives and those most closely connected with the cause. Standing before the coffins, white-faced Mary Donovan spoke the eulogy, five bitter paragraphs written by Gardner Jackson. "One of the blackest crimes in history," she declaimed in her rasping nasal voice. "Massachusetts and America have killed you—murdered you because you were Italian anarchists. . . . The minds of those who killed you are not blinded. They have committed this act in deliberate cold blood. . . . You, Sacco and Vanzetti, are victims of the crassest plutocracy the world has known since ancient Rome. . . .

"In your martyrdom we will fight on and conquer,"[29] she prophesied, her voice edged with hysteria. It was a prophecy already on the way to fulfillment. Those supporters in the funeral march from the North End to Forest Hills, those millions of marchers and protesters round the globe, had become followers, acknowledging Sacco and Vanzetti as martyrs whose blood was shed to redeem mankind from the sins of the capitalist world. Even before their execution the apotheosis had begun, the imagery of the Passion read into their particular fate. So the two anarchists in their last months had come to see themselves. Vanzetti, at his sentencing in April, accused his Plymouth lawyer of selling him "for thirty golden money like Judas sold Jesus Christ."[30] "Much have we suffered during this long Calvary," Sacco wrote in a farewell letter to his son Dante.[31]

Some of their more fervent admirers, most of them atheists, portrayed them as Christ-figures. Malcolm Cowley wrote:

> March on, o dago Christs, whilst we
> march on to spread your name abroad
> like ashes in the winds of God.[32]

A long-forgotten versifier, Vincent G. Burns, warned:

> Cruel men, beware! The Christs you kill
> Will walk in power with us still! [33]

One Clement Wood poeticized a "Golgotha in Massachusetts," as did Henry Reich, Jr., with:

> On new Golgotha the cross is set
> To slay these Christs.[34]

Ralph Cheney's America had become "My Judas Land." Jeannette Marks poeticized "Two Crucified." There would be no such outpourings of bad verse again until John Kennedy's assassination, though by Kennedy's time rhyme had fallen out of fashion.

For James Rorty, Sacco and Vanzetti had "indeed given us a new testament for our time."[35] John Haynes Holmes in reviewing the posthumously published *Letters of Sacco and Vanzetti* compared the book to Plato's *Apology* and *Crito* and certain passages of the Gospels. "They speak," he wrote, "like Jesus and Socrates."[36] In his impressionistic novel *The Passion of Sacco and Vanzetti*, Howard Fast saw their deaths as "your passion and mine. . . . It is the passion of the Son of God who was a carpenter."[37] Ben Shahn, who had come to Boston twice in the last days to join the State House picket line, gave the same title to the vast mosaic he created for the campus of Syracuse University. "Even as a youngster," he wrote, "I always regretted not having lived in some great historic time; the time of Lincoln or Washington, or even during the Crucifixion. Then suddenly it came to me—this was a crucifixion itself—right in front of my own eyes."[38] His Passion mosaic, sixty feet long and twelve feet high, on the east wall of the Huntington Beard Crouse Building, portrays their martyrdom for the ages, the legend's perdurable monument.

11

The Path of the Bullet

A few days after Governor Dukakis's 1977 pronouncement
vindicating Sacco and Vanzetti, I appeared on a television
program with, among others, his legal counsel, Daniel Taylor, on
whose advice he had issued his proclamation. A sallow youngish
man, Taylor had a politician's professional smile and a spasmodically
drooping eyelid, the combination giving him an oddly Mephistophe-
lian aspect. Grinning and winking, he told his listeners that Sacco
and Vanzetti had been tried in an atmosphere of "political hysteria"
and that there were "compelling grounds for believing the legal proceedings were permeated with unfairness." Television, I thought as I
watched him wink, was not his medium. He should have stuck to
radio.

After the program I asked him what his "compelling grounds"
were. Chiefly, he said, he based them on Captain Proctor's courtroom testimony that Bullet III was "consistent" with being fired
from Sacco's Colt whereas his real belief was that it had not been.
This alone, in Taylor's opinion, should have justified a new trial.

Originally Proctor had headed the South Braintree investigation
and he had never forgiven the district attorney for removing him. He
was equally disgruntled at having been passed over for appointment
as head of the newly established Massachusetts State Police Ballistics
Laboratory in favor of the more qualified Van Amburgh. When, after
the trial, he submitted a bill for $500 for his testimony, Katzmann
declined to approve it, maintaining that such testimony was part of
his official duties. From then on Proctor refused to speak to him. Two
years later Proctor was persuaded by a post-trial ballistics expert of
uncertain reputation, Albert Hamilton, to sign an affidavit shaped

by Thompson, who had entered the case for the limited purpose of arguing motions for a new trial. Submitted in support of the fifth supplementary motion, known as the Proctor-Hamilton motion, the affidavit stated that

> at the trial the District Attorney did not ask me whether I had found any evidence that the so-called mortal bullet passed through Sacco's pistol, nor was I asked that question on cross examination. The District Attorney desired to ask me that question, but I had repeatedly told him that if he did I should be obliged to answer in the negative. . . . Bullet Number III passed through some Colt automatic pistol, but I do not intend to imply that I found any evidence that the so-called mortal bullet had passed through this particular Colt automatic pistol and the District Attorney well knew that I did not so intend and framed his question accordingly. Had I been asked the direct question: whether I had found any affirmative evidence whatever that this so-called mortal bullet had passed through this particular Sacco's pistol, I should have answered then, as I do now without hesitation, in the negative.[1]

As all lawyers know, though few laymen realize, such affidavits are commonly construed by lawyers and merely signed by those supposedly making them. If Proctor had been asked whether he had found any evidence that the mortal bullet had *not* been fired from Sacco's pistol, he would also have had to answer in the negative. Stripped of Thompson's tendentious language, what the affidavit really says is that Proctor did not know one way or the other. Assistant District Attorney Williams described the incident in a counter-affidavit:

> He [Proctor] said that all he could do was to determine the width of the landmarks on the bullet. His attention was not repeatedly drawn to the question, whether he could find any evidence which would justify the opinion that this bullet came from the Sacco pistol. I conducted the direct examination of Captain Proctor at the trial and asked him the question quoted in his affidavit, "Have you an opinion as to whether Bullet 3 was fired from the Colt automatic which is in evidence?"
>
> This question was suggested by Captain Proctor himself as best calculated to give him an opportunity to tell what opinion he had respecting the mortal bullet and its connection with the Sacco pistol. His answer in court was the same answer he had given me personally before.[2]

Katzmann declared under oath that

prior to his testifying, Captain Proctor told me that he was prepared to testify that the mortal bullet was consistent with having been fired from the Sacco pistol; I did not repeatedly ask him whether he had found any evidence that the mortal bullet had passed through the Sacco pistol, nor did he repeatedly tell me that if I did ask him that question he would be obliged to reply in the negative.[3]

Proctor did not believe it was possible to match bullets fired from any particular gun, but he did believe it possible to determine the type of gun from which any particular bullet had been fired. In a 1915 case, when he was asked if two bullets taken from a dead man's body had been fired from a designated revolver, he replied: "I came to the conclusion that it *was consistent*—those two bullets with having been fired from this revolver or a revolver that had an imperfection exactly like it."[4]

Sacco-Vanzetti partisans have reiterated over the years that Proctor really believed Bullet III had *not* passed through Sacco's pistol, and that Katzmann and Williams had rigged his testimony to deceive the jury. It is a claim that has hardened into dogma. In 1971 Giuliano Montaldo, in his Sacco-Vanzetti film, had the dying Proctor make a lachrymose deathbed confession, although Proctor was in good health at the time of his affidavit.

As to "consistent," there was nothing so unusual in Proctor's use of the word, one he had used in previous cases and would use again in reference to Shell W. It is a word commonly employed by lawyers to express probability when they are not certain. The jurors, according to John Dever, their youngest, were not misled. Twenty-nine years after the trial Dever told the reporter Edward Simmons that "Sacco and Vanzetti were not convicted on the basis of Proctor's evidence."[5]

Judge Thayer, though much maligned, dealt with the matter reasonably enough. In denying the Proctor-Hamilton motion for a new trial he pointed out that the word *consistent* was chosen by Proctor, not Williams. He wrote:

> The questions propounded by Mr. Williams were clearly put, fairly expressed, and easily understood; they have been so commonly used by experienced trial lawyers throughout the Commonwealth for so many years that they have become almost stereotyped questions.[6]

Felix, one of the most coldly detached students of the case, considers Proctor's affidavit "a hairsplitting exercise by a man who did not know his subject; his affidavit offers too little substance for serious consideration."[7]

At the trial the experts had been more concerned with the bullets than with the shells, apparently unaware that the breechblock scorings on a shell base are as individual as fingerprints. Both sides agreed that the firing-pin indentation on Shell W differed from the indentations on the other three shells Bostock had given to Fraher. But whether the firing-pin mark on Shell W matched the firing-pin marks on the bullets tested in Lowell was a matter of dispute. When Williams asked Proctor if in his opinion the mark on the base of Shell W and the marks on the test shells were "consistent with being fired from the same weapon," Proctor replied: "I think so, the same make of weapon . . . there is a similarity between the W.R.A. [Shell W] and the other cartridges that were fired."[8] Van Amburgh found "a very strong similarity" between the firing-pin mark on Shell W and the other three Winchesters fired at Lowell.[9] Further than that neither would go. Henry Fitzgerald, the defense expert, contradicted them, saying flatly that the hole made by the firing pin in Shell W was "not the same" as in the test shells.[10]

The Proctor-Hamilton motion did give Moore the opportunity to reopen the ballistics question, reexamine the evidence, and sponsor new tests. He had placed Dr. Albert Hamilton in charge, a ballistics expert of tall claims whom he had met a few weeks earlier. Hamilton, after testing the bullets and shells, produced an extended affidavit in which he stated that Bullet III and Shell W in no way matched the Lowell test shells and bullets, and that they could not possibly have been fired from Sacco's Colt. Aware now of the significance of breechblock markings, he claimed that those on the base of Shell W bore no relation to the markings on the breechblock of Sacco's Colt. Shell W's firing-pin indentation differed, as well, from those on the test bullets. Concluding his involved explanation, he gave his "unqualified opinion" that the mortal bullet "was not fired through Sacco's pistol. . . ."[11]

Hamilton's findings were supported by Augustus Gill, professor of technical chemical analysis at the Massachusetts Institute of Technology, a specialist in the study of microscopy and microscopic measurements. After making extensive measurements of the lands and grooves on the Sacco pistol, on the mortal Bullet III, and on the Lowell test bullets, Gill in a brief affidavit stated that "I am absolutely convinced . . . that the so-called mortal bullet never passed through the Sacco gun."[12] Under Hamilton's direction Wilbur Turner, a Boston commercial photographer, made a series of photomicrographs of the exhibits. Countering Hamilton, Van Amburgh dealt with each of his claims point by point. At the trial he had been "inclined to believe." Since that time he had developed a device called a spiralgraph with which he was able to make strip photographs of bullets as they revolved on a turntable. By comparing the strips of two bullets, he maintained he could determine whether or not they had been fired from the same gun. Having taken and compared strip photographs of Bullet III and a Lowell test bullet and made additional comparison photographs of the breechblock markings, he was now unequivocal. "The facts which I have found from my entire investigation," he concluded, "are so clear that they amount to proof."

> I am absolutely certain that Shell W was fired in the Sacco pistol.* The score of the firing pin in the pistol is registered in the firing pin indentations in the Lowell Winchester shells and in Shell W. The impression of the breech block of the Sacco pistol is clearly shown on the primer surfaces of the Lowell Winchester shells and of Shell W. . . . I am also positive that the mortal bullet was fired in the Sacco pistol.[13]

Merton Robinson, a ballistics engineer for the Winchester Arms Company, in World War I a member of a special commission to observe the effectiveness and quality of ammunition furnished the troops, corroborated Van Amburgh. "From my careful examination and measurements," he wrote in a brief affidavit, "I am satisfied that Shell W . . . and the fired Winchester bullet known as the mortal bullet were fired from [Sacco's] Colt automatic pistol."[14]

Dr. Hamilton's doctorate was self-awarded. A druggist and concocter of patent medicines from Auburn, New York, with a morbid interest in crime, he advertised himself as a "microchemical investigator" and a qualified expert in chemistry, microscopy, handwriting, ink analysis, typewriting, photography, fingerprints, toxicology, gunshot wounds, guns and cartridges, bullet identification, gunpowder, nitroglycerine, dynamite, high explosives, blood and other stains, causes of death, embalming, and anatomy. In the then primitive state of ballistics knowledge, he had managed to insinuate himself into a number of trials—229, according to him. Not only were his findings at times fallible but even venal. In the 1915 trial of an illiter-

---

* In the transcript Shell W is referred to as Fraher Shell F4.

ate farm tenant for double murder, he had testified that the fatal bullets had been fired from the man's revolver. The tenant was found guilty and sentenced to death. Later it was demonstrated that the bullets were completely dissimilar and that the tenant's rusty revolver had not been fired in years.* In 1934 Hamilton would testify in a New York kidnapping case that a defendant's handwriting was completely different from the handwriting on certain ransom notes. But under cross-examination he was forced to admit that he had earlier been ready to testify for the prosecution that the handwritings were similar. Hamilton was, in brief, a voluble, many-faceted charlatan who had developed a certain expertise in ballistics.

Whatever his expertise, during the hearings on the fifth supplementary motion, Hamilton came close to overturning the Sacco-Vanzetti verdict. On the last day of the hearings he appeared in court with two .32-caliber Colt automatics and, without explaining what he was trying to prove, asked and was allowed by Judge Thayer to compare them with Sacco's pistol. Before judge and lawyers he stripped all three pistols and placed the parts in three piles on the table. Picking up the parts one by one, he explained their function and pointed out their interchangeability, although there seemed no relevance in what he was doing. Afterward he reassembled the pistols quickly, without anyone noticing that he had slipped the barrel of Sacco's pistol into one of his own. He then put his two pistols in his pocket, handed Sacco's to the clerk, and followed the lawyers out of the courtroom.

The Sacco-Vanzetti case might have ended then and there. Later, when additional tests would have demonstrated that Bullet III could *not* have been fired through the switched Colt barrel, the way would have been open to reverse the two men's convictions and set them free. But as Hamilton and the lawyers reached the threshold, Judge Thayer suddenly called out: "Just a minute, gentlemen!" They turned back, and Thayer told Hamilton to hand over his pistols. When he did so, Thayer impounded them. Shortly before his death the judge told Van Amburgh: "I don't know why I impounded those pistols. It just seemed the thing to do. I have thanked God many times since that I did so. And then the astounding discovery made later that the original barrel in Sacco's pistol was missing and an entirely different barrel substituted for it!"[15]

* This was the Stielow trial, which took place in New York. A full account is given in Edwin Borchard's book *Convicting the Innocent* (New Haven, Conn.: Yale University Press, 1932).

The impounded pistols were sealed in boxes and locked away by the clerk of court. At the close of the hearing Hamilton had requested permission to fire a hundred cartridges through the Sacco pistol to demonstrate the location of the firing-pin indentations. If, subsequently, he had managed to walk out of court with his two pistols and then later test-fired the Sacco pistol, such prolonged firing would have fouled the new barrel and blurred the evidence of any substitution. Judge Thayer's intuitive gesture intervened.

Three months after Hamilton's courtroom demonstration, Van Amburgh told Williams—who had now succeeded Katzmann as district attorney—that he had examined Sacco's Colt and found that the barrel was not the original barrel. Moore was notified. Two days later Sheriff Capen brought the pistols into court and they were taken from their boxes in the presence of Hamilton, Van Amburgh, and the lawyers for both sides. One of Hamilton's new Colts was found to have an "old, rusty and foul" barrel. Sacco's pistol had a new barrel, although the end of the muzzle had been artificially treated to make it look old. The question arose as to who might have made the substitution, inasmuch as the exhibits had been under lock and key since they were impounded. Williams maintained that the "tricky" substitution had been made by Hamilton with the aim of securing a new trial.

Hamilton brazened it out. Admitting that the barrel presently in Sacco's Colt belonged to the new Colt, he denied that the rusty and foul barrel had ever come from Sacco's pistol, and he accused Van Amburgh of making the switch in an effort to discredit him. Judge Thayer reserved judgment about who had made the substitution and whether it had been accidental, ruling merely that the fouled barrel was from Sacco's pistol and that it should be replaced without prejudice to either side.

The ballistics issue would not be raised again until the crisis summer of 1927, two months before Sacco's and Vanzetti's execution. Colonel Calvin Goddard, the inventor of the comparison microscope and one of three men in the country who had established firearms identification as a trustworthy element of legal proof, then came to Boston at his own expense and requested permission to demonstrate the effectiveness of his new instrument by testing the Sacco-Vanzetti ballistics evidence. The district attorney's office agreed to allow tests, but Thompson—who had now taken over the defense—refused to have anything to do with them.

The tests took place in the clerk of court's office in Dedham.

Ehrmann was present as an observer, along with several newspapermen and Professor Gill. Goddard proceeded to match Bullet III and Shell W with test shells and bullets. His findings were that Bullet III and Shell W "had been fired in Sacco's pistol and could have been fired from no other," and he invited those present to look at the matched bullets through his microscope. Gill, on looking through, remarked: "Well, what do you know about that!" Following Goddard's demonstration, Gill broke with the defense and repudiated his earlier findings. So did one of the defense's trial experts, James Burns. Ehrmann, after peering through the microscope, said nothing but refused to sign the report.

For Sacco-Vanzetti partisans to have accepted Goddard's conclusions would have meant accepting Sacco's guilt. Since Sacco by their definition had to be innocent, Goddard had to be wrong. But it took half a year of hectic research before they came up with a refutation. Goddard, they then revealed, had testified in a Cleveland murder trial that two bullets taken from a dead man's body matched two test bullets fired from a suspect's pistol. The suspect was nevertheless able to prove that he had bought his pistol *after* the murder. This, according to a *Nation* article, completely discredited Goddard as an expert.[16] He and his comparative microscope were not, however, at fault. It turned out that the Cleveland police had sent him mislabeled bullets. In accordance with the labels, he compared a death bullet with a death bullet and a test bullet with a test bullet. Obviously they matched.

After Goddard's findings, Hamilton conducted new tests and made additional photographs. But though devious, he was no fool, and however he might argue, he was again faced with persuasive evidence that Bullet III and Shell W had been fired in Sacco's Colt.

Hamilton did not announce the results of his tests, but Professor Morgan admitted, on examining the Hamilton photographs, that the scorings on the base of Shell W and the Lowell tests shells were identical.

Such was the quandary facing the defense in that final summer. At the hearings of the Lowell Committee, Thompson and Ehrmann, desperately trying to find their way around the Goddard report and the Hamilton photographs, for the first time raised the question as to whether a test bullet might have been substituted for the mortal bullet. Thompson began by asking Katzmann if he had noticed that scratchings made by the medical examiner on the base of Bullet III differed from those on the other three taken from Berardelli's body. Katzmann said that the question had never been raised. Ehrmann then brought in Turner, the photographer, who said he had recently examined the markings on the base of Bullet III and on the other three bullets. "There was a difference," he told the committee. "There was a tremendous difference in the marking, as though they were made with a different tool or scratched with a different instrument."[17] Through Ehrmann's eyes, bullets "1, 2 and 4 were marked in clean, parallel lines. No. 3 seemed obviously, even to the naked eye, to be marked by a clumsier hand and blunter instrument. . . . The fact is that they are completely different—that is obvious."[18]

Both Ehrmann and Thompson took almost exaggerated pains not to implicate Katzmann, Williams, or Dr. Magrath in any skulduggery. "I want to say at the start," Ehrmann told the committee, "that I share your abhorrence and incredulity at the thought that the District Attorney or Dr. Magrath would be party to substituting any exhibit."[19] Although he did not say so directly, he implied that Proctor—now dead—was the guilty agent. Since, he held, Proctor had admitted to one deception, he might indeed have been guilty of a far greater one. Ehrmann, in his final argument, suggested that

> something happened to one of the bullets. Understand, I do not say that either Mr. Katzmann, or Mr. Williams, or Dr. Magrath had anything to do with it. We have only the presumption in favor of Captain Proctor that it did not happen. . . . Now, I do not know what this Commission makes of Captain Proctor now. He apparently did something that he was mightily ashamed of. It was on his conscience.[20]

After Katzmann and Williams were dead, Ehrmann's abhorrence diminished. In 1969 he wrote:

> The trial record shows that Mr. Katzmann, in preparing his case, seized upon everything, no matter how flimsy, ephemeral or dubious, which might be made to prove, or even suggest, the guilt of the defendants. *Nevertheless, prior to the trial, after consulting his two experts, he abandoned any claim that Sacco's pistol had fired any particular bullet.* Later at the trial and in motions thereafter, he reversed his position entirely and claimed that Sacco's Colt had killed Berardelli. What caused such a drastic change in Mr. Katzmann's position? And is it possible that the physical evidence itself also underwent a change? [21]

Ehrmann was at least right in stating to the Lowell Committee that only Proctor was in a position to make any substitution, since the exhibits had been solely in his custody until the trial. At the trial Dr. Magrath, on examining Bullet III, identified it as the one he had taken from Berardelli's body. Consequently, any substitution would have had to have taken place during the Lowell test firings. But Bullet III was of the obsolete Winchester type unavailable at Lowell.

Beyond that, there is the question of motivation. What might have induced Proctor to have committed such a monstrous act in order to send two supposedly innocent men to their death? Neither Thompson nor Ehrmann supplied an adequate answer. If Proctor had made a substitution, his conscience might have troubled him afterward, but at least, when he testified at the trial, he could have dispensed with the qualifying "consistent," for he would have *known* that Bullet III had passed through Sacco's Colt. And if, when he signed his affidavit for Thompson, he had confessed to having made a bullet substitution, it would automatically have brought about a new trial. By implicating Katzmann and Williams he could not only have got even, he could have destroyed them. Morgan admitted that "until the hearing before the Lowell Committee there was no suggestion that Exhibit 18 [Bullet III] was not the fatal bullet, and there has not yet been disclosed anything that could reasonably be dignified as evidence to support any such suggestion."[22]

In 1961 I was able to examine the bases of the four bullets at the state ballistics laboratory and could see no real difference in the markings on Bullet III and on the other three bullets.* Partisans of Sacco and Vanzetti have continued to insist that there is. In 1982 Professor Regis Pelloux of the Massachusetts Institute of Technology, an expert in metallics, conducted tests on the four bullets to determine whether the numeric scratches on Bullet III differed from those on the other three bullets. He concluded that there were both differences and similarities, but that the differences could be explained by the deformation of Bullet III.[23]

Ehrmann, with a lawyer's ambivalence, continued to hold that: (a) the Goddard tests, and those I arranged in 1961, offered no conclusive proof that Shell W and Bullet III had been fired in Sacco's Colt; and (b) that Shell W and Bullet III were fraudulently substituted for the original shell and bullet. Shortly before his death in 1969 I wrote and asked him which he held to. Did he believe (a) that the tests were flawed? Or did he believe (b) that there had been a substitution of the original shell and bullet? If (a) was correct, I

---

* I then had the four bases photographed, the first photographs ever made of them.

wrote, (b) must be false. If (b) was correct, (a) must be false. Which was his choice? "Your letter," he replied, without indicating any choice, "is merely an exercise in logic."

In the agitation of the last weeks and following the executions, Sacco-Vanzetti partisans were not as scrupulous about connecting Proctor with Katzmann and Williams as Thompson and Ehrmann had been before the Lowell Committee. It would become part of the dogma that the district attorney had connived with Proctor in manipulating ballistics evidence to secure a conviction. But again there is the question of motivation. For Katzmann, the trial, at its beginning, was just another trial. If he had lost, he would have congratulated Moore and forgotten about it by the next session. He had no great stake in securing a conviction. His was merely the functioning of the adversary system. Before and after the trial he had an honorable if parochial career. Jerry McAnarney, though staying with the defense almost until the end, remained one of his half-dozen best friends. Those whom I talked with who knew Katzmann agreed that he was not a man who would have stooped to tampering with evidence. The liberal-minded former Massachusetts commissioner of correction, Eliot Sands, who lived for a number of years next door to Katzmann, told me it was impossible for him to have done such a thing. Paul Reardon, the retired chief justice of the Massachusetts Superior Court, knew both Katzmann and Williams. "A bit of a rough diamond, Katzmann," he told me, "but a thoroughly upright man. That talk of his plotting to substitute bullets is nonsense. And Williams as justice of our supreme court was one of the most respected lawyers in the state."

A man of polished integrity, Williams was so well thought of in Massachusetts that even Ehrmann could say nothing against him except that he was wrong about the Sacco-Vanzetti case. Throughout the years the two remained on courteous terms.

If Ehrmann and Jerry McAnarney had truly believed that Katzmann and Williams were accomplices in railroading their clients to death on false evidence, would they have tolerated the slightest association with them? Katzmann suffered the rest of his life from such accusations. In after years McAnarney was one day in Katzmann's office as Katzmann, with tears in his eyes, complained of the constant vilification he had undergone. "You were all right, Fred," McAnarney told him consolingly. "No matter what they said about you, you were all right."[24]

Though during most of the writing of my book I still remained convinced that Sacco and Vanzetti were innocent, I was faced with the categorical proposition that I later posed to Ehrmann. If Sacco was innocent, then either Goddard was in error or Bullet III and Shell W were fakes. My own feeling was that Goddard had somehow made a mistake. A new and more exact examination of the shells and bullets might, I believed and hoped, give other results, might indeed succeed where Hamilton had failed. But when I inquired after the Sacco-Vanzetti exhibits, they were nowhere to be found. The clerk of court at Dedham said they had been sent to the governor's committee in July 1927 and had never been returned. I wrote to Governor Foster Furcolo and after some delay received a reply from the attorney general that there was no record in the State House of the disposition of the exhibits after they had been seen by the committee. No one at the State Police Ballistics Laboratory seemed to have any idea what had happened to them.

The first time I visited there, I noticed two framed photographs hanging on the wall of the bases of Shell W and a test shell enlarged to about a foot in diameter. Side by side the photographs looked identical. I talked several times with Captain John Collins, the red-haired head of the laboratory, a man at odds with the whole adversary system. "I'm a gun expert," he told me, "that's all. All I care about is whether certain shells and bullets come from certain guns. What anyone does with the information after that is not my business. I don't take sides." At first he was reluctant to talk about the Van Amburghs. "Look," he finally said to me, "I know what happened to those Sacco-Vanzetti guns and bullets. Old Van Amburgh took them away with him when he retired. His son was head of the lab after that. The old man's dead now, but his son has the things. I never thought it was right, and that's why I'm tipping you off. But don't let on that I told you, don't even mention my name, or I may end up pushing a motorbike round the Pittsfield barracks."

Van Amburgh had groomed his son to succeed him and after the father retired in 1943 the son took over as head of ballistics. The younger Van Amburgh in turn retired in 1956 and moved to Kingston, on the fringe of Cape Cod. When I telephoned him to ask about the Sacco-Vanzetti exhibits, he was gruff, noncommittal. Did he have them? "Well," he said, "I have a lot of things." I told him I wanted to examine the ballistics exhibits to settle various unanswered questions, since I was writing a book on the case. "So am I," he said.

I wrote to Governor Furcolo again asking why any private person should have possession of such controversial evidence. To this letter I received no reply. Then I wrote to the *Boston Globe*. Several weeks passed, and my letter was never printed. Instead the *Globe*'s editor sent a reporter to see me—the rotund and amiable Bob McLean. He said the missing evidence was too important for just a letter to the editor. The editor wanted to build it up as a feature story. I told him what I knew.

The following Sunday the *Globe* ran Bob's article on the front page. Results were electric. According to Bob, the commissioner of public safety, Henry Goguen, had a tantrum, stamping round his office and shouting: "Get those goddam things back! Send two troopers down to Kingston! If Van Amburgh don't hand them over, arrest him!" Van Amburgh handed them over meekly enough. There was, of course, always the matter of his state pension.

I had thought Goguen would be grateful to me for having uncovered the missing exhibits and that there would be no difficulty at all in having new tests made. Instead of being grateful, he was furious. The Sacco-Vanzetti case was still a smoldering political issue in Massachusetts. He didn't want to be blamed for starting up the fire. "No tests!" he told me when I first went to see him, a gnomish, shredded man with the darting eyes of a chameleon. I remember he wore a sharkskin suit that peaked at the shoulders and a florid tie fastened with the state seal in silver. In his buttonhole he displayed the rosette of the Legion of Honor, awarded him *ex officio* as the head of L'Union St. Jean Baptiste d'Amérique, the largest French-Canadian fraternal insurance association in the United States—from which he still received a salary, although recently he had been conducting a campaign against moonlighting in his department. He was not well loved by his subordinates.

After I persuaded the editor of the *Boston Herald* to print an editorial, "Do Not Let Sleeping Bullets Lie," Goguen said I had misunderstood him, that what he really meant was that he didn't want any amateurs fiddling with the exhibits. He had no objection to tests made by qualified experts. When I presented him with the name of Jac Weller, honorary curator of the West Point Museum, he said that before any tests could be made they must first be approved by the attorney general's office. It took me several months to get this approval. Then Goguen said he must consult members of his department. Each time I went to see him he concocted a new excuse, awkwardly squirming in his chair, I wrote, as if he had pinworms—

another remark editors made me delete. A year went by. Finally he said that although he personally had no objection to further tests, his term of office was coming to a close and he did not want to commit his successor.

That successor, Frank Giles, though he later left office under a cloud, was straightforward enough and raised no objection to new tests. They were held at last in the ballistics laboratory on a rainy October day in 1961. Television cameras crowded the room. U.P. and A.P. representatives were there as well as local reporters. Weller, insisting that there must be at least two experts present, had brought along a more earthy type than himself, Colonel Frank Jury, former head of the Firearms Laboratory of the New Jersey State Police. "I have no idea how these tests will turn out," said Weller as we stood on the wet pavement in front of the Public Safety Building early that morning. "However they come out," Jury said, "we're bound to get a load of shit dumped on us."

During the tests Weller and Jury, each with a comparison microscope, sat on opposite sides of the room. While Jury compared Shell W with the Lowell test shells, Weller compared Bullet III with the test bullets. Then, without revealing their findings to each other, they unfocused their microscopes and changed places. Later they stated in individually submitted reports that Bullet III and Shell W had been fired in Sacco's Colt and could not have been fired in any other weapon. I myself looked through the microscope. That the markings of shell and bullet corresponded to those of the test shells and bullets was indisputable. As an afterthought Jury decided to fire additional shots through Sacco's Colt, even though the barrel had rusted slightly and he was not sure he could get a clear impression. But after two shots had cleared the barrel, the impression came clear and true. Comparing the 1961 test shells and bullets with Shell W and Bullet III, the two experts again concluded that Shell W and Bullet III had to have been fired in Sacco's Colt. As to the scratches on the base of the bullets, Jury and Weller found that the marks on Bullet III did not vary noticeably from those on the other three bullets. They also considered that Bullet III's deformity could not have been reproduced in a test firing.

Shortly after this Ehrmann telephoned to ask if he might see the test results. I told him I wasn't ready to make Weller's and Jury's findings public until my book came out, but I was willing to let him see the report if he would keep it confidential. The next time I was in

Boston I dropped in at his office and handed him the documents, expecting him to read them and hand them back. While I sat there, he excused himself and left the room briefly with the papers in his hand. What I did not realize was that he had gone out to photostat them.

For the next few months Ehrmann busied himself trying to counteract and disprove Weller and Jury. He brought in his own expert, Shelley Braverman, a man of as dubious reputation as Hamilton. Captain Collins snorted when he heard the name and told me he would not allow Braverman in his laboratory. The experts I met in the tests of 1983 were equally condemnatory. There are only a few hundred ballistics experts in the country, and they form what is really a guild. They all know each other and about each other, and once a year they get together to discuss recent ballistics developments. Braverman was never accepted by them.

In 1935 General Julian Hatcher published *Firearms Investigation, Identification, and Evidence,* at the close of which he included a number of case histories, devoting two pages to the Sacco-Vanzetti evidence. These pages were prepared for General Hatcher by Lieutenant George Roche of the Massachusetts State Police Ballistics Laboratory. Using the innovative comparison microscope, Roche had demonstrated with test cartridges that Bullet III and Shell W had been fired in Sacco's Colt. Hatcher's book was a technical one, and Roche's corroborative findings were little read except by law-enforcement officers. In 1957 Jury and Weller revised Hatcher's book to bring it up to date, expanding it but making no alterations in the old text. Braverman in his searchings came across the two Roche pages. Ehrmann now claimed, on the strength of Roche's insert, that Jury and Weller had committed themselves to Sacco's guilt before their tests and that consequently their findings were irretrievably tainted. He called their selection "a questionable choice since these gentlemen, *without making any examination of the bullets and shells, had already published their joint opinion* that Bullet III had been fired in Sacco's pistol."[25] When I sent this accusation to Weller, he wrote back that Roche's pages had been retained intact along with the rest of Hatcher's text and that by the time of the 1961 tests he and Jury had forgotten about them. Falling back on Ehrmann's second line of defense—fraudulent substitution—Braverman, by repeatedly firing a Colt automatic into a wooden plank, finally succeeded in producing a bullet misshapen much like Bullet III. What Ehrmann really believed, I was never able to find out.

Musmanno also made himself heard in efforts to discredit Jury and Weller. Although the Sacco-Vanzetti exhibits had been photographed many times, the first time shortly after the arrest of the two men, he maintained that there was no way of determining whether the guns, shells, and bullets taken from Van Amburgh were the same guns, shells, and bullets offered in evidence at the trial. The guns were, of course, identifiable by their serial numbers, the shells and bullets equally identifiable through the early photographs. I saw the whole ballistics collection shortly after it had been brought back to the laboratory. Shells and bullets were in their original official envelopes inscribed "Clerk of Court, Dedham." I do not think they had been opened since Van Amburgh took them away, for the metal clips securing the envelopes had rusted onto the paper. Musmanno vociferously insisted that, since the barrel of Sacco's Colt had rusted, it was no longer the same barrel. As for Bullet III, it was not the same bullet because it had been washed, "laundered," in Musmanno's equivocal term.

In March 1983, another examination of the Sacco-Vanzetti ballistics evidence took place, this one sponsored by a Boston television station, WBZ, in conjunction with a Sacco-Vanzetti program. The commissioner of public safety raised no objections to these tests. I think the WBZ people hoped, as indeed I had once hoped, that more extensive testings might overturn the old results and set the stage to establish at last that Sacco and Vanzetti were not guilty.

The March tests were held in Cambridge's Ramada Inn motel, the exhibits guarded by troopers of the Massachusetts State Police. Three independent experts—Anthony Paul, a firearms consultant from Pennsylvania; Marshall Robinson of the ballistics department of the Connecticut State Police; and George Wilson, the section-chief firearms examiner of the Washington, D.C., Metropolitan Police Department—spent three days examining each minute bit of evidence. They offered their services free to avoid any question of bias. Bluff, assured men, they had come to Boston solely in their capacity as ballistics technicians and they grew increasingly irritated as Bob D'Attilio questioned them about their knowledge of the background of the case. D'Attilio, one of the more reasonable Sacco-Vanzetti partisans, was nevertheless there to defend his cause. He had prepared several pages of questions he considered pertinent. The three experts did not. "Look, Mr. D'Attilio," the heavy-built, emphatic Wilson finally interrupted him. "We didn't come here to talk, we came here to make ballistics tests." When D'Attilio persisted, they cut him short, turned to me, and asked me what questions I had. I said I had one very simple one: Were Bullet III and Shell W fired in Sacco's automatic? "That," said Robinson, "is why we are here."

Their tests merely confirmed the earlier tests of Goddard, Roche, Gunther, Jury, and Weller. Bullet III and Shell W had come from Sacco's Colt and could have come from no other weapon. Rather testily, Robinson remarked, when he was interviewed on television: "Why do they keep running these tests over and over? They always come out the same."

"There's one thing we shall include in our report," Wilson told me at the conclusion of the tests, "though these television people missed it completely. Some of the cartridges found in Sacco's pocket were made on the same machine as two of those shells found at the scene of the crime. That is the one new thing that has come out. Let them make what they will of it!"

The head of the state ballistics laboratory, Lieutenant Jim McGuinness, as custodian of the Sacco-Vanzetti exhibits, was also there during the tests. "What did you think of them?" he asked me at the end.

"What I expected," I told him. "But I never knew that one could tell by the markings that bullets had been made on the same machine."

"Oh," he said, "we've known that for some years, though it wasn't known when Jury and Weller made their tests. Each machine puts its signature on the cartridge rim, just like a gun barrel or breechblock. Anytime you want to come over to the lab I'd be glad to show you."

Several days later I did go to his laboratory. He was at his desk behind a microscope of monumental complexity. "Lucky you came today," he told me. "Tomorrow and for the rest of the week I'll be in Springfield on a murder case. You wanted to see those cartridges made on the same machine? Wait a second and I'll get the exhibits."

He went to a side cupboard and came back with a medium-sized box, which he unlocked. Inside were Sacco's automatic and Vanzetti's revolver along with the various shells and bullets of the case in marked envelopes. "Here," he said, shaking out one envelope, "are the sixteen Peters cartridges found on Sacco and here, in this envelope, are the shells they picked up after the shooting—the Winchester, the Remington, and the two Peters. These six Peters cartridges and the two Peters shells were made on the same machine." He fitted a cartridge and a shell in the microscope and invited me to look. I could see the intricate threadings around the rim of shell and cartridge as they were brought together; they matched as if they were a single piece. Then, with the same deft precision, he matched the second Peters shell and the other five Peters cartridges. Each time the rim lines matched as if they were one.

"Now," McGuinness said, "we'll take the other ten cartridges and try them out with the same shell." I looked again. This time the multiple threadings in no way coincided. Shell and cartridge remained two distinct units.

"There you have it," he concluded, patting his microscope.*

That Sacco had a mixture of Peters, Winchester, Remington, and U.S. cartridges on him at his arrest, and that the four spent shells that Bostock had picked up were Peters, Winchester, and Remington, went far beyond coincidence. But that six of Sacco's cartridges and the two Peters shells had been turned out by the same machine was a fact that even an Ehrmann could not subvert. As I went down the steps of the State Police Building into the spring sunshine and walked up Commonwealth Avenue toward Boston University, I was filled with a curious sense of finality. At last I had come to the end of the ballistics road. Tests, each more extended than the previous one, had proved beyond further dispute that Bullet III and Shell W had been fired in Sacco's Colt. Now it was equally clear that the two Peters shells and the six cartridges had a common origin. Sacco and the unidentified gunman who had fired the five other shots had drawn their ammunition from the same cache. Here, in the identity of manufacture, was the culminating evidence. Faced with it, any theory of substitution collapses. Sacco's was the murder weapon.

There still remains the matter of Vanzetti's revolver. Was it the "white gun" that the shoe cutter Peter McCullum saw a bandit take from the prostrate Berardelli? The guard customarily carried a Harrington & Richardson revolver. Five days before his murder he had shown it to Jimmy Bostock. According to Fraher, the Slater & Morrill superintendent, Berardelli had originally got the revolver from him.

* It would have been interesting to determine whether the Peters cartridge taken by Police Inspector Brouillard from Boda's automatic had been manufactured in the same machine as Sacco's six Peters. Unfortunately I could find no trace of the Boda cartridge in the state archives although it is listed among Captain Proctor's exhibits.

On March 20, 1920, Berardelli had left his revolver in Boston at the Iver Johnson Sporting Goods Company to be repaired. Lincoln Wadsworth, in charge of the Iver Johnson repairs, tagged it as a "38 Harrington & Richardson revolver, property of Alex Berardelli," number 94765, and sent it up to the gunsmith. When shown Vanzetti's revolver at the trial, he testified that it "answered the description of the revolver brought in that day."[26]

The gunsmith, George Fitzmeyer, testified that he had received a Harrington & Richardson revolver with the repair number 94765. In his records he had noted "New Hammer and repairs. Half an hour." On being handed Vanzetti's revolver, he said that it had a new hammer. The firing pin did not show "of ever being struck."[27]

James Jones, the firearms department manager, told the court that to the best of his knowledge the revolver had been redelivered, although sometimes the delivery records were faulty. Guns not called for were sold at the year's end. An absolute record was made of every weapon sold. There was no record, said Jones, of any sale of the Berardelli revolver. "That gun was not sold from our store," he said emphatically.[28] But it was no longer there.

Berardelli's widow, Sara, said that while her husband's revolver was being repaired, Parmenter had lent him another one. In October 1919 Parmenter had bought a .32-caliber Harrington & Richardson revolver in a Brockton hardware store, and this was no doubt the one Berardelli carried while his own was being repaired. Sara Berardelli, a sad, confused woman, did say that her husband had originally been given his revolver by Parmenter. But according to Fraher, Berardelli had originally got the revolver from him. This leaves a certain ambiguity. Fraher, who did not see the Vanzetti revolver when he testified in court, told his brother of the scorings he had seen on the butt before the crime, a feature not considered or remarked on elsewhere. Vanzetti's Harrington & Richardson, which I examined in 1961 and again in 1983, had such scorings.

Here one must leave fact for surmise. Orciani gave or sold a Harrington & Richardson revolver to Falzini, who in turn gave or sold it to Vanzetti. Although present at the Dedham trial, Orciani refused to take the stand. Gambera's evidence is conclusive enough to establish Vanzetti's innocence, though not the innocence of his revolver. Ultimate proof is lacking, but the signs point to Orciani as the gunman who took the revolver from the dying guard.

12

The Roads to Providence and Needham

I
Providence

In mid-May of 1926 Thompson had engaged Ehrmann as his associate counsel. For the rest of Ehrmann's life the Sacco-Vanzetti case would remain his preoccupation. Not only would he write two books elucidating his role and his findings, he would also write a Sacco-Vanzetti play that would run briefly in New York. Two days after Madeiros's second conviction, Ehrmann set out on the old Boston Post Road to Providence to check up on the confession.

Intuitively he anticipated what he was going to find. Who were the four Italians with Madeiros in the murder car? Madeiros had refused to name them, but that was just the gangster code.* The answer, Ehrmann was certain, lay in the city just over the horizon. Madeiros's story, for all its gaps and hesitancies, was true.

His intuition was confirmed when he talked with the chief inspector at Providence's dingy Fountain Street police headquarters. Yes, the inspector said, there was indeed a local gang engaged in robbing freight cars. Known as the Morelli Gang, from five brothers who formed its core, it consisted of the leader, Joe Morelli; his brothers Patsy, Fred, Butsy, and Mike; and—beyond the Morellis—Bibba Barone, Joseph Imondi (a mild pick-lock known derisively as "Gyp the Blood"), Paul Rossi, and Tony Mancini. During the preceding two years they had been hijacking freight-car shipments of shoes and clothing routed through the Providence yards. The Morellis were petty thieves, pimps, gamblers, receivers of stolen goods, cowardly,

* The code had not kept Madeiros from naming Harry Goldenberg as the fourth—and still fugitive—participant in the Wrentham holdup-murder for which Madeiros and two others had been convicted.

shying away from violence, not the holdup kind, not—as later described by Ehrmann—"typical gangsters and gunmen of the worst type."[1]

In October 1919 Joe, Patsy, Fred, and Butsy had been indicted on fifteen counts of possession of stolen goods. The eighth count charged that they had unlawfully and feloniously bought, received, and had in their possession seventy-eight pairs of men's shoes, part of an interstate shipment from Slater & Morrill in South Braintree to the Potter Shoe Company in Cincinnati. Four more counts charged them with unlawful possession of 605 pairs of ladies' shoes shipped from South Braintree's Rice & Hutchins plant to Chicago. The remaining nine counts concerned shipments looted from other companies in other cities. These shipments had been stolen haphazardly from freight cars in Providence, and—as Robert Montgomery pointed out—they are "absolutely the only evidence linking any member of the Morelli gang with South Braintree."[2]

For Ehrmann the inspector's story was a glowing confirmation. There was a notorious gang of freight robbers just as Madeiros had said. Though Madeiros had named no names beyond Bill and Mike, Ehrmann already anticipated that they were Morellis. All that was needed was to determine which of the gang might have been in South Braintree, a matter of deduction.

Ehrmann proceeded to form his cast of characters. Fred and Bibba he could eliminate because on April 15, 1920, they were in jail. Patsy could prove he had been elsewhere and Gyp the Blood was too timid. He picked Joe as the lead, the man who had fired the shot killing the guard. This deduction he made chiefly because Joe possessed a Colt of the same caliber as Sacco's. Unfortunately for this hypothesis, a deputy searching the Morelli house before April 15 had confiscated the Colt. But Ehrmann assumed that Joe must have had a second Colt. Ehrmann next selected Mancini as his second murdercar passenger, the only real killer in the gang, then serving time for a 1921 New York street murder. According to police records, the pistol Mancini used was a Star. Although no one at the Sacco-Vanzetti trial had attempted to identify the South Braintree bandit who had fired five shots into the bodies of the guard and paymaster, Ehrmann decided that he must have been Mancini. The trial experts had testified that the five bullets had been fired either in a Savage or a Stehr, and Ehrmann concluded that a stenographic error in the record had transformed the Star into a Stehr.

On April 24, 1920, Butsy Morelli had attracted the attention of a

New Bedford police sergeant by driving by in a Cole touring car with the same license plates that two weeks before had been seen on a Buick driven by his brother Mike. This was coincidence enough for Ehrmann to place Butsy in the murder car. To choose the driver was not so easy. Madeiros had said in his affidavit that he had been picked up in Providence "by four Italians who came in a 5 passenger touring car."[3] But the witnesses at South Braintree had described the car's driver as pallid, thin, not an Italian. After several leading talks with Ehrmann and Thompson, Madeiros in a deposition a month later stated:

> Well, I might say that there was one fellow was not an Italian. . . . I believe Polish or Finland . . . a kind of slim fellow with light hair. That is the way I can tell he was not an Italian.[4]

At first Ehrmann thought he had located his driver in a young sneak-thief, Ray McDevitt, who although not a member of the Morelli Gang knew Joe and was thin and fair. But after talking with Madeiros, Ehrmann decided that McDevitt would not do. A pal of Madeiros appeared a more likely candidate, one Steve Benkoski, known as "Steve the Pole," recently killed in a hijacking operation. "After considering all the available data," Ehrmann wrote forty years later, "we finally surmised that Madeiros's young friend had been the driver."[5] The available data did not amount to much: three witnesses who had seen the getaway car and six years later recalled some resemblance between the driver and a newspaper picture of Benkoski. Nevertheless, with Steve the Pole Ehrmann satisfied himself that he had accounted for the five passengers of the murder car. The man waiting in the Randolph Woods with the second car was, no doubt, Mike Morelli, and the car had to be the Buick Mike had been seen driving through New Bedford a few days earlier.

Ehrmann traced the hypothetical course of the Hudson on its two morning trips from Providence to Boston. Madeiros's story, to his mind, fitted every particular. The five or more witnesses who *thought* they had seen the Buick in Braintree that morning with its five passengers were simply mistaken and must have seen some other car. According to Ehrmann's reconstruction, Steve the Pole drove the Hudson to the Randolph Woods. There he, Mancini, Madeiros, and Joe and Butsy Morelli changed to Mike's Buick and went on to the Braintree speakeasy to while away the time before the holdup. After the robbery they returned to the Randolph Woods, switched the

Buick license plates to the Hudson, and then headed for Providence, followed by Mike in the Buick. Ehrmann became almost lyrical in his vision of that journey back:

> I could see Mike Morelli, the New Bedford brother, bring the Buick to the meeting place. I could picture the hasty return of the Buick from South Braintree, the switching of the money boxes and number plates, and then Mike's leisurely and unsuspected drive from Randolph to New Bedford. Under cover of night the pleasant roll to the Manley Woods would be accomplished with another car trailing to take Mike away from the abandoned evidence of his complicity.[6]

Of course, Madeiros's story made no sense, and I have often wondered if Ehrmann in his later years continued to believe it. That the sly and calculating Morellis would have aimlessly driven back and forth twice from Providence to Boston—a total distance of 180 miles—is as incongruous as it is to imagine with Ehrmann that no one saw the Buick, with its passengers, cruising through Braintree that morning. Equally incongruous is having the Morellis kill time in a speakeasy either in South Boston or South Braintree. Nor can one imagine the astute Mike making a return drive that evening through miles and miles of empty land to abandon the Buick so close to Puffer's Place. Closely examined, Madeiros's confession is a shifty concoction by a man of limited intelligence, cunning but ill-informed. A month after he had written his confessional note, his mother and sister Mary visited him. Talking in Portuguese, Madeiros told them: "You think I am tough because I am in this case—well, there is a fellow in here over five years who killed two men on a job."[7]

Assiduously Ehrmann collected affidavits, going as far afield as Leavenworth, Kansas, and Auburn, New York, where he visited Joe Morelli and Mancini in their respective prisons. Joe in ungrammatical indignation denied he had had anything to do with the Braintree crime. Mancini had nothing to say.

Like Ehrmann, Thompson remained stubbornly convinced that the Madeiros confession marked the solution to the Sacco-Vanzetti case. Even as he was preparing his new trial motion, he telephoned Assistant District Attorney William Kelley to tell him that the case would be cleared up in a few days. All that remained was to gather together the corroborating details.

Judge Thayer's denial of the Madeiros motion outraged Thompson. Of course, the judge could merely have denied the motion without explanation, but because of the sensational nature of Madeiros's confession and the rising agitation over Sacco and Vanzetti, he decided he must give his reasons at length. Pointing out the many discrepancies in Madeiros's story and explaining how he came to his decision, he is logical and exact, though something of his testy nature is reflected in his twenty-five-thousand-word opinion. The state supreme court justices sustained his decision on every point.

Professor Morgan, in reviewing Ehrmann's *The Untried Case: The Sacco-Vanzetti Case and the Morelli Gang,* called the Madeiros confession "a wholly worthless story from an utterly untrustworthy source."[8] Before the execution, Governor Fuller, in examining the evidence, came to the same conclusion, as did the members of his advisory committee.

Ehrmann had taken the high road to Providence, convinced that it would lead to the vindication and freedom of Sacco and Vanzetti. Instead, although he could never in later years face the fact, his high road had ended in a cul-de-sac. Yet singularly enough, the many little back roads of the case, for the most part overlooked, led to a main road.

II
Needham

The day before Christmas 1919, a Needham police officer telephoned George Hassam at his garage behind the Needham town hall to tell him that the license plates seen on a getaway car used in a Bridgewater holdup that morning had been identified as his. Hassam at first could not believe it. That particular set of plates, Mass. 011730, had been attached to an R. C. Hupp runabout in the rear of the garage. When he went to look, he found the plates missing.

The runabout belonged to a young Italian, Joe Miele, a clerk in a Needham grocery store. On the previous Thursday, Miele had come to Hassam to ask if he might borrow a pair of license plates. He explained that he had just bought a runabout that needed to have the gears fixed. As yet he had not registered it. Hassam lent him the plates, and half an hour later Miele drove up with the runabout, which he left in the front of the garage. He had fastened the plates loosely with picture wire. On Saturday Hassam moved the runabout to the rear of the garage next to a truck.

Hassam had been running his garage for several years. He had two mechanics working for him, seventeen-year-old Julius Chamberlain and Clarence Linn, a man in his fifties, both reliable mechanics. On Monday Miele dropped in to ask about his car. That same afternoon a swarthy foreigner came to the garage on foot. In broken English he asked to borrow a set of plates for an automobile he said he had bought in Wellesley. After Hassam turned him down, he walked away muttering. Hassam had never seen him before and never saw him again, but he described him to the police as "stocky build, black hair, dark sallow complexion, black mustache, clipped close."[9] At the Plymouth trial, witnesses identifying Vanzetti as the shotgun-wielding bandit described him as having a trimmed mustache, a description that more realistically fits the foreigner who tried to borrow Hassam's plates.

On the day after Christmas, two Pinkerton operatives, who signed themselves H.H. and J.J.H., came to Needham to question those connected with the garage. Hassam told them that whoever stole the license plates must have been familiar with the building, since the runabout was in the rear and hidden by a truck. He added that he had seen Miele in the garage on Monday and again on Tuesday. Linn told Operative J.J.H. that Miele had been there on Tuesday and explained that he was not working because of a toothache. Chamberlain told the same operative: "I am positive that Joe Miele was at the garage on Tuesday afternoon and think he went into the rear of it. . . . Fred Taylor, a local jitney man was here at the time. Wednesday night Joe and I had a talk about the holdup and then he made a remark which made me think he knew something about it."[10] Taylor corroborated Chamberlain, telling J.J.H. that on Tuesday afternoon at about two o'clock "I saw Joe Miele working in the rear part of the Needham Garage on his car and saw a spark plug in his hand."[11] Miele's landlady said he left the house at quarter to two on Tuesday afternoon and returned about half-past three.

Miele was questioned that evening by the Needham police chief at the town hall, with the Pinkerton operatives present. He denied that he had ever been at the garage on Tuesday. "I did not take the plates at any time," he told the chief, "and had no knowledge that they were gone until I read of the holdup."[12]

"Next Julius Chamberlain was brought in," H.H. noted, "and while awaiting Chamberlain's arrival, Miele lost his composure and showed that he was very nervous, but when he learned that Chamberlain could not tell us much he regained his composure and stuck to his statements."[13]

Before the operatives left Needham, they went over the garage carefully. H.H. reported that "the car is at the rear of the garage where it would seem impossible for a stranger to go unnoticed and Mr. Hassam and his employees say that strangers never go to that part of the garage."[14]

In spite of Miele's flustered denials, four independent witnesses—Hassam, Chamberlain, Linn, and Taylor—insisted that they had seen him in the garage on Tuesday. No stranger could have known that the runabout, with its easily detachable plates, was there or could have got to the rear of the garage unobserved. The foreigner who tried to borrow the plates on Monday may or may not have known Miele, but he would neither have known where the plates were nor have had the opportunity to steal them. Only an insider could have taken them away unnoticed. Reluctant though Miele may have been, all the evidence points to his being the thief.

Always, in and out of the various investigations, one is brought back to Needham, the small, isolated Boston outer suburb where any stranger, any strange car, would be at once obvious. The Braintree Buick turned out to have been stolen on the evening of November 20, 1919, from in front of a house on Fair Oaks Road, Needham, not far from Hassam's garage. Later that same evening a Dedham policeman, Warren Totty, spotted a touring car hurtling through Dedham Square at fifty miles an hour. He stepped out to stop it but scrambled back onto the sidewalk as the driver swung toward him. The car then speeded on under the railroad bridge in the direction of Hyde Park. Totty managed to get the license number. It was the same as that of the stolen Buick. Operative J.J.H. reported on December 27 that "it looks very much now as though the Bridgewater bandits used a Buick car and it may well be the one stolen in Needham in November."[15] The Buick plates in the Braintree holdup had been stolen from a Ford in a private garage on Webster Street, Needham, on January 6, 1920.

Needham, as it came out briefly several years after the trial, appears to have harbored the Braintree Buick's mysterious driver, a professional car thief, a man of many aliases, known mostly as William Dobson. From 1917 to 1919 he had worked off and on in a Needham garage, living close by with his wife Jessie, who continued to live there after he had left her.

Dobson, a sallow-faced man, roughly fitted the South Braintree witnesses' description of the getaway-car driver. Never mentioned as a Braintree suspect, he had come to the attention of the Bureau of Investigation through his interstate theft of cars, a federal offense. On December 6, 1921, Bureau Agent Donald Casey went to Needham to talk with Jessie. Naïvely voluble, she said her husband told her he had driven the car containing the men who shot the guard and paymaster in South Braintree. Casey passed the information on to Captain Proctor without result. Some months later Jessie sued Dobson—then in jail—for divorce. She confided to a Hearst reporter that her husband had given her $800 of the thousand he had received for driving the Braintree bandit car. Hearst's *Boston American* printed the story with embellishments, but neither the district attorney's office nor Moore showed any real interest in it. The issue was never again raised. Dobson continued his career of theft, dying in jail during the Second World War.

Needham even crops up, briefly, in the Lowell Committee hearings. Rosina Sacco, in her testimony there, mentioned that her husband sometimes used to go shooting with a man from Needham named Rossi. The remark was incidental, but the place-name emerged.

The Hudson touring car that Madeiros had driven in the Wrentham holdup, he had stolen in Pawtucket, a bleak industrial city adjacent to Providence. With its massed anonymous streets, it was a relatively easy and safe place to steal a car. It would have been an equally easy source for the light-fingered Morellis. To think that they would drive so many miles north through a series of intervening towns to steal a car in such a backwater as Needham makes as little sense as Madeiros's claim that he and the gang had driven back and forth twice from Providence to Boston on the morning of the Braintree murders. And there are of course the contrary statements of Ensher and MacDonald that they had seen Boda driving a Buick touring car in West Bridgewater in the spring.

Yet, if Ehrmann's version is accepted, it was the Morellis who came to Needham in November to steal the getaway Buick, then returned six weeks later for the Braintree license plates. Ehrmann preferred to disregard the theft from Hassam's garage, maintaining that the Bridgewater holdup attempt was the work of amateurs, whereas the equally amateurish South Braintree robbery was committed by skilled professionals. Why all these thefts in Needham, why the Morellis' obsession with that obscure town, he never tried to explain.

When Officer Totty saw the stolen Buick speed through Dedham

Square, it was headed for Hyde Park, and Hyde Park was where Boda was then staying with Orciani. Until then he had lived in a small Italian enclave on the outskirts of Needham next to Wellesley, where he and his brother had worked in a dry-cleaning shop. The foreigner who had tried to borrow Hassam's plates had obviously not walked from Providence, but he could easily have come from Needham's Italian colony. The ambivalent Miele, Dobson the car thief, and Boda were all linked to Needham. The Buick, along with the Bridgewater and Braintree license plates, had been stolen in Needham. There the diverse roads of the Sacco-Vanzetti case converged. The trail did not run to Ehrmann's fantasized Providence but to disregarded Needham.

13

The Road to Washington

A few months after the Dedham trial a defense pamphlet, *The Challenge*, circulated by Friends of Freedom—a group of Italian anarchists and the Union of Russian Workers—accused the Department of Justice's Bureau of Investigation* of "fastening this crime on Sacco and Vanzetti . . . to achieve two victories: to prejudice the public against social rebels and to cover up its own criminal action."[1] Five years later Thompson expanded this accusation in a supplementary motion for a new trial. Among the affidavits he filed were two from former Boston agents of the bureau, Lawrence Letherman and Fred Weyand, accusing the bureau of conniving with the prosecution to convict the two anarchists. On these affidavits Frankfurter based one of the most telling charges of his seminal book, claiming that

> the case against Sacco and Vanzetti for murder was part of a collusive effort between the District Attorney and agents of the Department of Justice to rid the country of these Italians because of their Red activities. In proof of this we have the affidavits of two former officers of the Government . . . both of whom are now in honorable civil employment. The names of Sacco and Vanzetti were in the files of the Department of Justice . . . the Department was eager for their deportation, but had not enough evidence to secure it, and inasmuch as the United States District Court of Massachusetts had checked abuses in deportation proceedings the Department had become chary of resorting to deportation without adequate legal basis. The arrest of Sacco and Vanzetti, on the mistaken theory of Stewart, furnished the agents of the Department of Justice their opportunity.[2]

* The Bureau of Investigation did not become the Federal Bureau of Investigation until 1935.

Weyand stated under oath that he had been a special agent of the Bureau of Investigation's Boston office from 1916 until he resigned late in 1924. According to his affidavit, Sacco and Vanzetti some time before their arrest had appeared in the files of the Department of Justice as radicals to be watched.

The Boston files of the Department [Weyand continued] including correspondence, would show the date when the names of these men were first brought to the attention of the Department. Both these men were listed in the files as followers or associates of an educated Italian editor named Galleani. . . . The suspicion entertained by the Department of Justice against Sacco and Vanzetti was that they had violated the Selective Service Act, and also that they were anarchists or held Radical opinions of some sort or other.

A man named Feri Felix Weiss was transferred from the Immigration Bureau to the Department of Justice in Boston in the year 1917, and remained a special agent of that Department in Boston until 1919, I think. . . . In 1925 Weiss returned to the Immigration Department, where he is at the present time.

William J. West, who is now a Special Agent of the Department of Justice, became such in July or August, 1917. Prior to that he was Immigration Inspector with Feri Weiss. Since his appointment as a Special Agent he has spent most of his time in the Boston office of the Department of Justice, having in charge during the past seven years the so-called Radical Division of the Department of Justice, which has been in operation since about 1917. . . .

Shortly after the arrest of Sacco and Vanzetti on the charge of the South Braintree murders, meetings began to be held by sympathizers, and I was assigned to attend these meetings and report to the Department the speeches made. . . . Mr. West was also attending meetings of Sacco-Vanzetti sympathizers during the same period. The original reports thus obtained were sent to the Washington office of the Department of Justice, and duplicates kept in the Boston office, where I believe they now are. . . .

Shortly after the trial of Sacco and Vanzetti was concluded I said to Weiss that I did not believe they were the right men, meaning the men who shot the paymaster, and he replied that that might be so, but that they were bad actors and would get what they deserved anyway.

Instructions were received from the Chief of the Bureau of the Department of Justice in Washington from time to time in reference to the Sacco-Vanzetti case. They are on file or should be on file in the Boston office.

The understanding in this case between the agents of the Department of Justice and the District Attorney followed the usual custom, that the Department of Justice would help the District Attorney to secure a conviction, and that he in turn would help the agents of the Department of Justice to secure information that they might desire. . . . The Boston agents believed that these men were anarchists, and hoped to be able to secure the necessary evidence against them from their testimony at their trial for murder, to be used in case they were not convicted of murder. There is correspondence between Mr. Katzmann and Mr. West on file in the Boston office of the Department. Mr. West furnished Mr. Katzmann information about the Radical activities of Sacco and Vanzetti to be used in their cross-examination.

From my investigation, combined with the investigation made by the other agents of the Department in Boston, I am convinced not only that these men had violated the Selective Service rules and regulations and evaded the draft, but that they were anarchists, and that they ought to have been deported. By calling these men anarchist I do not mean necessarily that they were inclined to violence, nor do I understand all the different meanings that different people would attach to the word "anarchist." What I mean is that I think they did not believe in organized government or in private property. But I am also thoroughly convinced, and always have been, and I believe that is and always has been the opinion of such Boston agents of the Department of Justice as had any knowledge on the subject, that these men had nothing whatever to do with the South Braintree murders, and that their conviction was the result of co-operation between the Boston agents of the Department of Justice and the District Attorney. It was the general opinion of the Boston agents of the Department of Justice having knowledge of the affair that the South Braintree crime was committed by a gang of professional highwaymen.[3]

Letherman made his affidavit a week after Weyand:

I live in Malden, and am in the employ of the Beacon Trust. I was in the Federal service for thirty-six years, first in the railway mail service for nine years; then three years as local agent for the Department of Justice in Boston in charge of the Bureau of Investigation. I began the last named duties in September, 1921.

While I was Post Office Inspector I cooperated to a considerable extent with the agents of the Department of Justice in matters of joint concern, including the Sacco-Vanzetti case. The man under me in direct charge of matters relating to that case was Mr. William West, who is still attached to the Department in Boston. I know that Mr. West cooperated with Mr. Katzmann, the District Attorney, during the trial of the case, and later with Mr. Williams, the Assistant District Attorney.

I know that before, during, and after the trial of Sacco and Vanzetti Mr. West had a number of so-called "undercover" men assigned to this case, including one Ruzzament and one Carbone. I know that by an arrangement with the Department of Justice, Carbone was placed in a cell next to the cell of Sacco for the purpose of obtaining whatever incriminating information he could obtain from Sacco, after winning his confidence. Nothing, however, was obtained in that way. . . .

The Department of Justice in Boston was anxious to get sufficient evidence against Sacco and Vanzetti to deport them, but never succeeded in getting the kind and amount of evidence required for that purpose. It was the opinion of the agents here that a conviction of Sacco and Vanzetti for murder would be one way of disposing of these two men. It was also the general opinion of such of the agents in Boston as had any actual knowledge of the Sacco-Vanzetti case, that Sacco and Vanzetti, although anarchists and agitators, were not highway robbers, and had nothing to do with the South Braintree crime. My opinion, and the opinion of most of the older men in the Government service, has always been that the South Braintree crime was the work of professionals. . . . The letters and documents on file in the Boston office would throw a great deal of light upon the preparation of the Sacco-Vanzetti case for trial, and upon the real opinion of the Boston office of the Department of Justice as to the guilt of Sacco and Vanzetti of the particular crime with which they were charged.[4]

In the last months before Sacco and Vanzetti were executed, Thompson wrote to J. Edgar Hoover—in 1924 promoted to head of the Bureau of Investigation—demanding access to the bureau's files "dealing with the investigations made by the Boston agents *before, during and after* the trial." Following this request Hoover asked the Boston bureau head, John Dowd, for a summary of all the information in the files about Sacco and Vanzetti, particularly as to when they had come to the bureau's attention. Dowd replied in an eight-page letter marked "Personal & Confidential":

Special Agent West, of this office, who at the time was thoroughly conversant with the trend of such matters in this district, never heard of either defendant, either in or out of the anarchist organizations, in this district up to the time of their arrest and never knew that such persons existed. In fact all of the information was secured after the formation of a so-called "Defense Committee" in the summer of 1920 and after the trial in 1921. . . .

It is not our intention to claim that the names of either or both never appeared in any report emanating from the Boston Office prior to April of 1920, as such a name or names might have appeared incidentally in connection with an investigation of similar nature, and the files of this office at that time contained merely an index of the caption of the report. It can be said, however, that they were certainly not sufficiently active to come to the attention of the office up to that time in any matter of importance. . . . Not one agent of this office ever conducted any investigation of the crime for which these men stand convicted and not one scintilla of evidence ever came to the files of this office which offered any basis for any individual opinion expressed or entertained by any agent on the guilt or innocence of these men.[5]

The Boston office, Dowd informed Hoover, had a drawerful of reports of anarchist activities during and after the trial, "none of which so far as we can ascertain has any bearing upon the facts at issue between the Commonwealth and the defendants."

Hoover ordered Dowd to go with West and discuss the matter with Thompson. When Dowd telephoned for an appointment, Thompson asked him if he was ready to turn over the files. Dowd said he had no such instructions. At that Thompson told him angrily that he did not want to see either him or West. Dowd then dispatched a coded telegram to Hoover:

Thompson stated that he did not want to talk to West unless prepared to tell the truth and that he had affidavit showing number of agents who had worked on case and number who covered trial and that our files were full of information and that we had placed spies in the jail. He interspersed his remarks with considerable profanity and angry words and inquired if I thought I could railroad people to jail and kill them because they were anarchists. Inquired if he would specify what he wanted in the files and he responded as best I can quote him. Quote: Specify nothing I want every damn thing in your files and you better telephone Washington without delay. Unquote.

Hoover refused Thompson anything more than a summary, on the grounds that the complete files were "confidential and could not furnish anything in the nature of new evidence." Such a summary was finally released to the press the day before the executions. The files themselves remained sealed. When, a third of a century later, I wrote to Hoover suggesting that after so many years the files on Sacco and Vanzetti should be opened as a matter of history, I received the stock reply that FBI files were not available to the public. In writing a biography of Warren Harding, I had asked to examine the Secret Service files on a Professor Chancellor, a crackpot teacher

at Wooster College, Ohio, who at the time of the Braintree murders
had written a scurrilous book about Harding. Harding's Attorney
General, Harry Daugherty, had sent out Secret Service agents to con-
fiscate the plates and all copies of the book that they could find. At
my request the Secret Service Division in 1965 not only gave me
permission to see the files but sent them on from Washington to Boston so that I might examine them there. But the FBI files were to
Hoover his cherished personal property and he denied all outside access to them. Not until the passage of the Freedom of Information
Act in 1975 was I able to get permission from the current FBI director, Clarence Kelley, to examine the pertinent files.

In writing *Tragedy in Dedham* I had assumed that the affidavits
furnished Thompson by the two former bureau agents were accurate.
Even when I had begun to develop doubts about the innocence of
Sacco, I had no doubts about the integrity of Letherman and
Weyand. The bureau's Sacco-Vanzetti files, however, showed Letherman and Weyand in an entirely different light, stripped of any integrity. Letherman had been appointed to the bureau in October
1921 by his old crony William J. Burns of the Burns Detective
Agency, who had been made head of the Bureau of Investigation by
his crony, Attorney General Daugherty. In March 1922 Burns made
him head of the Boston office. A boozy elderly man verging on senil-
ity, a drug addict, Letherman was even at his best indolent. Once installed in Boston he became a close friend and drinking companion of
Weyand. In the shake-up of the Department of Justice following
Daugherty's forced resignation in 1924, Letherman's removal was
recommended because of "neglect of duty, failure to maintain discipline and to properly supervise the work of his division." He was
shown among other derelictions to have falsified expense accounts
and efficiency ratings, and to have left the administration of the office to subordinates. In 1923 and 1924 he visited the office only a few
times. His confidential report concluded that he was "suffering from
senile dementia caused by old age and debauchery."

Weyand had begun his career in 1917 as a bureau informant. In
February 1919 he was made a special agent and assigned to the Boston office. Although that same year he had apparently defrauded his
creditors in a bankruptcy proceeding, he continued in the bureau.
While an agent he engaged in smuggling liquor to bootleggers in
Maine. In spite of rumors of his illegal activities, Letherman protected him. Often the two held after-hours drinking bouts in Lether-

man's office. When Hoover became director, Special Agent Hanrahan was assigned to investigate Weyand. He reported that Weyand had "either been extremely negligent in making investigations or had deliberately falsified reports . . . reporting [his] interviewing persons whom he had not seen and calling at places where he did not call."

Since its inception the Bureau of Investigation had been a loose, not to say lax organization, as Hoover himself later wrote, "made up largely of untrained and undisciplined political appointees." Hoover as incoming director in 1924 introduced training and discipline into the bureau while making a clean sweep of the unqualified and incompetent. Among the agents dismissed in his initial purge were Weyand and Letherman. Trading on the resentments of these disgraced and disgruntled men, Thompson persuaded them to make the affidavits that he himself shaped and formed.

In the aftermath of the Weyand and Letherman affidavits, Hoover asked Dowd for further clarification. Dowd replied that a thorough search of the file indexes showed no reference to Sacco or Vanzetti before the date of their arrest "with the possible exception of a small card bearing the name of Bartolomeo Vanzetti which was found long after the arrest of this defendant in a lot of rubbish in the office and is presumed to have been a card taken in some anarchist raid back in 1918." West, according to Dowd, was not in communication with District Attorney Katzmann during the trial. He conferred once with the district attorney about placing an informer in the jail with Sacco in the hope of picking up information about the Wall Street bomb explosion. Weyand's claim of an understanding between the district attorney and the Department of Justice was false. At his conference with West, Dowd wrote, Katzmann had merely asked if there had been any sudden increase in the bank balance of the Italian Workers' Defense Committee that might account for the $15,000 stolen at South Braintree. The New York office reported that there had been none. "Further than this, the only communications appearing in the Boston office in reference to the Sacco-Vanzetti case either from or to the district attorney is a letter from Special Agent in Charge Hanrahan to Frederick G. Katzmann inclosing translations of articles appearing in radical publications at that time, and a letter from Mr. Katzmann thanking him for the same."

Letherman had sworn that as a postal inspector he had cooperated with Department of Justice agents in various matters, including the Sacco-Vanzetti case, but Dowd pointed out that Letherman had left the postal service nine years before the case occurred. After indicating other discrepancies and fabrications in the Letherman affidavit, Dowd took up the charge that the bureau's Boston agents were of the opinion that convicting Sacco and Vanzetti for murder would be one way of disposing of them.

> This statement is a most vicious one and can only be characterized as a figment of imagination, or else that of a displeased former employee stooping to this in order to appease his wrath against the Department as a whole. . . . Sacco and Vanzetti were apparently unknown to this office up to the time of their arrest. . . . The office never communicated with the presiding justice or any member of the jury, never interviewed any witness in relation to the case, never assisted the county prosecuting attorney to prepare the case, and never had anything to do with the defendants, other than an investigation of so-called radical activities on their behalf which arose after their arrest.

Following Thompson's demand for access to the files, Hoover asked Dowd and West to go over them once more. They reported that "there was nothing in the files that in any way reflected upon the guilt or innocence of Sacco and Vanzetti." But the reiterated insistence of the Sacco-Vanzetti Defense Committee that some dark secret inimical to the two men was buried in the depths of the Department of Justice continued to plague Hoover. In January 1927 he again sent West back to the files, and again West reported that "there is *absolutely nothing* in the files that would shed any light upon the guilt or innocence of the defendants."

Shortly before Sacco and Vanzetti were executed, Hoover ordered the Boston, New York, and Washington bureau offices to check all their files and to submit detailed reports on whether there was anything to give any indication of the two men's guilt or innocence or of any collusion in the case between federal and state authorities. He also asked for a list of the files' contents. The Washington and New York files contained nothing, the Boston branch only two irrelevant items.

West, in Boston, expanded his document search to include the wartime files. He reported that his first intimation of the existence of Sacco and Vanzetti came nine days after they were arrested when the division superintendent notified him of their arrest and that their names had appeared in the list of subscribers to *Cronaca Sovversiva*.

West did manage to unearth a few more scraps of information from earlier files. He now called attention to a report on *Cronaca Sovversiva* compiled by the New York office in April 1918:

That report was found today in Boston. . . . It reports the following communication received on August 10, 1916, reading as follows:—"In whatever concerns the Cronaca, I am with you. Yours for the revolution. (signed) F. Sacco, Milford, Mass." That no doubt is a communication from Nicola Sacco. The undersigned saw it for the first time today when he unearthed it in one of the war period files.

In the same file we found a list of communications taken under search warrant process at the plant of the "Cronaca Sovversiva," Lynn, Mass., on February 22, 1918, by the U. S. Marshal's office. That list contains mention of a postcard from F. Sacco to R. Schiavina, August 10, 1916, and two letters from B. Vanzetti to "Cronaca Sovversiva" dated Sept. 14th and 24th, 1916.

West also found Vanzetti's name among a collection of several hundred index cards, relating to subscriptions to *Cronaca Sovversiva*, that were uncovered in the walls of a demolished barn in Newton, Massachusetts.

Keeping in mind the bombings that followed Luigi Galleani's deportation, West concluded that "a review of the files, including the reports of agents from the New York City office who were working in the Boston district in March and April of 1920, fails to show any reference therein to either Sacco or Vanzetti, and it is fair to assume that had the Boston office then the knowledge that it has now with reference to the connection of Sacco and Vanzetti with Luigi Galleani, they would have been surely the subjects of inquiry at this time." He apologized to Hoover for his lengthy communication but considered it necessary "to bring to the attention of the Bureau every scintilla of evidence or information which might in any manner be interpreted to indicate any connection between the Federal and State governments in the prosecution of that case."

The bureau's files on the Sacco-Vanzetti case contain forty open folders plus thirteen labeled "Confidential," 781 pages in all. Most of the material records the post-trial agitation here and abroad, the ephemeral meetings, the activities of the defense committee, the various and varied threats of violence. But scattered between propaganda leaflets and repetitious accounts of meetings are memoranda and confidential reports on what the bureau knew about Sacco and Vanzetti, where the information came from, how it was used, and whether in any way it indicated guilt or innocence. It is now clear from the files that the Boston bureau agents were not aware of Sacco and Vanzetti before their arrest. Although the bureau had collected information about a number of Massachusetts anarchists, the Plymouth fish peddler and the Stoughton shoe worker were too obscure to have come to the bureau's attention. The bureau did not aid the prosecution and had no opinion as to guilt or innocence in a crime it considered outside its jurisdiction.

"Just think of attacking Weyand and Letherman because they betrayed secrets, departmental secrets, the very thing I say they have told us!" Thompson exclaimed melodramatically in arguing an amended bill of exceptions before Judge Thayer. "Secrets! And when I want to know what those secrets are, I am told I cannot have them, no matter what the consequence may be to Sacco and Vanzetti."[6] But the real secret of the Bureau of Investigation files on Sacco and Vanzetti is that there was no secret.

14

The Road to Norwood

When I went to see the Brinis in Plymouth, still living in the Suosso's Lane house where Vanzetti had boarded, they talked about those days without hesitation. Disarmingly warmhearted, they still clung to the memory of their old friend. LeFavre, as a girl a Plymouth witness for Vanzetti, showed me several letters he had written her parents. She insisted on my having coffee and cakes. A small grandson wanted me to see the toy gun he had got for Christmas. Her brother Beltrando, who testified that he was delivering eels with Vanzetti on the day of the Bridgewater holdup, had become a schoolteacher and was principal of an elementary school in Wollaston, a seaside suburb adjacent to Boston. Equally willing to talk, equally friendly, he was also equally insistent that he really had been with Vanzetti in Plymouth on that far-off December morning. After spending an evening with him, I was convinced he was telling the truth. This I still believe.

With the Brinis, doors opened readily. But with the Sacco family, the door remained closed. That was what Upton Sinclair discovered when he came to write *Boston*:

> I had visited Sacco's family and I felt certain that there was some dark secret there. Nobody would be frank with me, and everybody was suspicious even though I had been introduced and vouched for by Mrs. Evans, a great lady of Boston who had led and financed the fight for freedom of these two Italians.[1]

In the decades when I concerned myself with the case, I never tried to approach Sacco's son Dante. Others have. Felix once telephoned him, and Dante replied with frigid politeness that he did not care to discuss the matter. More recently, an editor of *Paris Match* tried to arrange an interview with Rosina through her son. "Nobody stands a dog's chance of interviewing my mother," Dante told him. When the poet Kenneth Rexroth intruded on him, presuming on a mutual bond of anarchy, Dante chased him from the premises with a revolver.[2]

Two years after Sacco's death Rosina became the common-law wife of Ermano Bianchini, a member of the defense committee who had fallen in love with her during the time of Sacco's imprisonment.* Dante was then sixteen years old. He and his sister Inez moved with their mother into Bianchini's four-room bungalow on one of the almost anonymous streets of Watertown, an obscure industrial suburb of Boston. During the Depression years he worked as a deliveryman, first for a local grocer, then later for Filene's, the large Boston department store. In 1939 he eloped with a girl five years younger than himself, a waitress whom he had met in an ice-cream bar in an adjoining suburb. She was Swedish by descent. To avoid any publicity they were married in the village of Friendship, Maine, 175 miles north of Boston.

The war that banished the Depression was his opportunity. He found an outlet for his natural mechanical bent as an airplane mechanic. His reserved occupation kept him out of the armed forces. Before the war ended he had become parts manager for the local airport in Norwood, Massachusetts, four miles south of Dedham. In 1947 he moved to Norwood. He bought a brown six-room Dutch colonial house with a sun porch, like the other houses on its maple-shaded side street, where the yards run into one another, flags are displayed on public holidays, and a basketball hoop is hung above most garage doors.

His life could have been that of any average American in the now somewhat archaic pattern of the small town as illustrated by Norman Rockwell. For twenty-seven years he worked as parts manager. He had three sons. By the mid-sixties the oldest was married, the next one had just been admitted to membership in the First Congregational Church, and the youngest was still in college. He belonged to the Norwood Chamber of Commerce and the Businessmen's Bowling League. Sundays he ushered at the neocolonial brick Congregational Church, with its soaring white spire that recalled the arch-pattern of

---

* Anarchists do not believe in formal marriage vows except for practical ends. Twenty years later Bianchini would marry Rosina, possibly for Social Security reasons.

the New England meeting house. His wife was the church's financial secretary, which meant that she sorted out and kept track of all the pledge envelopes.

Bearing his father's name, he must have been looked at with curious, hostile eyes when he first came to Norwood. In time he became accepted in that small open community whose Main Street is no more than a pause on the old road from Boston to Providence. Yet everyone in town was aware of the shadow, and he knew that they knew. He kept the knowledge from his children as long as he could. Some years after his death his son Spenser told Brian Jackson that he himself was twelve before he learned about his Grandfather Sacco.

> My daddy was a wise man. He kept us blissfully out of the Sacco-Vanzetti thing. Then one night he was out at a PTA meeting, and I was downstairs making a model airplane. We had this landlord then, and his son came back drunk, very drunk. "Your grandfather was the bastard who went to the electric chair." *He* knew. It all spilled out and I just didn't understand. But I was frightened and rang up my parents.
>
> They hustled back and daddy said "come upstairs" and he explained it all. He was right to keep us out of it as long as possible, but in the end, if you are a Sacco, there is no escaping it.[3]

Periods of quiescence, when the volumes of the Sacco-Vanzetti trial record gathered dust on library shelves, were invariably succeeded by intervals of revived discussion and agitation. In 1959 Tom O'Connor's vindication committee succeeded in getting a bill introduced in the Massachusetts legislature to grant a posthumous pardon to the two anarchists. The bill, sponsored by a florid Italian-American representative from Melrose, Al Cella, got a thin reception from the legislative committee, in spite of the silvered oratory and tossing silver mane of Judge Musmanno, who had come from Pennsylvania to be the principal speaker for the measure. Dante, approached by Felicani—one of the few who could approach him—not only refused to endorse the bill but objected even to its having been introduced. He wanted nothing to do with any Sacco-Vanzetti revival. The only time I ever saw Felicani really angry was before that hearing in the State House when he learned of Dante's refusal.

Throughout the years Dante remained apart. Sacco-Vanzetti dogmatists and fanatics would have made him a peripatetic evangelist, dragging him from platform to platform, from forum to meeting hall to radical assembly, to hear him shriek his father's name and denounce his father's murderers. In that name he could have commanded worldwide audiences. He would have none of it nor of those who would have used him. Scholars, radicals domestic and foreign, professed revolutionaries, his father's comrades, appealed to him periodically to break his silence. He did not answer.

By the time of their deaths Sacco and Vanzetti had at least the cold consolation of martyrdom. Dante they saw as their continuity, their life-to-come, their vindicator, to whom they would pass on the bright torch of anarchy. Two days before he died Sacco wrote his son, then fifteen, a letter that was at the same time a public testament.

> . . . Remember always, Dante, in the play of happiness, don't use all for yourself only, but down yourself just one step, at your side and help the weak ones that cry for help, help for the prosecuted and the victim, because they are your better friends; they are all the comrades that fight and fall as your father and Bartolo fought and fell yesterday for the conquest of the joy of freedom for all and the poor workers. . . .
>
> Dante, I say once more to love and be nearest to your mother and the beloved ones in these sad days, and I am sure that with your brave heart and kind goodness they will feel less discomfort. And you will also not forget to love me a little for I do—O, Sonny! thinking so much and so often of you.[4]

At about the same time Vanzetti also wrote to Dante, tenderly, but with similar public intent:

> I write little of this because you are still too little-boy to understand this things and other things of which I would like to reason with you.
>
> But if you do well, you will grow and understand your father's and my case and your father's and my principles for which we will soon be put to death.
>
> I tell you now that for and of all I know of your father, he is not a criminal, but one of the bravest men I ever knew.
>
> One day you will understand what I am about to tell you; that your father has sacrificed everything dear and sacred to the human heart and soul for his fate in liberty and justice for all. That day you will be proud of your father; and if you come brave enough, you will take his place in the struggle between tyranny and liberty and you will vindicate his (our) names and our blood. . . .
>
> Remember, Dante, Remember always these things; we are not criminals; they convicted us on a frame-up; they denied us a new trial; and if we will be executed after seven years, four months and 17 days of unspeakable tortures and wrongs, it is for what I have already told you; because we were for the poor and against the exploitation and oppression of the man by the man.

The documents of our case, which you and other ones will collect and preserve, will proof you that your father, your mother, yourself, Inez, I and my family are sacrificed by and to a State Reason of the American Plytocratic reaction.

The day will come when you will understand the atrocious sense of the above-written words, in all its fullness. Then you will honor us.[5]

Dante, to the bewilderment and dismay of Sacco-Vanzetti partisans, remained apparently unmoved by these passionate appeals of his doomed blood.

In Maxwell Anderson's verse play *Winterset*, shaped by the Sacco-Vanzetti case, Mio Romagna, the son of an innocent man executed for murder, gives his life to tracking down the real criminals. As he tells a friend he meets in his wanderings across America: "For my heritage they've left me one thing only, and that's my father's voice crying up out of the earth. . . . I've tried to live and forget it—but I was birthmarked with hot iron into the entrails."[6]

It is Mio's compulsion to search out the men who had committed the crime for which his father died, a compulsion that brings him to his death. Dante Sacco did not feel that visceral urgency to vindicate his father's name and avenge his blood. The desperate eloquence of those final letters, the memory of the man who loved him and whom he as a thirteen-year-old had visited in the death house did not drive him into the ranks of that struggle "between tyranny and liberty."[*]

He was seven years old when his father was arrested, nine when he sat beside his mother in the Dedham courthouse and heard her cry out after the jury brought in its verdict. Through the years of his growing up he went regularly with her to the Dedham jail, bringing his father Italian food and delicacies. It was from that jail that Sacco plaintively recalled the time when he lived with his family in their Stoughton bungalow, how after visiting friends in the evening he and Rosina would come back with Dante asleep in his arms. "Those day," he wrote Cerise Jack, "they was a some happy day."[7] Dante would never have been able to forget that slight, dark man in the

---

[*] Commenting on an article of mine on Dante's enigmatic silence, John Braine wrote: "I doubt whether Dante cared whether or not his father was guilty. I believe that he took the view that the majority of us would take: he personally had nothing to do with the Sacco-Vanzetti case, the dead were dead, and he wanted no part in it one way or another. He wanted to live his own life. He didn't wish to find himself on public platforms, sitting on committees, being interviewed, and all the rest of it. What I'm getting at is that this is the silent majority's position, the private person's position. I honestly doubt if Dante ever even read about the case or discussed it or thought about it. The disquieting thing is the gap between the intellectual and the nonintellectual majority."

prison jacket who had carried him. He must have loved his father, yet he could not escape the shadow. A less honorable man might have shouted out his father's innocence to applauding crowds. He could not. His father's cause was not his. Nicola Sacco was an Italian, an anarchist, a revolutionary. Dante was an American who wanted nothing more than to be a member of the solid small middle class that Alfred North Whitehead maintained was the strength of America. But he was caught. If, like Al Capone's son, he had changed his name and fled to some far-off city, it would have been an admission of his father's guilt. So he lived his years in Norwood almost within sight of the courthouse where his father had been condemned.

While I was living in Wellesley, at the close of the sixties, my friend and neighbor Joseph Murray—the first doctor to have performed a kidney-transplant operation—told me that his mother had just read *Tragedy in Dedham* and wanted to talk to me. As Mary De-Pasquale she had first taught Sacco English. She had also been friendly with Rosina Zambelli, Sacco's future wife, when the Zambellis rented the upper apartment of her father's house.

Mary Murray, widow of a Worcester judge, still lived in Milford, still remembered the bright and attentive young man who had come to her evening classes so long ago. Never could she believe that young man guilty of anything as sordid as the Braintree murders. When I first talked with her she said she did not agree with my book's conclusions, but reading it had brought back many old memories. She asked me if I knew what had become of Rosina and her children. I told her Dante lived in Norwood a dozen miles away and that Rosina had married an anarchist friend of Sacco's named Bianchini and lived in West Bridgewater.

That town seemed an ironic choice for the Bianchinis to end their days. Once on my way from Cape Cod to Boston I had driven past their house, on the town's outskirts, a small boxlike ranch house, neat but somehow forlorn. Its venetian blinds were drawn, and as I went by I saw a shadow briefly against a blind, wondered if it might be Rosina. Through the years she had lived with the man she had chosen, a recluse, never once speaking out in defense of the man who had been her husband. After Bruno Richard Hauptmann was executed for the murder of the Lindbergh baby, his widow Anna never ceased insisting on his innocence. "All of my life I have prayed that the truth will come out," she told a friendly interviewer forty years later.[8] But with Rosina there was only silence.

Mary Murray said she was going to write Dante and ask about his mother. She thought perhaps the three of us might one day have lunch together. I told her I doubted if Dante would answer her letter, much less be willing to see me. Shortly after our talk she did write him. When I saw her a few weeks later she said she had not got a reply. Then on September 15, 1970, I had a letter from her, and from September to November of that year I received seven more letters, the last on November 30, all dealing with Dante and Rosina.

Yesterday I got the surprise of my life [she wrote in her first letter]. You will never guess who came out to see me. Dante Sacco and wife called on me.

Remember I wrote him, no reply. Well it seems he drove to Milford another time—no one at home then. He is a fine fellow, in the aviation field business—is an aviator himself. More later. I mentioned his father, told him about your book and he showed me some pictures of his family, mother Rosina, and his stepfather. Told him I wanted to see her again soon. When he read my letter to her, she knew who I was instantly, he observed.

Well, we have a foot in the door now. I must not rush him but I will get some news now from his mother and himself.

A week later she wrote to say she had just written a letter to Rosina telling her how much she had enjoyed Dante's visit. Then in October she wrote that

tonight, Dante and wife Mildred called on me again. Of course I was delighted to see them both. However, it seems he was and looked disturbed and soon I found out the reason. His mother thought he should not have given me *her address*, etc. for fear I would broadcast it to anyone and although he did not say so, I think she must have chided him for coming to see me. *I am not sure of the latter.* When I assured him that no one would know her address through me, he looked relieved. Poor fellow, he did not wish to tell me about his mother or hurt *my* feelings but, when I told him I understood her reluctance to have anyone know her whereabouts, he was himself *again*.

Perhaps I made a mistake in writing to her at all, but I did. However, I was so careful not to open old wounds, just wrote that I often thought of her, remembering her as a beautiful girl, convent-bred, of her father, mother, family and ended by saying I would love to see her *once more* before I died—that I was 79 yrs old, etc.

No answer to this note but Dante called instead. The door is shut now I guess, but Dante and wife are still my friends and I hope will continue to be.

According to them, the mother and her husband are recluses, never go any place, never see anyone. In fact, even the son hardly ever sees her, twice in the last six months. . . .

After another two weeks, she wrote:

No, not a word from Dante! I suppose his mother warned him not to talk, for I really think left to himself he would have said something. In fact, he let slip out once, there was his stepfather to consider, a good man, etc. What an excuse! . . .

If Sacco had been my father I would have moved heaven and earth to clear his name all those years and would have proclaimed it from the roof-tops.

For me Dante's persistent silence carried an implication of his father's guilt. Yet, I told myself, he might not have known. He might merely have been motivated by his wish to be divorced from the whole tragic affair, to free himself from his inherited burden, to live his own instead of his father's life, to be the best bowler in Norwood rather than the embodiment of a lost cause. After several more talks with Mary Murray, I at last wrote him a letter but let her read it first to see if she thought I ought to send it. She said that I should. I wrote:

Dear Mr. Sacco:

It is only after a great deal of hesitancy that I have finally decided to write you. As you know, some years ago I wrote a book about the Sacco-Vanzetti case. During the writing of it I knew that you lived in Norwood, and in the State House records I learned about your mother's remarriage. Also I believe it was Aldino Felicani who told me she lived in Bridgewater. But I have never tried to approach any of you because I felt that this dark and enormous tragedy had shadowed your lives through no fault of your own. If you wanted to keep silent, that was your right.

Oddly enough our paths have crossed indirectly several times. My friend Henry Beston told me he had once rented his Outermost House to you for the summer and said you had been married in Friendship where I spent many summers. Also Mrs. Mary DePasquale Murray is a friend of mine. Her son lived for years next to us, and her granddaughter is my own daughter's godmother. She told me much about your father as a young man when she used to teach him English, and although our views of the case differ we remain understanding friends.

I am afraid what I must next say is painful, but once having written you I cannot avoid it. I am shortly getting out a new edition of my book to mark the fiftieth anniversary of the Dedham trial. After the bullet tests that I sponsored in 1961 and that I personally supervised, I could only conclude that the Colt found on your father at his arrest was the one that fired a fatal bullet in South Braintree. Who might have pulled the trigger then is another matter. But I cannot look on him as an innocent man. I may be wrong. So much has always been indeterminate in this case. Yet in the silence of the Sacco family is, at least to outsiders, an implication of guilt. That is the only conclusion that I can draw. In the case that I may be wrong I finally decided to write you.

When years ago I visited the Brinis in Plymouth, where Vanzetti used to board, they overwhelmed me with good will in the memory and defense of their old friend. And the son Beltrando, now a teacher in Wollaston, spent an evening talking with me as openly as a man can talk even though the case has warped his life. With Vanzetti's friends everybody talks. With your family there is silence. The conclusion may be cruel, but it is inevitable.

The case has really been the great American case of the century, transcending the individuals involved. My book with its flaws is a minor matter. Your own feelings are a major matter, and I expect you could many times have wished the whole thing out of your life. Yet it does become a part of history, and even as a part of history it remains vague. The Dreyfus case, to which it has been compared, at least had a conclusion. Dreyfus was the innocent victim of a frame-up. We now know how and why. But the Sacco-Vanzetti case is something to which history cannot yet supply an unequivocal answer. There are those still alive, a few at least, who know just what did happen on that April afternoon in South Braintree half a century ago. For the sake of history it is another tragedy that they should die without making it clear.

What I am prepared to ask you is something you have never done and perhaps never will do. But I wonder if once for the sake of history you will be willing to make your own statement about the case. If the conclusion that the silence of the Sacco family is an implication of guilt is wrong, I should like to be able to say so. Only this has persuaded me to write you, assailed as you must have been by the fanatics of both sides.

I have spent years in making up my mind to send this letter to you. And I can well understand that you may choose not to reply to me or to anyone else. But I in turn have to draw what conclusions I can from every aspect of the case, not for my own vanity or any other reason than that in my imperfect way I feel I have an obligation to history.

To this letter, as I told Mary Murray, I never received a reply.* In her last letters to me she wrote that

* This was my sole attempt to communicate with Dante. I never wrote again nor tried at any time to get in touch with him, although Carey McWilliams has accused me of "hounding" him ("Massachusetts Pays Its Debt," *The Nation*, August 20, 1977).

after thinking it over I decided that if he [Dante] ignored your letter, he would throw mine in the waste paper, so I did nothing more.

He is a queer individual, but realizing what he went through as a child and young man under the guidance of his mother (I know nothing of his step-father), I am not much surprised that he acts as he does, You and I would have acted differently but he—

Perhaps I never should have written to his mother, then I could have continued to see Dante and perhaps after he knew me better would have spoken more freely. . . . Then, again, his mother, I think, influences him and must have told him to remain silent. . . . The mother, I think, has the key to the truth, but if she did not even approve of Dante's giving me her address you can readily see that she will not talk or even wants anyone, myself included, to write or reach her.

Sixteen months after I wrote to Dante, he died of a pulmonary embolus, a blood clot on the lungs. He was fifty-eight years, three months, and fourteen days old; a good husband, a good father, a good citizen, a loyal employee, a faithful churchman. The pastor said so in his eulogy. Every seat in the church was taken at his funeral.

Within a year of his death his son Spenser broke the family's self-imposed silence to emerge publicly in defense of his executed grandfather, bobbing up at an assortment of conferences and meetings. He was then an instructor in music at Salve Regina, a Catholic women's college in Newport, and on Sundays a church organist. A short, prematurely bald, mild-featured man, he had come to terms with his background in ways that would have surprised his grandfather.

I first saw him at a Sacco-Vanzetti conference of the American Italian Historical Association held in November 1972 at the North Bennett Street School in the North End.* To balance the program, its organizers had picked me as *advocatus diaboli*, among the half-dozen speakers the one challenger to the dogma of innocence betrayed. Somebody had to take the opposite side. Walking through the Italian district on that sullen, rainy Saturday afternoon, I realized that I was on my way to face a hostile audience. How hostile remained to be seen.

The school's auditorium, painted a rancid green and smelling faintly of floor oil and vanished humanity, was almost full by the time I made my way to the platform. Below me I could see a scattering of

---

* Formerly the North Bennett Street Industrial School, its founding purpose was to give vocational training to immigrants. Today it specializes in teaching such crafts as wood carving and violin making. Though its auditorium is used for occasional local meetings, it is no longer concerned with the surrounding Italian community.

familiar if not exactly friendly faces: Ehrmann's widow; Clem Norton, amiable enough in his checkerboard suit; a son of Felicani; Roberta Feuerlicht, her face twisted in a grimace; directly in front of me, Al Cella. Al had grown fatter in the dozen years since I had seen him at his State House–sponsored posthumous-pardon hearing. The next year he had been defeated for reelection. But the Massachusetts legislature looks after its own. Ex-members, if they can do nothing else, are appointed doorkeepers, with the result that the Massachusetts State House has more keepers than doors. Al, after his defeat, was made a Boston municipal judge. I do not know the details.

I realized at once that this was more a testimonial meeting than a conference. But I did spot one friendly face, that of Tony Di Cecca, a criminal lawyer from Somerville. While I was writing *Tragedy in Dedham*, he had persuaded a reluctant ex-convict to take a lie-detector test that was one of the factors impelling me to change my mind about the Sacco-Vanzetti case. Tony had various underworld and Mafia connections. Moving among thieves, he had often touched pitch, without ever being defiled. An honest man, whose friendship went beyond ethnic loyalties. As he caught my eye, he waved encouragingly.

Louis Joughin was the lead speaker, a bearded academic with a withered face. As I walked across the platform, he glanced at me contemptuously. According to his version, the Sacco-Vanzetti case must remain the enduring concern of every right-minded American. New vistas, he said, were opening. Nevertheless, the revisionism of the previous decade had made its mark. He was willing to admit—as he would never have done in his 1948 *Legacy of Sacco and Vanzetti*—that no one could definitely say whether or not Sacco and Vanzetti were guilty. That was no longer the point. Guilt or innocence had become subsidiary to the larger issue of the whole judicial process. Further studies were required: analyses of the FBI files, the Lowell papers, Judge Thayer's public and private correspondence, Katzmann's papers, Moore's papers, and so on—a formidable list. Moore he dismissed as an "incompetent fool." As he talked on and on, the other panel members grew restive, worried that he was intruding on their time. But when he at last wound down, the applause was resonant.

When I, in turn, began to speak, I could sense the tenseness. I explained that, being neither lawyer nor professor, I had concerned myself more concretely with the question of guilt or innocence. Judging by the record, I did not consider the trial unfair even though there were aspects one might take exception to. I mentioned Moore's and Tresca's doubts. "Bullshit!" someone bellowed. When I concluded, the silence was deafening. The moderator asked if there were any questions.

First on his feet was Al Cella, squarely in front of me, his face red, his body expanding as if he were blowing himself up. In a voice raucous with emotion he accused me of doing more than anyone to foul the waters of the Sacco-Vanzetti case. A mouse with one eye, he said, could see that it wasn't a murder case, it was a fix-up by the politicos. I had turned facts on their head. I had written dozens of insulting letters to Sacco's son. I had viciously libeled such noble spirits as Herbert Ehrmann and Judge Musmanno. What Al's question was I never did find out.

Even as Al was speaking, Clem Norton had jumped up, waving his arms for attention until he finally got, or rather seized, the floor. He was angry, not at me, but because he had not been included among the speakers on the platform. "I have documents in my hand," he announced sonorously, holding up what may have been his Boston Public Library card or his senior citizen's subway pass, "to prove the villainous conspiracy that District Attorney Katzmann was engaged in. Proof at last!" Then, as if he had lost his thread of thought, he sat down.

From the shadowy back of the hall a slight man began haranguing me in a reedy indistinct voice. It took me some moments before I grasped that this vague figure was Sacco's grandson Spenser. His tone was mild, his words vituperative. Where did I get my misinformation about his family? he asked. What was I doing snooping about the back streets of Norwood? My writings were lies, gossip, innuendo. What did I know? Nothing.

He now explained that his father had kept silent because of his family. Holding up his right hand and ticking off each finger, he said that his father had been protecting his own mother, his wife, his three sons. I had written an article for *Metro Boston* in which I concluded that Dante's silence might be taken as an imputation of guilt. This article Spenser now compared to a red light hanging over a brothel. I presume someone like Al Cella had written his speech for him. He seemed too soft a man for what he was saying. Of course, he could not explain why he was not as concerned about protecting his fivefold family as his father had been, or why he had never broken his own silence until after his father's death. When he finished, I said nothing.

Tony Di Cecca came forward to meet me after the meeting. Someone pushed ahead to confront me on the stairs. "Come along," said Tony, slipping his bulk between us. "Come along. Let it pass."

The rain was beating down, the pavement glistening as we walked along empty Hanover Street. Tony had recently lost his father and was still grieving over his loss. We talked about Spenser's tirade, and I asked him what he would have done if his own father had been executed for a murder he never committed.

"I'd try to find out who the real murderer was," he said.

"Even if it took the rest of your life?" I asked him.

"Yes," he said, "I'd keep on trying just the same. I'd never stop."

"But supposing your father was guilty and you knew it?"

"Then," said Tony emphatically, "I'd shut up."

15

The Road to Cambridge

Several years after the execution of Sacco and Vanzetti, a group of their supporters met to view a selection of newsreels on the case pieced together under the title of *The Good Shoemaker and the Poor Fish Peddler*. Among the viewers were William Thompson, Herbert Ehrmann, and Felix Frankfurter. As the mournful spaniel features of Harvard's President Lowell appeared on the screen, Thompson remarked with deliberate loudness: "There is the real villain of the piece!"[1]

So Lowell would remain, fixed in the eyes of Sacco-Vanzetti partisans and sympathizers. Public opinion did not concern him. He himself was impervious to criticism. In the 1919 strike of the Boston police he had urged Harvard undergraduates to enroll as strikebreaking volunteer policemen, and several hundred did just that.[2] During that strike Harold Laski, then a Harvard instructor in political science, addressed a public meeting in defense of the striking policemen. Boston papers denounced him as a traitor and a Bolshevik and many Harvard alumni—including some of the university's most generous benefactors—demanded his dismissal. This the governing boards had a right to do, since Laski lacked tenure. But Lowell informed them that if they dismissed Laski—whom he did not happen to admire—his own resignation would immediately follow.[3]* When Frankfurter's book first came out as an article in the *Atlantic Monthly*, the Harvard overseers objected to its appearance while the Massachusetts Supreme Court was still hearing the appeal for a new trial. Lowell rebuffed them, asking: "Would you have wanted Frankfurter to wait in expressing his views until the men were dead?"[4]

* A few months later Laski received a call to a professorship at the University of London.

Such was Abbott Lawrence Lowell, such was the autocratic presence who took over the chairmanship of the committee of which he was supposedly merely a member. The Governor's Advisory Committee was at once taken for granted as the Lowell Committee. Governor Fuller had said that if the members failed to agree, he would consider it a reasonable doubt. But it did not seem within reason that Judge Grant and Massachusetts Institute of Technology President Stratton—an outsider from Illinois—would fail to agree with Lowell. In the summer of 1927 Lowell held the fate of the two condemned Italians in his hands, the one man in Massachusetts who could reverse the Dedham verdict.

In what amounted to a second trial, the Lowell Committee read the stenographic record, interviewed witnesses, some of whom had not testified at the trial, ballistics experts, ten of the eleven jurors, Judge Thayer, and District Attorney Katzmann. This second trial, beginning on June 1 in the Massachusetts State House, lasted almost two weeks longer than the original six-and-a-half-week Dedham trial. Summarizing their report, the committee saw

> no evidence sufficient to make them believe that the trial was unfair. On the contrary they are of the opinion that the Judge endeavored, and endeavored successfully, to secure for the defendants a fair trial; that the District Attorney was not in any way guilty of unprofessional behavior; that he conducted the prosecution vigorously but not improperly; and that the jury, a capable, impartial, and unprejudiced body, did, as they were instructed, "well and truly try and true deliverance make."[5]

The report did nothing to mollify Sacco-Vanzetti partisans. Lowell was vilified, called a murderer, a cold-blooded reactionary willing to sacrifice the lives of two alien radicals in defense of his caste and the Massachusetts judicial establishment. Walter Lippmann, as chief editorial writer for Pulitzer's *New York World*, after consulting with Frankfurter, devoted his entire page to expressing his doubts and dissent. In the same paper Heywood Broun wrote bitterly that "if all the venerable college presidents in the country tottered forward and pronounced the men guilty they would still be innocent." Subsequently he grew so violent in his comments on Lowell's "throwing the switch" and on Harvard as "hangman's house" that Pulitzer finally suspended his column. In an eight-hundred-word open letter to Lowell, John Dos Passos accused him of being a collaborator in judicial murder. "As a Harvard man," he wrote, "I want to protest most solemnly against your smirching the university of which you are an officer with the foul crime against humanity and civilization to which you have made yourself an accessory."

In the years after the executions Lowell continued to be attacked. One versifier, in a "Ballade of the Crime Wave," asked why thieves and pimps should be punished when

> Webster Thayer still sits on the bench,
> A. Lawrence Lowell is still at large.[6]

At the Harvard tercentenary celebration in 1936, six Harvard alumni—including Heywood Broun, Gardner Jackson, and Granville Hicks—distributed *Walled in This Tomb*, a pamphlet condemning Lowell and his committee, "for special consideration by the alumni of Harvard University." e. e. cummings described Lowell to Edmund Wilson as "going round everywhere with a little poodle, whose balls trail on the ground and make the letter H—that's what he's like."[7]

To the mounting attacks made on Lowell after the publication of the committee's report, to the repeated allegations that his files contained information that would have exonerated Sacco and Vanzetti, he never publicly replied. As he had always done, he declined to be interviewed, refused any comment. He kept all his Sacco-Vanzetti papers intact. When he died in 1943 he left his private papers to his Harvard colleague and biographer, Henry Yeomans, and his former secretary, Norma Dwyer. His Sacco-Vanzetti papers were sealed and deposited in the Harvard University archives on December 9, 1948, with the stipulation that they were not to be opened until December 9, 1977.

They remained in the archives, even though one researcher brought legal action to get access to them under the Freedom of Information Act as public documents. Finally, on the morning of December 18, 1977, in Harvard's semisubterranean Pusey Library, the two-foot-square package containing the papers was brought out. Under the glare of television-camera lights, before photographers, television and radio announcers, reporters, representatives of the foreign press, historians and would-be historians, the curator of the archives, Harley Holden—with the director emeritus of the Massachusetts Historical Society beaming in the background— flourished a pair of scissors to cut open the package, then read out a list of the contents. But as Holden explained to his disappointed audience, the actual papers were not yet available for inspection. First they had to be classified and microfilmed. That would take at least a month.

Late in January I was finally able to go through them. No ultimate secrets have been buried there, no startling revelations, nothing to alter partisan opinions, though the papers do enlarge on how Lowell's committee came to its conclusions. Half the papers have long been part of the public record: the governor's and committee's reports; the transcript of the committee hearings; newspaper clippings; letters from Lowell reprinted in Yeomans' 1948 biography. During the hearings Thompson had been allowed to be present and to cross-examine witnesses, but when the jurors and Judge Thayer were interviewed, he was excluded, as was apparently the stenographer, and these deliberations remained secret. Disappointingly, there are no minutes of them in the papers, no explicatory references to Judge Thayer.

It is clear that Thayer, whose judicial conduct before the Sacco-Vanzetti trial had never been questioned, became unnerved by the persistence and virulence of the attacks he had to endure over the years, the threats to himself and his wife and family. That these threats were not idle was demonstrated in 1932 when his house was dynamited and his wife injured. The case became his obsession, and he talked about it compulsively when he was off the bench and after the trial. Just what he did say is uncertain, since the evidence is hearsay, two or three times removed. The original report concluded that

> the judge was indiscreet in conversation with outsiders during the trial. He ought not to have talked about the case off the bench, and doing so was a grave breach of official decorum. But we do not believe that he used some of the expressions attributed to him, and we think there is exaggeration in what the persons to whom he spoke remember. Furthermore, we believe that such indiscretions in conversation did not affect his conduct at the trial or the opinions of the jury, who, indeed, so stated to the committee.[8]

A hint of what transpired in the committee's interview with Thayer is given in Judge Grant's autobiography, written in his eightieth year. "The evidence that he had been grossly indiscreet in his remarks off the bench was cumulative," Grant wrote.

> I was amazed and incensed that any Massachusetts judge could have been so garrulous. That he had talked he did not deny, but he declared under oath with convincing emotion that several of the accusations

against him—notably of having rehearsed a part of his charge to the jury—were untrue. . . . When we came to consider the language of our Report, I was asked, as the one who ought to know how a judge should conduct himself, to suggest the words of censure. They were used, and if my associates felt a shade less outraged by his unseemly conduct, it was from a due sense of perspective.[9]

The substance of the Lowell Papers is in the 233 letters about the case sent or received by Lowell. To his well-wishers he replied with a form letter. Friends and more significant acquaintances he answered at some length, even when they protested his conclusions. "Have you not been carried away by the mob-psychology provoked by energetic propaganda?" he replied to a challenging letter by J. A. Williams. "I had not my present opinion when appointed to the commission for I had, like yourself, an impression derived from the attitude common in the public; but a careful reading of all the evidence convinced me that the popular impression of the case was quite wrong, that the verdict was due to overwhelming evidence of guilt, mostly circumstantial and little known to the public,* that the class and political prejudice has been worked up since."

R. G. Allen, of the Harvard class of 1905, demanded that Lowell resign as president of the university, adding that "we can stand anything but a murderer and you can be described only by such a term." To such letters—one from Paris even addressed to "Hangman's House"—he did not reply. Shortly before the executions an old friend, Julia Sartori, wrote him from Italy expressing her doubts. On August 29 he wrote back:

> We who were appointed by the Governor a Committee to inquire into the fairness of the trial, and the guilt of the two men, studied all the evidence with great care. This almost no one has done, and when we had done so, there was no doubt in our minds that the trial was fair and the men were guilty. We felt that any impartial person who studied all the evidence would come to the same conclusion. It was a task that we undertook with great repugnance, but felt that as good citizens we could not refuse. The seven long years in prison has been inexcusable, but it has been due mainly to the lawyers for these men who have made repeated requests for a new trial for reasons that did not justify it.

In December 1928 Lowell explained to Marshall Best (whose Viking Press was publishing the letters of Sacco and Vanzetti):

* The committee had the results of Colonel Goddard's test available as well as other ballistics evidence.

The evidence of guilt would have been regarded, I think, by everyone as sufficient for convicting any American citizen in whose favor there was not violent prejudice. The mere fact alone would have been enough that two weeks after the murder the two men were arrested, one of whom had on his person the weapon with which the murder was committed (as is proved by the possession of a Colt automatic and the obsolete bullets exactly like the fatal one), and the other [had] on [his] person a pistol taken from the dead murdered man (as seemed clear to the committee from the fact that the accused first lied about the way he got it; that he did not know how many of the chambers the pistol had and had no ammunition for it save what it contained).

Among the Lowell Papers' documents are the initial and final drafts of the committee's report, with various emendations, mostly matters of style or elaboration, made in Lowell's handwriting. In the final draft the sentence "The evidence against Vanzetti is more varied" has been altered from the first draft's "The evidence against Vanzetti is less strong." Both drafts contain the sentence "On the whole, we are of the opinion, beyond reasonable doubt, that Vanzetti was also guilty, though with much less assurance than in the case of Sacco." Before the typescript went to the printer, the words "though with much less assurance than in the case of Sacco" were crossed out. Even at that, Lowell's adversaries fell on the phrase "on the whole" as indicating doubt. To the troubled query of his friend in England, Sir Horace Plunkett, Lowell explained that

> the use of the words "on the whole" appears to have been unfortunate though I used them deliberately. The evidence against Sacco was partly direct, partly circumstantial. . . . The evidence against Vanzetti was wholly circumstantial. Therefore "on the whole" indicates a putting together of circumstances no one of which alone would be conclusive. If the result left in my mind had not been a conviction beyond reasonable doubt, I should not have said so. Our final impression was that Vanzetti was the plotter and Sacco an executioner.

There is an iteration of Lowell's thoughts even when he writes to his more intimate friends. Keeping men in jail for six years awaiting execution is, he admits, outrageous, "but it was done in the main because their counsel took advantage of these methods." Again and again he expresses his conviction that the case was greatly misrepresented by Sacco-Vanzetti partisans, that "no impartial person could fail to come to the same conclusion that we did." The worldwide protest he sees as "a curious instance of mob psychology artfully influenced by not too scrupulous methods."

For all Lowell's public aloofness, attacks on his integrity nettled him. A year and a half later he wrote wryly to Plunkett:

> I have long felt that the belief in the innocence of Sacco and Vanzetti would, like the belief that Bacon wrote Shakespeare, continue forever, wholly unaffected by the evidence. The start in both cases is made with the facts to be proved, and then everything must be reconciled with that assumption.
>
> The logical process is something like this: the prisoners were Reds. There was violent prejudice against Reds in the United States. Therefore the men were unfairly tried. Therefore they were innocent. Therefore it was a judicial murder for political reasons.

Nothing changed his opinion in the years to come. Although Professor Frankfurter had been made to seem his adversary, their academic relationship remained cordial. When Frankfurter was appointed to the Supreme Court, Lowell wrote to congratulate him, adding that "although I suppose I might not agree with all the decisions you will render, I know that you will be no man's tool, but stand squarely upon your own legal principles." In reply Frankfurter wrote how deeply touched he was by Lowell's good wishes.

In 1932 Lowell retired as president of Harvard. Four years later, at the time of the Harvard tercentenary, he was again publicly assailed for his action in the Sacco-Vanzetti case. That same year he made what was in brief his apologia:

> After nine years' history [he wrote Bruce Bliven], I am perfectly satisfied with the position our Committee took in the Sacco-Vanzetti case. I have seen no reason to change my mind that the evidence proved these men guilty of the crime of which they were charged.
>
> If I could re-live that part of my life with the knowledge that I have now, that I should suffer persecution for doing my duty as a citizen, I should nevertheless do it as I did before.

16

The End of the Road

I

SACCO and VANZETTI: their linked names have continued to echo across the years, symbol of man's injustice to man. Enlightened world opinion, shaded somewhat by the revisionism of the last few years, has held almost unanimously that they were innocent and that the real guilt lay in those who prosecuted and tried them. Their case became a "cause, a passion, a heartbreak; it defined the term 'liberal,' "[1] their innocence so much an article of faith that to doubt it would have been to doubt one's own integrity. As David Felix explained in his illuminating study, intellectuals, identifying themselves with two portrayed idealists in rebellion against Philistines and Pharisees, were caught up in an act of faith. Believing in "innocence and betrayal through a burst of revelation, they began with pure emotion and applied their best intelligence to the proof of it. . . . The case became the private drama of the intellectuals."[2]

Why is this so? Why did a trial in a lesser Boston suburb of two inconspicuous aliens for a holdup murder enlarge to such an earth-shaking event that it still reverberates three-quarters of a century later? Innocent men are killed daily, injustice is commonplace in our era. Why should these two Italian anarchists have become symbols?

The answer is manifest in the two lawyers who so variously defended them, Fred Moore and Felix Frankfurter. Moore had given the Sacco-Vanzetti case its first international impetus. Frankfurter's polemic made it chic. Few who demonstrated and protested so fervently in the spring and summer months of 1927 knew much more about it than Frankfurter's tendentious essay that swept over the intellectual community like a tidal wave.*

In Frankfurter there was much of the abrasiveness of the self-made man. When he was twelve his immigrant parents had brought him from Vienna to New York. At first knowing no English, he learned quickly and was soon heading his classes in the Lower East Side public schools and subsequently in that haven for the upwardly mobile, the College of the City of New York. Entering Harvard Law School in 1903, he stood first in his class for three years, becoming editor of the *Law Review*, the law school's highest honor. Ten years after graduation, having served as assistant to the secretary of war, he returned to Harvard as a law school professor. Brilliant, scathingly self-confident, he refused an appointment to the Massachusetts Supreme Court. In 1939 his Washington friend Franklin Roosevelt would appoint him to the United States Supreme Court. As Felix wrote, "despite his Jewish background, he had made himself half-acceptable in Boston by his position at Harvard, his important friends in government, his great abilities, and his marriage to a Massachusetts lady."[3]

Frankfurter's Sacco-Vanzetti article, subtitled "A Critical Analysis for Lawyers and Laymen," sounded a clarion call to all liberal minds, all academics, all concerned citizens. To the case that had been smoldering for six years, his denunciation gave a sudden blazing illumination. For many it was a kind of lay conversion, a stand against the dark forces of reaction and bigotry. Such were the hard-bitten liberals who liked to proclaim the statement misattributed to Voltaire that though they might disagree with you they would defend with their life your right to speak. Yet, for all that, once they had embraced a cause they did not expect disagreement. I doubt if anyone could have continued living in the Elizabeth Peabody House in my Aunt Amy's day who held that Sacco and Vanzetti were guilty.

As hierophant of the case, Frankfurter brooked no deviance from his position. Not long after the publication of his 1927 article he met a lawyer friend in the Boston subway. "That was a wonderful brief

---

* In an acid comment on Frankfurter's role a reviewer in the *Times Literary Supplement* of July 26, 1963, wrote that "the chief cause of the case becoming known was probably the (to British minds impossible) article by the then Professor Frankfurter in the March, 1927, *Atlantic Monthly*. He attacked the whole case. He called in question the two men's arrest, the selection of the jury, Judge Thayer's 'patriotic rhetoric,' various procedural details. . . . One scintilla of such comment before the decision on appeal in a British court would have landed an editor in gaol for contempt, and a commentator who was a professor of law in gaol for a very protracted term."

you had in the *Atlantic*, Felix," the friend told him. "Brief!" Frankfurter replied before turning abruptly away. "No! It was a precise
statement of the facts."[4] And the two men parted on the ruins of a
friendship.[*]

On the night of the executions, shortly before midnight, Frankfurter and his wife Marion were walking aimlessly along the dark and
narrow streets of Beacon Hill. Suddenly from an open window a radio
blared out, "Sacco gone, Vanzetti going." Marion Frankfurter collapsed and was caught up by her husband and a friend who was with
them. Frankfurter did not speak.[5] The urbane and understanding
Judge Learned Hand, seeing him the next day, recalled that "he was
like a madman. He was really beside himself. I wouldn't have thought
of trying to talk to him."[6] Two days later his friend and associate,
Supreme Court Justice Louis Brandeis, wrote him consolingly that "the
end of S.V. is only the beginning. 'They know not what they do.' "[7][†]

At a memorial meeting after Frankfurter's death, one of his former law clerks remarked that "there never was a better friend or un-
fairer enemy."[8] His law-school colleague Roscoe Pound so
considered him. Pound, dean of the Harvard Law School and a me-
ticulous legal scholar, had been one of the dozen nationally known
lawyers, including Frankfurter, who publicly protested against the
Department of Justice's illegal acts in the 1919 roundup of aliens. In
1927 he was among those who petitioned the Massachusetts governor
to appoint a committee to review the Sacco-Vanzetti case. His interest in it continued over the years. In 1962 he often had lunch with
the legal scholar and former diplomat George Jackson Elder, then at
Harvard writing a book for the law school. One day the case came up
in their conversation. Pound told Elder that he had read "every bit
of evidence in the Sacco-Vanzetti case and that there was not the
slightest doubt of Sacco's guilt—that Felix (Frankfurter) was completely wrong and that his humanitarian instincts had distorted his
judgement. Vanzetti was almost certainly an accessory, if not a principal, but the evidence was not conclusive."[9]

---

[*] Ehrmann in his defensive recapitulation, *The Case That Will Not Die*, insisted forty
years later that Frankfurter's "complete accuracy has never been successfully challenged."

[†] As professor at the Harvard Law School, Frankfurter became Brandeis's political alter
ego. Brandeis paid him an annual subsidy to keep him politically informed. In June 1927,
he wrote Frankfurter: "I have long realized that S[acco]. V[anzetti]., inter alia, must have
made heavy demands for incidental expense, as well as time, and meant to ask you when we
met whether an additional sum might not be appropriate this year."

Why any particular case, among so many others scarcely noticed, should cause such ferment is owing in part to the sensational nature of a crime, the personality of the accused, the coincidence with the public mood, and the gap between the trial and the carrying out of the sentence. Caryl Chessmann, the cruising "red light bandit and rapist," under sentence of death in California for twelve years, his execution repeatedly postponed by adroit legal maneuverings and appeals, finally died in the gas chamber to a burst of world protest, partly because of the time-gap and the doubts it engendered, partly because he wrote several moving books during those years, and such a literary *tour de force* always exerts a certain fascination on intellectuals.

Massachusetts has had several cases to rival that of Sacco and Vanzetti in controversy and emotion. One of the earliest was that of Jason Fairbanks, tried at Dedham in 1801 for the murder of fourteen-year-old Betsey Fales.[10] Jason, a frail and ailing boy of sixteen with a withered arm, lived in the low, gabled Fairbanks house built by his Dedham ancestors in 1636, a remnant of Gothic New England.* For some time he had been keeping company with Betsey, his neighbor. Sometimes she would slip away from her family to spend the night with him in the rambling homestead. On one afternoon they met at the edge of a pasture behind the Fairbanks house. Half an hour later Jason appeared suddenly at the Fales house, wild-eyed and bleeding from a dozen wounds, a ten-cent knife in his hand. "Betsey has killed herself!" he gasped to the girl's mother, "and I have killed myself too!"

Betsey was found lying on the grass in a "loose gown" and a green skirt, stab wounds in her breast, arms, and back, her throat cut. Jason did not die. When he had recovered sufficiently he went on trial for murder. Feeling against him in Federalist Dedham ran high, and he was denounced as a "Liberty Pole Boy," a reader of the infidel Tom Paine, capable of any crime.

In a "Solemn Declaration," dictated shortly before his execution, Jason acknowledged that he had "possessed Betsey's person, and received the pledge of her attachment." After she had questioned him and he admitted that he had told some of his friends of their "connection," she turned on him in blind anger, exclaiming, "Oh! You are a monster! Give me that knife, I will put an end to my existence, you

---

* The house, within living memory occupied by members of the Fairbanks family, is now a museum, but the attendants make no mention of the murder.

false-hearted man! For I had rather die than live!" She then seized the knife he had been whittling with and stabbed herself repeatedly. Seeing her dying, he had tried to kill himself.[11]

Jason was defended by John Lowell, a fiery self-styled rebel, conservative of conservatives in his rebellion, detesting Napoleon, Jefferson, and Madison. Lowell the rebel came to accept Jason's story, in the end believing so passionately in his innocence that the case became his dominant and enduring preoccupation. In an eloquent defense before the Dedham court he narrowly escaped cutting himself while demonstrating with a knife how Betsey had stabbed herself in the back. It took the jury an extra day to agree, but they found Jason guilty. When he was publicly hanged in Dedham, Lowell all but collapsed.

> Profoundly convinced of Jason's innocence . . . he felt as millions the world over were to feel a century and a quarter later of another trial in Dedham Court, that the verdict, sentence and execution was, quite simply judicial murder. The practice of law, at which he was making nine thousand dollars a year, became distasteful to him and his health further deteriorated. When in the spring of 1803, his physicians ordered him to take a long rest, he retired from the bar forever.[12]

Late in the same century the controversy-ridden trial of Lizzie Borden took place in Fall River, Massachusetts, for the ax murder of her father and stepmother. Her case remains an American legend, preserved in a ballet, embellished in a mnemonic jingle.* Undoubtedly she was guilty. Undoubtedly no jury in 1893 would have convicted such a respected and respectable woman, a Sunday-school teacher, of many charities, a doer of good works. Following her arrest and indictment, cohorts of determined if vaguely informed supporters sprang to her defense. Such militants for women's rights as Susan Fessenden, president of the Women's Christian Temperance Union, the elderly Lucy Stone, organizer and president of the Woman's Suffrage Association, and organizations like the Woman's Auxiliary of the YMCA rushed to aid and comfort her "so ecstatically as to leave doubt whether they were acting from logic or emotion. . . . Blatantly they abused the Judge, the District Attorney and the police."[13] The judge's conduct in sitting on the bench after pre-

---

* Lizzie Borden took an axe
  And gave her Mother forty whacks;
  When she saw what she had done,—
  She gave her Father forty-one.

siding at the inquest, they assailed as "indecent, outrageous and not to be tolerated in any civilized community."[14]

Reaction, even after Lizzie had been found not guilty, was sharply against the prosecution, in the opinion of the *New York Times* "a condemnation of the police authorities of Fall River and of the legal officers who secured the indictment and conducted the trial." That trial, in language to be heard a generation later, was "a shame to Massachusetts."[15]

Still another Massachusetts case with repercussions similar to that of Sacco and Vanzetti occurred in 1905 with the trial of Charles Louis Tucker for the murder of Mabel Page, a forty-one-year-old spinster of Weston who had been discovered on the floor of her bedroom stabbed to death. Tucker, a local odd-job man at the time jobless, was not at first a suspect, though on the day of the murder he had been seen riding through Weston in a fish wagon. Later the driver had found a leather sheath on the wagon floor and had turned it over to the police, telling them Tucker might have dropped it.

Questioned a week later, Tucker at first denied owning a sheath but, on being shown the one found in the fish wagon, admitted it was his, saying he had put it in his pocket *three days* after the murder. Though he denied he had ever owned a knife to go with it, the police discovered fragments of a blood-stained blade in his overcoat pocket as well as a stickpin that a maid testified had belonged to Miss Page.

His arrest caused a sensation in the press. The Hearst papers in particular took up the cause of "the boy Tucker," vociferously denying his guilt and assailing the prosecution. To their readers it soon seemed that "the only blood-guilty person was the chief law officer of the Commonwealth and his assistants."[16] One of Tucker's lawyers was John Vahey, who fifteen years later would defend Vanzetti in the Plymouth trial. Like Vanzetti, Tucker declined to take the stand in his own defense. The jury brought in a verdict of guilty. After Tucker's execution Vahey felt that the public should know the reasons for his client's failure to testify.

The question gave us great concern throughout the trial ... [he explained]. While the whole matter had remained in abeyance, I think we all had a feeling that the defendant would take the stand.

Judge Sherman asked me if I wanted any advice from him on the matter. I said I would be glad to receive it. He told me he thought it advisable from long experience to state all the reasons for and all the reasons against his testifying to the defendant and his people and let them decide.[17]

Tucker's lawyers filed various motions for a new trial and even submitted a writ of errors to the United States Supreme Court. When all these were unsuccessful, appeals poured in to the governor. "Agitation grew to enormous proportions. . . . A tumult almost unprecedented in the history of the state. They [Tucker's partisans] were willing to attack and traduce any officer of the Commonwealth; persecute and vilify any witness whose testimony was unpalatable to them; pursue with slander the family of the dead woman."[18]

After giving an extended hearing to the petitions and consulting with the two judges who presided over the trial, the governor declined to set aside the jury's verdict.

> Only a few days remained before the time set for execution of the sentence, but the Tucker party continued its agitation. . . . As the hubbub increased, and as some of the more reckless writers and speakers tried to blacken the character of everyone connected with the Government, brighter and more shining in their estimation grew the personality of Tucker. He was a martyred boy, a model for youth, a hero, a saint being hounded to his death by bloodthirsty men. . . . A day or two before his execution there was a meeting in his behalf in Faneuil Hall. Somebody sent out a telegram to the President of the United States, alleging that he had the right to intervene under some Federal law and urging him to do so. . . . [19]

The next day a clergyman made a final appeal. Tucker was executed the following night.

There are even more pronounced ideological parallels between the Sacco-Vanzetti case and two of the twentieth century's earlier cases: the trial in Boise City, Idaho, in 1907 of Big Bill Haywood, Charles Moyer, and George Pettibone of the Western Federation of Miners for the murder of ex-governor Frank Steunenberg; and the 1911 trial of John and James McNamara, of the Iron Workers Union, charged with the bombing of the *Los Angeles Times* Building. Before both trials, friends and associates of the defendants launched massive publicity campaigns charging that the men were innocent victims of a "fiendish plot" to discredit and destroy organized labor. As the trial dates neared, tremendous demonstrations took place in cities throughout the United States. In Europe the cases became front-page news. Partisans of the miners and the McNamara Defense League raised thousands of dollars. Eugene Debs called the Boise City trial "the greatest legal battle in American history."[20] Just before the trial opened, over a hundred thousand New Yorkers marched in protest, carrying banners, red flags, torches, and Chinese lanterns. From time to time they set off roman candles, while bands played the "Marseillaise." The marchers blocked traffic along Fifth Avenue from sundown well into the night. Haywood, Moyer, and Pettibone *had* to be innocent. Millions would insist with equal vociferousness on the innocence of the McNamara brothers.

In both cases Clarence Darrow was retained as defense counsel, the miners' federation alone paying him $200,000. That federation, the most violent labor body in the United States, would later form the backbone of the Wobblies, the revolutionary Industrial Workers of the World. Though Moyer was the union's president, the one-eyed Bill Haywood was its dominant figure—a flaming personality, a bare-knuckle fighter, a boozer, a radical for whom violence was a concomitant of the class struggle. As a strike leader he was undoubtedly responsible for the dynamiting of the Idaho Bunker Hill Company's quarter-of-a-million-dollar mill in 1899. Following the mill's destruction, Governor Steunenberg appealed for federal troops to control the riotous miners. Six years later Steunenberg was blown to bits by a trip bomb that went off as he opened his front gate.

A manager of the Pinkerton Detective Agency, sent to investigate the murder, finally apprehended Harry Orchard, Moyer's sometime bodyguard and undercover man. After several days in solitary confinement and long hours of relentless questioning, Orchard broke down, confessing not only to the Steunenberg murder but to twenty-five others, all, he said, instigated by the miners' inner circle of Haywood, Moyer, and Pettibone. He had followed their orders. They were the brain; he was merely the hand.

"The most monumental liar that ever existed," was Darrow's reply to Orchard's confession.[21] Partisans portrayed the coming trial as a farce, a travesty of justice. Socialists and labor radicals referred to judge and prosecution as "a corporation of vultures and vipers." Debs demanded a Great National General Strike.[22]

Darrow, in his nine-hour address to the jury—made up mostly of farmers—appealed to their inherent populism and denounced "the spiders and vultures of Wall Street" who "wish to get rid of agitators and disturbers" and are ready to imprison anyone "who fights for the poor and against the accursed system upon which the capitalists lived and grew fat."[23]

Orchard's uncorroborated testimony was not enough. Though the jurors admitted afterward that they considered Haywood and his associates guilty of complicity, conclusive evidence was lacking. In compliance with the judge's instructions, the jury acquitted them. Darrow doubled back on his own words. "The trial has been fair," he now said, "the judge impartial and the counsel considerate."[24] Anthony Bimba, in his *History of the American Working Class*, claimed that Haywood, Moyer, and Pettibone "were saved from the gallows by the militant section of the working class."[25]

John McNamara and his brother James were not to fare so well. Their Iron Workers, violent in temper as the Western Miners, had been equally ready to resort to dynamite "in an emergency." The anarchist Johann Most's slogan, "Dynamite . . . that's the stuff," could have been John's motto. As the union's secretary-treasurer he made the tactical decisions. His brother James, "handy with the sticks," carried them out. From his headquarters in unionized San Francisco, John had sent strong-arm squads to open-shop Los Angeles, where the virulently union-hating General Harrison Gray Otis, publisher-editor of the *Times*, commanded the anti-union forces from his office-citadel. The McNamaras' plan was to blow up the *Times* building and make it appear that Otis himself had done it in an attempt to place the blame on the unions and drive them out of town. On October 1, 1910, a bomb demolished the *Times* plant. Unexploded bombs were found under Otis's house.

With the *Times* building in ruins, with twenty dead and over a hundred injured, rewards of $300,000 were offered to apprehend the bombers. The mayor of Los Angeles engaged William J. Burns, head of the detective agency of that name, to investigate. Even before the *Times* explosion, Burns had been aware of James McNamara's dynamiting activities. For further evidence he waited until McNamara and his assistant, Ortie McManigal, did a few more "jobs," then arrested them. McManigal, like Orchard before him, confessed, admitting that he and James had blown up the *Times* building on orders from John McNamara. Following McManigal's confession, John was taken into custody.

The arrest of the McNamara brothers made their case a national issue, transforming them into symbols of labor's struggle against predatory capitalism. The case against them was denounced as a frame-up, a reactionary conspiracy. Millions were convinced of their innocence. Great demonstrations took place in Los Angeles, San Francisco, San Diego, Portland, Seattle, Cleveland, St. Louis, Chicago, Indianapolis, and many cities of the East. From his cell John McNamara sent out a "Labor Day Message to the Toilers of America." Debs telegraphed:

> Sound the alarm to the working class! There is to be a repetition of the Moyer-Haywood, Pettibone outrage upon the labor movement. The secret arrest of John McNamara, by a corporation detective agency, has all the earmarks of another conspiracy to fasten the crime of murder on the labor union officials to discredit and destroy organized labor in the United States. . . . Arouse, ye hosts of labor, and swear that the villainous plot shall not be consummated![26]

Even Samuel Gompers, as head of the American Federation of Labor, announced that he had investigated the entire case and that "Burns has lied. . . . The whole affair smacks of well-laid pre-arrangement."[27]

At the trial it took eighteen days for the first two jurors to be picked, and a month later the jury box was only half-filled. At one point Darrow and the district attorney almost came to blows. Yet before the trial was really under way, Darrow withdrew the not guilty pleas. James now admitted to dynamiting the *Times* building, John to blowing up the Llewellyn Iron Works. The prosecution had agreed to recommend mercy if they pleaded guilty, and this plea at least saved their lives. Afterward Darrow told reporters: "We didn't see any way around it. They had it on us. The county had a complete case. There was no loophole. No loophole."[28] Gompers, on being told, is said to have cried.

Partisans of those accused, when there seems to be no other loophole, periodically fall back on the claim that the prosecution has rigged the evidence. It is a common tactic. Supporters and sympathizers, starting with the conclusion that their defendants must be innocent, work backward. If the facts do not fit, then the facts must be a fraud. Sacco's Colt could not have fired the fatal bullet, therefore the experts were wrong or there had to have been a bullet substitution. In the Alger Hiss case, when Whittaker Chambers produced top-secret State Department documents that had been copied on Hiss's Woodstock typewriter, Hiss accused the FBI of constructing a Woodstock simulacrum to counterfeit the documents. Despite all proofs of their guilt, the Rosenbergs had to be innocent, the charges against them a frame-up. According to their lawyer, the FBI—among other machinations—forged a hotel registration card as vital evidence against them. Echoing its earlier Sacco-Vanzetti propaganda, the American Communist party called the Rosenbergs' execution "a brutal act of fascist violence" planned by our "desperate rulers" and abetted by a "terrorized" jury. "The world speaks its admiration for this humble and obscure couple whose souls were as pure as their executioners were vile."[29]

When, during the First World War, Roger Casement was executed by the British for treason, Irish patriots could not accept the fact that in private life he was a pathic. He had to be a high-minded patriot, a martyr among the Irish martyrs. His incriminating *Black Diaries*, which reveal his private perversions, were for his partisans despicable forgeries. Yeats, in the challenging verses of his Casement poem, castigates the accusers:

> Afraid they might be beaten
> Before the bench of time,
> They turned a trick by forgery
> And blackened his good name.[30]

In such emotionally weighted cases the charge of fraud or forgery is a last despairing effort to nullify what cannot be explained away. So it was, and so it remains preeminently, in the Sacco-Vanzetti case. David Kaiser, with the late William Young the author of *Postmortem: New Evidence in the Case of Sacco and Vanzetti*, arranged for the 1982 metallurgical tests on Bullet III in the hope it could be determined that the scratches on the base had been made with a different instrument than the scratches on the other three bullets. Although the tests proved nothing of the kind, *Postmortem*—published three years later—goes to byzantine lengths in attempting to demonstrate that the Bullet III and Shell W offered in evidence at the trial had been substituted by Captain Proctor, with the connivance of District Attorney Katzmann and Assistant District Attorney Williams. "Sacco and Vanzetti," the authors conclude, "two innocent men, most probably were framed for a murder they did not commit."[31]

Through the decades the Sacco-Vanzetti case has remained a living issue, a fixture in the intellectual mind. Books on it continue to be published—six since Governor Dukakis's proclamation—all, except for the record of the 1983 ballistics tests, holding to the legend of innocence betrayed.*

* Roberta Feuerlicht's *Justice Crucified* (1977); Katherine Anne Porter's *The Never-Ending Wrong* (1977); Brian Jackson's *The Black Flag* (1981); The Trustees of the Boston Public Library's *Sacco—Vanzetti: Developments and Reconsiderations* (1982); Young and Kaiser's *Postmortem* (1985); The Select Committee on Sacco and Vanzetti's *Examination of Firearm-Related Evidence: The Nicola Sacco and Bartolomeo Vanzetti Case* (1985).

In the feverish months of 1927 the case became a rallying point for the intellectual and academic commonality that in many cases set the tone for their entire lives. As a vehicle of protest it filled a need. To intellectuals in their postwar sense of isolation and alienation, it gave a community of spirit, the pentecostal feeling of belonging, as well as the unadmitted satisfaction of identifying themselves with an elite. Their indignation was itself liberating, a catharsis of the emotions, a commitment of faith where the need to believe became the will to believe.

Sacco and Vanzetti, from anonymous alien workmen—"two wops in a jam"—had within their seven years' imprisonment emerged as world figures. Both saw their fate obsessively. "I never knew," Sacco said at his sentencing, "never heard, even read in history anything so cruel as this court. . . . You know it, Judge Thayer,—you know all my life, you know why I have been here, and after seven years that you have been persecuting me and my poor wife, and you still today sentence us to death."[32]

The more eloquent Vanzetti followed Sacco. In a forty-five-minute speech to the court, he accused judge and district attorney of doing "all what it were in your power in order to work out, in order to agitate still more the passion of the juror. . . . We have proved that there could not have been another judge on the face of the earth more prejudiced and more cruel than you have been against us. . . . Eugene Debs say that not even a dog—not even a dog that kill chickens would have been found guilty by an American jury with the evidence that the Commonwealth have produced against us."[33]

During his prison years Sacco made one suicide attempt and experienced at least one psychotic episode, during which he refused to eat because he said poison was being put into his food and poisonous vapors blown into his cell. With obsessive anger he at one point rejected the mothering women who had adopted him, turned savagely against Moore, who had kept him alive, and, in the weeks before the Lowell Committee met, he twice discharged Thompson, though each time Thompson returned because, as he explained to the committee, "I believe he has been dealt with unfairly." Nevertheless he considered Sacco a "fanatic."[34]

Vanzetti suffered equally obsessive interludes. Several times during his confinement he lost his mental balance. Late in 1925 he took to barricading his cell door each night for fear, he explained, that his enemies might overpower the guards and kill him. He told the state psychiatrist that at his trial perjurers and Fascists had been out to get him and he needed a gun for protection. In the death house at Charlestown, when he learned that the last legal appeal had been denied, he broke briefly, scrawling an almost illegible note to Thompson and dating it "New Era Year I":

> I hope you have radiocasted at once my order of mobilization to all the nations of the world. Big corps of men are in march. . . . Take all the protective measures to the crossing of Rio Grande and Panamal Canal; lent me the coasts most you can. Renew my notes to the King of Italy and the Pope. . . . Informe me by wireless, and immediately, of each move and particular.[35]

Always he remained convinced of the malign conspiracy against him. Thayer was "a bloodthirsty murderer," his Plymouth trial an obscene farce in which a defender-lawyer has sold to a Court-Ring his client, the defendant—as a rabbit is sold at a market." To Roger Baldwin he wrote on May 23, 1926: "we will ask for revenge and rivindication. I will put fire into human breaths."*

At the conclusion of Sacco's last defiant statement he told the court: "Judge Thayer know all my life, and he know that I am never been guilty, never—not yesterday, nor today nor forever."[36] For him to have admitted his guilt might have saved his comrade, but it would have betrayed the high cause of anarchy. He and Vanzetti were prepared to die for that cause. "Both of them want to be martyrs," Thompson wrote to a friend in November 1926, "and Sacco for two years has been especially desirous of having all defense dropped so that he may go to the electric chair as a martyr to what he calls 'the Cause.' I think it would be perfectly easy for me to get both of these men to write me a letter saying that they did not desire any further services from me or from any other lawyer."[37]

Vanzetti was not as intransigent in his martyr role as Sacco. During his Charlestown years he was even planning to escape, for him the only way to freedom he could take with honor. Early in the case he was offered the chance of freedom, but Sacco would have had to pay the consequences. As Moore told Upton Sinclair:

> I had a great temptation when I was making my closing arguments. There was so little evidence against Vanzetti—almost none in fact—I believed that there was a good chance of an acquittal if I should push home the fact. But I felt sure, in that case, Sacco would be found guilty.

---

* In the published letters "revenge" and the "fire into human breath" have been deleted.

I thought there was a fighting chance the jury would disagree as to the two but if they acquitted one I knew enough of juries to feel sure they would soak the other. So I put it up to Vanzetti: "What shall I do?" and he answered, "Save Nick, he has the woman and child."[38]

Sacco saw himself as a soldier of the revolution. Those on the capitalist side of the barricade were the enemy. Anarchists were at war with society. As he saw it syllogistically, killing was justified in wartime. He was an anarchist. He was justified in killing for anarchism. By any anarchist measure robbery was not robbery but expropriation for the need of harassed and persecuted comrades. The cause justified and clarified the means. Sacco and Vanzetti, like Hiss and the Rosenbergs, were to themselves innocent, accepting the yoke of martyrdom, guilty only in the eyes and by the laws of the society they rejected. To insist on their innocence, however incontrovertible the facts, was their moral obligation.

Vanzetti, according to Felicani temperamentally incapable of violence, nevertheless accepted it theoretically. "It only remain to us to sweep it [bourgeois capitalism] from the earth's face," he wrote. "To destroy for to create."[39] The subtleties of common law were beyond him. If he had not been in South Braintree on the day of the crime, how could he have been an accessory? Was the mere knowing a crime? What he knew primarily was that he was innocent. Beyond that lay the code of silence—and the cause. In the end Sacco could have talked and saved him. Neither was willing to pay that price.

It is possible, as Brian Jackson briefly suggested, that Sacco came to believe in his actual innocence. Our minds are compartmentalized, and over the years the image of the guard and the paymaster sprawled in the gravel may have been overlaid by the events in the Dedham courthouse, where the Sacco-Vanzetti case had taken root. The legend nurtured by their partisans had been absorbed by Sacco and Vanzetti. Whether Sacco was guilty, whether Vanzetti knew, were questions they had thrust aside. They sensed themselves to be larger than life. By their own definition they had to be innocent.

II

For over three decades the roads of the Sacco-Vanzetti case have crisscrossed my life, from those first May mornings when I used to head through Needham to the Dedham courthouse, to that November afternoon with the swans reflected in Sandwich's Shawme Pond.

So many twistings and turnings and culs-de-sac it took to bring me on another April afternoon to this last road, the expressway to Boston's Logan Airport. Yet even the impersonally labeled Route 3 had its haunted aspect. At North Plymouth a green-and-white sign pointed to the Cherry Street exit, the street where Vanzetti had lived just before his arrest. Twenty-five miles farther on, where the expressway bypasses Braintree, I could see the slender brick tower of Thayer Academy like a gnomon, shadowing the spot on Pearl Street where in 1920 the paymaster and his guard had lain dying in the gutter. And at the end of Route 3 was California.

Two weeks earlier I had telephoned Ideale Gambera to ask if I might see him. What he was, who he was, I had no idea, but his voice was friendly and reassuring. Yes, he said, he would be happy to see me. If I let him know when I was coming, he would meet me at the airport. I must stay with him. At first I said no. But the next day, when I thought over arriving alone in an unfamiliar city, I called again and said if it would not be inconvenient I would stay with him. I then gave him the flight number and the time when my plane was arriving.

The twilight was gathering in by the time I reached Logan, lights beginning to flicker in the cubelike buildings across the harbor. Our flight itself was in darkness. Except for a few bumps it was as if we weren't moving at all, the miracle of flight reduced to six encapsulated hours, an encapsulated air meal and a grade-B film. Then, as we neared San Francisco, the hum of the jet engines faded. Through the night I could see striations of lights, ribbons, necklaces, galaxies, pinpoints like stars marking the individuality of a street, a house, a family—white, yellow, amethyst, the sequence of lights patched with darkness. Such a sight was commonplace enough from any night plane arriving in any city. Not worth the looking up. Only if one saw it for the first time would the wonder and the mystery be apparent. As the plane dipped down, I felt the pressure in my eardrums. Below me, a few minutes away now, was a soft-voiced stranger who held within himself the secret of the most enigmatic case of the century. San Francisco's myriad lights came closer. What should I find? What indeed?

He was there beyond the gate, a short, bearded smiling man. I knew him at once. As I saw him standing beside his wife, I sensed a reaching out, an instantaneous friendship. We drove from the airport over the bridge and across the bay to his house on a hill beyond Sausalito, not large but light and airy, full of books and a sense of living. On the way he told me about himself, his growing up in Boston, his family's move to California, where he had gone to college, taken a graduate degree, and become in time a teacher of English and American studies.

We sat talking in his study until after two California time, first light in Sandwich. How did he happen to write me in the first place? I asked him.

"I read your book when it came out," he said. "Of all the books written about the case it seemed to come closest to what I knew was the truth. I wanted to write you then and there, but I couldn't, not while my father was alive. What he told us was our family secret. That code of silence, *omertá*, he kept as a Sicilian and an anarchist. But after his death I could see no further reason to keep his silence. Those connected with the case, those who might be hurt, were all dead. Felicani was the last. It is part of history now."

"Do you think Felicani knew the truth?" I asked him. "It's so hard for me to imagine him knowing and never giving a sign. Those times when I used to sit talking with him in his little office, the plaster bust of Tresca on the filing cabinet. I keep thinking of that, of seeing him look up smiling as I crossed the threshold. He seemed so ingenuous. When I knew him he said he didn't believe in violence for political ends anymore."

"Of course he knew. But he was part of the cause and the cause was part of him. He had to defend Sacco and Vanzetti. He couldn't do anything else. He and my father both thought the trial was a swindle. They both believed that De Falco woman. My father thought if the defense committee had paid her the money, Sacco and Vanzetti would have gotten off, got sent back to Italy instead of to the electric chair. That was what he kept on thinking. He never changed. He did change in some ways, though, once he came to California. After he was some years here he took out papers and became an American citizen. He even served on a jury, and when he got some sort of certificate for it, he was so proud he had it framed. In the bits he wrote about the case he couldn't bring himself to put down on paper that Sacco was guilty. I suppose he feared the written record, that it might get outside the family. He told us. That was all. But I did get him to repeat it on a tape recorder. I'll let you hear it later."

We talked through the night until we both grew bone-weary. Yet as I finally lay in bed in my downstairs room, I could not sleep. T. S.

Eliot somewhere said that anyone could fly the Atlantic in six hours, but it took a soul three-and-a-half days. If that was true of the North American continent, my soul was somewhere near Buffalo, New York. Finally sleep did come to me. I woke to bland sunshine and an orange tree outside my window.

I spent the morning in Ideale's study going through his father's papers. They were scant, a dozen lined pages written at random in halting English, the superficial and repetitive mixed with the revealing. Most consequent were the four pages he entitled "Defense Committee Records." It was there he had referred to Vanzetti's "not much knowledge" of the Bridgewater holdup, without realizing the implication of what he wrote. Through the pages I kept coming across the name Donnaruma, apparently some sort of North End ward boss who "since the 'proibition Era' had a deep and 'import' connections with High political and 'High pressure' 'influence' in Massachusetts and other States." Donnaruma promised that he would use his influence to free Sacco and Vanzetti and get them deported as anarchists. When Moore came to Boston he at once met with Donnaruma and may have received money from him. Ideale said he had heard of Donnaruma and thought he might have had links with the Mafia, but knew no more about him.

Gambera gave three pages to what he called the "Mrs. De Falco Bribe Offer." He had been present with Felicani, Guadagni, and Moore at their conference with her.

> Mrs. De Falco was quite nervous . . . but after we assured her, in Italian language and particular by Prof. Guadagni, in their native Dialect she, calmed, and particular . . . when she was informed that Donnaruma was informed of our presence—at this meeting. . . .
>
> Assured by our friendly and patriottic feeling De Falco stated That 'the acquittal" of "Sacco and Vanzetti" would be assured, by depositing the etire sum of $15,776,51/100—from the 'South Braintree' hold up, plus, a $5,000.00— . . . or . . . may be $10,000 for various "payment fees,—for those who would help" in Deporting Sacco" and Vanzetti" to ITALY"—as "Anarchists" only"—. . . .
>
> She was told, that such big Sum, was not in the funds of the "DE-FENCE COMMITTEE" and as soon as such sum was collected by the Committee we would notify Mr. 'Donnaruma," and the meeting was closed—in a hopeful friendly spirit—

Obviously Moore, without knowledge of Italian, did not gather what was going on—and when he found out, he had Mrs. De Falco arrested—but Gambera, writing in his old age, sometimes confused time sequences, mentioning, for example, that Madeiros had already been sentenced before the De Falco incident, whereas he did not commit his holdup-murder until four years later. Gambera's last five pages, consisting of an inconsequent comparison of the case of Angela Davis and that of Sacco and Vanzetti, plus what he called "condensed notes" of the Bridgewater and Braintree holdups, are of no significance.

By the time I had finished my copying, the morning had worn away. Ideale then drove me to San Francisco for a ramble through the to-me-unfamiliar streets and a quick sandwich at Fisherman's Wharf. Afterward we drove back across the Golden Gate Bridge and up the winding road to Wolfback Ridge, where we stopped to look out over the bay below us and the white city edging the horizon. From such a height the sea-landscape stretched out, as stylized as an eighteenth-century aquatint: green-gray water streaked with cumulus shadowings and dotted with tiny white sails that scarcely seemed to move at all. On this transparent afternoon the tawny bridge below us seemed no more than one of those children's snap-together toys. From my hill prospect I could see the gleaming skyline of the alabaster city, its everydayness, the incongruities of its recent architecture transfigured by distance. And in that poised interval between past and future, the time-pendulum ticked to a stop, as if there never could be anything but this immediacy, the glaucous sail-dotted bay, San Francisco's towers and turrets beyond, and the quiet self-contained man beside me who through all the years of turbulence and lacerating indignation had been the keeper of the Sacco-Vanzetti mysteries. He had held the key to the enigma that had persisted for two generations without a resolution, and he had honored his father's secret until that time when—with a scholar's abstract love of truth—he knew it must be told.

The afternoon shadows were lengthening now and it was time for us to go. But on this high hill beyond the Golden Gate, I knew that the roads of the Sacco-Vanzetti case had at last reached their end.

Appendix A. *The Eloquence of Vanzetti*

Vanzetti, for all his limited education and rigidity of outlook, had the gift of words. Perhaps his imperfect command of English gave his speech an adventitious eloquence. Somehow he was at times able to capture the underlying rhythms of the English tongue. Telling phrases came spontaneously to him, vivid, unforgettable. He saw his judge as "a black-gowned cobra." To the native American anarchist Leonard Abbott, he wrote: "Try to save us from the flameless fire of the twentieth century." From the confines of his cell he recalled his open days in Plymouth: "Oh, that sea, that sky, those fresh and full of life winds of Cape Cod! Maybe I will never see, never breath, never be at-one with them again." Sometimes he would overreach himself, drifting from the eloquent to the absurd, as when at his sentencing he told the judge that "not even a leprous dog would have his appeal refused two times." But in that same speech, counterbalancing his words, in his peroration he achieved a massive and moving dignity:

> My conviction is that I have suffered for things that I am not guilty of. I am suffering because I am a radical and indeed I am a radical; I have suffered because I was an Italian, and indeed I am an Italian; I have suffered more for my family and for my beloved than for myself; but I am so convinced to be right that if you could execute me two times, and if I could be reborn two other times, I would live again to do what I have done already.*

Part of his address, a eulogy for Sacco, he had overlooked, and when he attempted to add it as a postscript, the judge cut him off. The next day he wrote it out; the most important thing, he told Thompson, that he had to say:

> I have talk a great deal of myself but I even forgot to name Sacco. . . . Oh yes, I may be more witfull as some have put it. I am a better babbler than he is, but many, many times in hearing his heartful voice ringing a faith sublime, in considering his supreme sacrifice, remembering his heroism I felt small, small at the presence of his greatness and found myself compelled to fight back from

* *Transcript of the Record*, 4904.

my eyes the tears, and quanch my heart trobling to my throat not to weep for
him—this man called thief and assasin and doomed. But Sacco's name will live
in the hearts of the people and in thier gratitude when Katzmann's and yours
bones will be dispersed by time, when your name, his name, your laws, institutions, and your false god are but a deem rememoring of a cursed past in
which man was wolf to the man.*

Vanzetti's most quoted statement is the one he made to Phil Stong, a journalist
who visited him in the Dedham jail in the summer of 1927. At the end of their
informal interview, Vanzetti "nodded his fine head, and suddenly his voice was
stern":

If it had not been for this thing, I might have live out my life among scorning
men, I might have die, unmarked, unknown, a failure. Now we are not a failure. This is our career and our triumph. Never in our full life can we hope to
do such work for tolerance, for joostice, for man's understanding of man, as
now we do by an accident.
Our words—our lives—our pains—nothing! The taking of our lives—lives
of a good shoemaker and a poor fish peddler—all!
The moment that you think of belong to us—that last agony is our triumph!

This is the version that Stong gave in his 1949 article, "The Last Days of Sacco
and Vanzetti,"† claiming he had jotted down the words in shorthand. But his earlier *New York World* version differed in several places. Originally he had written
"these thing" and "I might have live out my life talking at street corners to
scorning men." He later also admitted that he had added the "good shoemaker"
and the "poor fish peddler" for clarity. Edward Shanks, an English writer,
thought that these paragraphs compared with the Gettysburg Address but
doubted that Vanzetti ever uttered them. Undoubtedly Vanzetti said something
of the kind, but how much is his and how much Stong's remains an open question.

---

* The Vanzetti quotation ending "man was wolf to the man" is in *The Letters of Sacco
and Vanzetti*, 379–80.
† Included in *The Aspirin Age* (Isabelle Leighton, ed., New York: Simon & Schuster,
1949).

Appendix B. *The After Years*

Several years after *Tragedy in Dedham* was published, the German television producer Peter von Zahn, who had earlier transposed Reginald Rose's lachrymose two-part Sacco-Vanzetti melodrama, came to Boston to make a documentary on the case. He interviewed various surviving partisans, including Clem Norton and Felicani. I spent an evening trying to persuade him to present both sides of such a controversial issue, showed him enlarged photographs of Shell W and a matching test shell, informed him of Moore's doubts and Tresca's devastating statement, but his mind was set. Sacco and Vanzetti had to be betrayed innocents; there were no two sides to that. I felt as if I were talking to a resurrected Weimar liberal, a ghostly survivor, as if the Hitler years and World War II had never intervened. In the end I did make a brief statement before his camera, but this was omitted from the documentary when shown. Opinion in Germany remained adamant on the innocence of Sacco and Vanzetti. *Tragedy in Dedham* was never published there, although it appeared in England, France, and Brazil, and was even a book-club selection in Italy. Only the negligible *Justice Crucified* was subsequently translated into German.

Von Zahn was followed by an Italian television team that came to Sandwich for a day and set up cameras in my library. The director, an amiable young man in a mink jacket, spoke no English but was much taken with my three-year-old daughter. "Bella! Bella!" he exclaimed as he picked her up after she had tripped over the equipment wires. The segment I recorded then appeared duly on Italian television but has somehow been deleted from the copy in the Boston Public Library.

After Giuliano Montaldo arrived to survey the ground for his film, I urged him to present both sides, but like von Zahn his mind was fixed. When I had earlier made this suggestion, one of Dino De Laurentiis's assistants replied that even if what I said was true, entrenched liberal opinion held Sacco and Vanzetti to be innocent victims—and that was the way the film makers wanted it to be.

In 1962, when I was in East Berlin, I picked up a fictional autobiography of Vanzetti, a booklet put out, oddly enough, by the East German military publishers. Four years later, in Leningrad, I came across a poster showing the Statue of Liberty with an inverted torch, and the names Sacco and Vanzetti underneath.

They have remained a living issue in the Soviet Union. A Russian naval destroyer is named *Vanzetti*, and a pencil factory still produces red-and-blue pencils with the linked names stamped on them. There is a Sacco-Vanzetti street in Tula and no doubt there are other streets I do not know of so named.

In the United States, Group W of the Westinghouse Broadcasting Company sponsored a 1963 Sacco-Vanzetti television play, "The Advocate," that was at the same time presented on Broadway. Governor Dukakis's proclamation was featured on "Today." Boston station WBZ produced a documentary in connection with its 1983 ballistics tests. Another documentary was shown in 1985 by WCVB.

Recently, a number of Sacco-Vanzetti publications have been reprinted. Joughin and Morgan's book was reissued by the Princeton University Press, there has been a new edition with photographs of Sinclair's *Boston*, Octagon Books republished *The Letters of Sacco and Vanzetti*, and the massive six volumes of the *Transcript of the Record* were reprinted with a prefatory essay by Supreme Court Justice William Douglas.

Appendix C. *The Perjury of Ramuglia*

In August 1962 I received a letter from the labor writer Paul Jacobs, who had recently read my Sacco-Vanzetti book. He had read much of the case's history and knew many of those involved. He wrote:

> I think you might like to know one item of corroborative evidence for your feeling that perhaps Sacco was guilty. Years ago, when I was still a union representative, I had a close friend, Anthony Ramuglia, who was also a union representative. Tony was a good many years older than me and had been an anarchist in his youth, moving from there to the Communists and eventually to the Trotskyists. We were both discouraged and disheartened by what had happened to the union movement, but while I was able to break away and become a writer, Tony was trapped by his age and lack of other skills into remaining a union official. One day, he came to me and said he had a story he wanted me to write. I think it must have been 1952 or 1953. The story was that when he was a young man around the anarchist movement in Boston, he had been approached to be one of Sacco's witnesses for his alibi in the restaurant at lunch. My friend Tony agreed, and, evidently, was carefully coached in what he was to say, when suddenly he remembered that on the day in question he had actually been in jail in St. Louis and so might obviously be found out as a perjurer. He told someone about this and was relieved of his responsibilities. He told me then that they had to get someone else to act as the alibi and asked me to write the story that he had been carrying around for thirty years.
>
> At the time, I felt it would have been wrong to write it without going into the kind of detailed analysis of the case which you did so ably. I asked Tony whether he thought Sacco and Vanzetti were really guilty, and he replied in much the same way as you quote Tresca. "Sacco could have done it but Vanzetti was never capable of such a thing."

Ramuglia's story is to a degree corroborated by an anonymous memorandum in the Boston Public Library's file entitled "Mrs. De Falco re-called." On any count Mrs. De Falco is a devious witness, but what she related here was apparently in confidence to her lawyer after her trial:

Felicani said Yes Vanzetti gave a share of money from Braintree hold up and it was in treasury of Defense Committee and that Sacco had $10,000 that belonged to the Committee and that he gave it to Mrs. Sacco which she had it buried in a tin box and that it was ten feet away from the house—buried underground. Guag [Guadagni] also said they had frame up witnesses and that he was going to say that Sacco had been to dinner with them in that same restarant on the day of the Braintree hold-up. Guag said that the Italian consul was going to be another witness that was going to say at the time of the Braintree hold up Sacco was in his office and wanted to return to Italy.

I had in mind to tell Katzmann the whole story. . . . Sacco Vanzetti defense told by Fel [Felicani] and Guad.

All conversations with Fel and Guad about Sacco and Vanzetti is in this statement. Told Bailey her counsel and no one else. My family or anybody else.

Mrs. De Falco's mention, months before the Dedham trial, of the lunch alibi, the contrived witnesses, and the Italian consul, does seem to demonstrate that initially she was party to some of the defense committee's secrets. According to Ideale Gambera, his uncle, Angelo Monello, had also agreed to give perjured testimony.

Another curious corroboration of Sacco's guilt and Vanzetti's guilty knowledge is recorded in a book by the late anarchist historian Louis Mercier Vega. In *L'Increvable Anarchisme* he writes that "a very few anarchists knew the identity of those who had actually led the holdup attack. And among those who knew were Sacco and Vanzetti." A short time before his death he confided to Ronald Creagh that one of those involved was an anarchist who was then sent hurriedly to Latin America. This militant—presumably Boda—returned to Italy several years later.

Notes

1. The Roads of the Sacco-Vanzetti Case

1. Eugene Lyons, *Assignment in Utopia*, 32.
2. G. Louis Joughin and Edmund M. Morgan, *The Legacy of Sacco and Vanzetti*, 511.
3. "The Sacco-Vanzetti Case Reconsidered," *Commentary*, January 1962.
4. *The Nation*, December 5, 1928.
5. *The New Leader*, September 26, 1960.
6. David Felix, *Protest: Sacco-Vanzetti and the Intellectuals*.
7. *The American Heritage History of the 20's & 30's*, 149.
8. *Boston Globe*, August 24, 1977.
9. Brian Jackson, *The Black Flag*, 96.
10. Boston Public Library Conference Proceedings. *Sacco-Vanzetti: Developments and Reconsiderations*, 102.
11. *The Black Flag*, xii.
12. Ibid., 97.
13. Ibid., xii.
14. "Massachusetts Pays Its Debts," *The Nation*, August 20, 1977.
15. *The Legacy of Sacco and Vanzetti*, vii.
16. *Tragedy in Dedham: The Story of the Sacco-Vanzetti Case*, anniversary edition, xxii–iii.

2. The Road to Sandwich

1. *Sacco-Vanzetti: Developments and Reconsiderations*, 50.
2. Tape-recording made by Felicani in 1957 for the Boston Public Library.
3. *Developments and Reconsiderations*, 4.
4. Ibid., 46.

3. The Road to Boston

1. *Controcorrente*, July–August 1962.
2. "The Fishpeddler and the Shoemaker," *Institute for Social Studies Bulletin*, II, Summer 1953.

3. *Assignment in Utopia*, 12.
4. Ibid., 4.
5. *The Great Interlude*, 123–24.
6. *Il Martello*, October 23, 1921.
7. " 'This Is Our Agony . . . ' ", September 26, 1960.
8. "Carlo Tresca and the Sacco-Vanzetti Case," *The Journal of American History*, December 1979.
9. Ibid.
10. "The Sacco-Vanzetti Case," *Kansas City Law Review*, 1962–63.
11. *The Journal of American History*, December 1979.
12. *Developments and Reconsiderations*, 103–4.
13. *The Journal of American History*, December 1979.

4. The Road to Friendship

1. Ethelbert Grabill, *Sacco and Vanzetti in the Scales of Justice.*
2. *Transcript of the Record of the Trial of Nicola Sacco and Bartolomeo Vanzetti*, 2241.
3. Ibid., 2251.
4. Ibid., 2263.
5. "Tragedy in Dedham," *The Antioch Review*, Winter 1955–56.

5. The Road to Braintree

1. *Transcript of the Record*, 1341.
2. Ibid., 1157.
3. *The Rise and Fall of the Luftwaffe*, 314.
4. *After Twelve Years*, 397.
5. Ibid., 397.

6. The Road to Brockton

1. Ensher's testimony is in the *Transcript of the Record*, Supplementary Volume, 143. MacDonald's statement is in Moore's papers in the Boston Public Library.
2. *Transcript of the Record*, Supplementary Volume, 382.
3. Ibid., 386.
4. Herbert B. Ehrmann, *The Case That Will Not Die*, 102.
5. *Transcript of the Record*, 2120.
6. Files of the Massachusetts State Police.

7. The Anarchist Road

1. My information about Gambera and his early life derives from talks with his son.
2. Gambera memoir.
3. Ibid.

4. *Developments and Reconsiderations*, 83.
5. Ibid., 81.
6. Ibid., 82.
7. Ibid., 65–66.
8. Bartolomeo Vanzetti, *The Story of a Proletarian Life*, 6.
9. Ibid., 6.
10. Ibid., 9.
11. Conversation of the author with Beltrando Brini.
12. *Developments and Reconsiderations*, 80.
13. Robert K. Murray, *Red Scare*, 69.
14. *Boston Herald*, March 2–3, 1919.
15. "An Unhappy Lot," *National Review*, July 18, 1975.
16. Files of Department of Justice.
17. "The Case Against the Reds," February 1920.
18. Department of Justice report.
19. *Transcript of the Record*, 4986.
20. *Developments and Reconsiderations*, 88.
21. Ibid., 72.
22. Ibid., 60.
23. Ibid., 61.
24. The Sacco-Vanzetti Case Papers, Harvard Law School Library. Unless other-wise indicated, letters are from the Law School collection. This letter, to Virginia MacMechan, is dated August 26, 1923.
25. *Developments and Reconsiderations*, 89.

8. The Road to Dedham

1. *The Legacy of Sacco and Vanzetti*, 46.
2. *The Murder and the Myth*, 39–40.
3. *Transcript of the Record*, Supplemental Volume, 333–34.
4. *The Legacy of Sacco and Vanzetti*, 44.
5. William Young and David E. Kaiser, *Postmortem: New Evidence in the Case of Sacco and Vanzetti*, 36.
6. "Background of the Plymouth Trial" and "Awaiting the Hangman," *Sacco-Vanzetti Defense Committee Bulletin*, 1926.
7. *The Legacy of Sacco and Vanzetti*, 49.
8. *Protest*, 51.
9. Gambera memoir.
10. *Protest*, 18.
11. "Eels and the Electric Chair," *The New Republic*, December 29, 1920.
12. *Assignment in Utopia*, 22.
13. Ibid., 35.
14. *Collected Poems*, 129.
15. *Assignment in Utopia*, 35.
16. *The Never-Ending Wrong*, 37–38.
17. Ibid., 35.

18. *The Bostonians*, 35.
19. *Boston*, 174.
20. *New Bedford Standard-Times*, November 12, 1950.
21. *Transcript of the Record*, 1902.
22. Ibid., 896.
23. Ibid., 896.
24. *Protest*, 156.
25. *Transcript of the Record*, 1721.
26. Ibid., 1745.
27. Ibid., 1835.
28. Ibid., 5057.
29. *Developments and Reconsiderations*, 88.
30. *Boston*, 458–59.
31. *Transcript of the Record*, 1876–77.

9. The Road to Charlestown

1. *Transcript of the Record*, 2010.
2. *The Murder and the Myth*, 117.
3. *The Legacy of Sacco and Vanzetti*, vi.
4. *Red Scare*, 241–42.
5. *Boston Herald, Boston Post*, April 24, 1920.
6. *Holmes-Laski Letters*, 975.
7. *Transcript of the Record*, 5524.
8. This and subsequent quotations from the jurors are taken from Simmons' article.
9. *Protest*, 154.
10. *Boston Herald*, June 12, 1921.
11. "Sacco-Vanzetti—A Reasonable Doubt," *The Nation*, September 28, 1921.
12. *Protest*, 147–50.
13. *Transcript of the Record*, 2175–2176.
14. Ibid., 4957.
15. Ibid., 4982.
16. Files of Massachusetts State Police.
17. *Holmes-Laski Letters*, 1265.
18. FBI files.
19. Ibid.
20. Moore Papers, Boston Public Library.
21. *Protest*, 22–23.
22. Ibid., 21.
23. Letter of Sinclair to Herbert Ehrmann, January 1928. Ehrmann Papers, Harvard Law School Library.
24. *Protest*, 114.
25. Letter to Moore, August 18, 1924.
26. Letter of Elizabeth Evans, September 12, 1924.
27. Letter to the author.

... Iris

10. The Road from Charlestown

1. *Protest*, 135.
2. Letter to Elizabeth Evans, August 2, 1925.
3. Letter to Cerise Jack, July 20, 1924. Ibid., 126. *The Letters of Sacco and Vanzetti*, Gardner Jackson and Marion Frankfurter, eds.
4. Letter to Elizabeth Evans, Early Spring 1922.
5. Letter to Elizabeth Evans, July 14, 1927.
6. Letter to Maude Pettyjohn, December 11, 1926.
7. Letter to Alice Stone Blackwell, September 15, 1924.
8. Letter to Alice Stone Blackwell, November 13, 1925.
9. Letter to Alice Stone Blackwell, February 27, 1924.
10. *Developments and Reconsiderations*, 72.
11. Letter to Mary Donovan, April 14, 1927.
12. *Transcript of the Record*, 4638.
13. Ibid., 4544.
14. Ibid., 4724.
15. Ibid., 4748.
16. Told to the author by James Burnham.
17. *The Case of Sacco and Vanzetti*, 46.
18. Ibid., 65.
19. Ibid., 104.
20. Leonard Baker, *Brandeis and Frankfurter*, 260.
21. Ibid., 260.
22. Henry Knox Sherrill, *William Lawrence: Later Years of a Happy Life*, 84.
23. *Transcript of the Record*, 5378.
24. Granville Hicks, *Small Town*, 35–36.
25. *The Never-Ending Wrong*, 23–25.
26. Ibid., 25.
27. Ibid., 17–19.
28. Files of Massachusetts State Police.
29. *Boston Globe*, August 29, 1927.
30. *Transcript of the Record*, 4900.
31. *Letters of Sacco and Vanzetti*, 71. The original is not available.
32. "For St. Bartholomew's Day," *The Nation*, August 22, 1928.
33. *The Legacy of Sacco and Vanzetti*, 383.
34. *The Sacco-Vanzetti Anthology of Verse*, 17.
35. *The Nation*, December 5, 1928.
36. *Unity*, February 4, 1929.
37. *The Passion of Sacco and Vanzetti: A New England Legend*, 143.
38. *The Passion of Sacco and Vanzetti*, 12.

11. The Path of the Bullet

1. *Transcript of the Record*, 3642–3643.
2. Ibid., 3682.
3. Ibid., 3681.

4. Lowell Papers.
5. Interview with Edward Simmons, *New Bedford Standard-Times*, November 12, 1950.
6. *Transcript of the Record*, 3699.
7. *Protest*, 56.
8. *Transcript of the Record*, 895.
9. Ibid., 919.
10. Ibid., 1473.
11. Ibid., 3633.
12. Ibid., 3650.
13. Ibid., 3666.
14. Ibid., 3676.
15. Charles J. Van Amburgh and Fred H. Thompson, "The Hidden Drama of Sacco and Vanzetti," *True Detective Mysteries*, April–September, 1935.
16. Arthur Warner, "A Sacco-Vanzetti Revolver [sic] Expert Revealed," *The Nation*, December 7, 1927.
17. *Transcript of the Record*, 5225.
18. Ibid., 5317.
19. Ibid., 5314.
20. Ibid., 5320.
21. *The Case That Will Not Die*, 254.
22. *Harvard Law Review*, January 1934.
23. Files of Massachusetts State Police. Letter from David E. Kaiser to Commissioner of Public Safety Frank J. Trabuco.
24. Conversation with Katzmann's partner, Michael Dray.
25. *The Case That Will Not Die*, 285.
26. *Transcript of the Record*, 816.
27. Ibid., 820.
28. Ibid., 834.

12. The Roads to Providence and Needham

1. *Transcript of the Record*, 4791.
2. *The Murder and the Myth*, 244.
3. *Transcript of the Record*, 4416.
4. Ibid., 4631–4632.
5. *The Case That Will Not Die*, 424.
6. *The Untried Case*, 60.
7. *Transcript of the Record*, 4573.
8. *Harvard Law Review*, January 1934.
9. *Transcript of the Record*, Supplemental Volume, 341.
10. Ibid., 372.
11. Ibid., 376.
12. Ibid., 373.
13. Ibid., 371.
14. Ibid., 371.
15. Ibid., 377.

13. The Road to Washington

1. FBI files.
2. *The Case of Sacco and Vanzetti*, 68–69.
3. *Transcript of the Record*, 4500–4504
4. Ibid., 4504–4506.
5. This and subsequent quotations in this chapter, unless otherwise indicated, are from the FBI's Sacco-Vanzetti files.
6. *Transcript of the Record*, 4389.

14. The Road to Norwood

1. "The Fishpeddler and the Shoemaker."
2. Letter to the author from Rexroth's widow.
3. *The Black Flag*, 101.
4. *The Letters of Sacco and Vanzetti*, 72–74. The original of this moving letter written five days before Sacco's execution is not available.
5. Death House letter to Dante Sacco, August 21, 1927.
6. *Winterset* in *Twenty Best Plays of the American Theatre*, 10.
7. Letter to Cerise Carmen Jack, December 6, 1923.
8. Anthony Scaduto, *Scapegoat*, 472.

15. The Road to Cambridge

1. Conversation with Judge Lurie, who was also present at the showing.
2. For a full account of the strike, see *A City in Terror*.
3. Ferris Greenslet, *The Lowells and Their Seven Worlds*, 351–52.
4. *Developments and Reconsiderations*, 18.
5. *Transcript of the Record*, 5378n.
6. Cato, *Lantern*, II, July 1929.
7. *Developments and Reconsiderations*, 24.
8. *Transcript of the Record*, 5378-i.
9. *Fourscore*, 372.

16. The End of the Road

1. *Brandeis and Frankfurter*, 256.
2. *Protest*, 240.
3. Felix, "How Boston Almost Saved Sacco and Vanzetti," *Boston Review*, August 1984.
4. *Protest*, 159.
5. Liva Baker, *Felix Frankfurter*, 129.
6. *Brandeis and Frankfurter*, 269.
7. Bruce A. Murphy, *The Brandeis-Frankfurter Connection*, 80.
8. "How Boston Almost Saved Sacco and Vanzetti."
9. Letter from George Jackson Elder to the author, March 30, 1985.
10. A full account of the Jason Fairbanks case is given in Ferris Greenslet's *The Lowells and Their Seven Worlds*.

11. *The Solemn Declaration of the Late Unfortunate Jason Fairbanks*, 8.
12. *The Lowells and Their Seven Worlds*, 98.
13. Edmund L. Pearson, *Studies in Murder*, 68.
14. Ibid., 66.
15. Ibid., 109.
16. Ibid., 247.
17. Ibid., 260.
18. Ibid., 251.
19. Ibid., 158–59.
20. Louis Adamic, *Dynamite: The Story of Class Violence in America*, 149–50.
21. Ibid., 151.
22. Ibid., 151.
23. Ibid., 153.
24. Ibid., 153.
25. Anthony Bimba, *The History of the American Working Class*, 242.
26. *Dynamite*, 216.
27. Ibid., 217.
28. Ibid., 230.
29. Ronald Radosh and Joyce Milton, *The Rosenberg File: A Search for the Truth*, 421.
30. William Butler Yeats, *Last Poems and Plays*, 24.
31. *Postmortem*, 9.
32. *Transcript of the Record*, 4996.
33. Ibid., 4898, 4900.
34. Ibid., 5279.
35. Letter to William Thompson, August 19, 1927.
36. *Transcript of the Record*, 4896.
37. Harvard Law School Library.
38. Moore Papers.
39. Letter to Alice Stone Blackwell, June 5, 1925.

Bibliography

The books and articles included here are those I have used in the present work or those that have appeared since the 1962 bibliography of *Tragedy in Dedham*.

BOOKS

Adamic, Louis. *Dynamite: The Story of Class Violence in America*. New York: Viking, 1934.

American Heritage History of the 20's & 30's. Edited by American Heritage Editors. New York: American Heritage–McGraw-Hill, 1970.

Anderson, Maxwell. *Winterset*. In *Twenty Best Plays of the Modern American Theatre*. Edited by John Gassner. New York: Crown, 1953.

Baker, Leonard. *Brandeis and Frankfurter*. New York: Harper & Row, 1984.

Baker, Liva. *Felix Frankfurter*. New York: Coward-McCann, 1969.

Bimba, Anthony. *The History of the American Working Class*. Westport, Conn.: Greenwood Press, 1973.

Chambers, Whittaker. *Witness*. New York: Random House, 1952.

Creagh, Ronald. *Sacco et Vanzetti*. Paris: Editions La Découverte, 1983.

Dickenson, Alice. *The Sacco-Vanzetti Case*. New York: Franklin Watts, 1972.

Draper, Theodore. *The Roots of American Communism*. New York: Viking, 1953.

Ehrmann, Herbert B. *The Case That Will Not Die*. Boston: Little, Brown, 1969.

———. *The Untried Case: The Sacco-Vanzetti Case and the Morelli Gang*. New York: The Vanguard Press, 1933.

Fairbanks, Jason. *The Solemn Declaration of the Late Unfortunate Jason Fairbanks*. Dedham: The Minerva Press, 1802.

Farrell, James T. *Bernard Clare*. New York: The Vanguard Press, 1946.

Fast, Howard. *The Passion of Sacco and Vanzetti: A New England Legend*. New York: The Blue Heron Press, 1953.

Felix, David. *Protest: Sacco-Vanzetti and the Intellectuals*. Bloomington: Indiana University Press, 1965.

Feuerlicht, Roberta. *Justice Crucified*. New York: McGraw-Hill, 1977.

Frankfurter, Felix. *The Case of Sacco and Vanzetti: A Critical Analysis for Lawyers and Laymen.* Boston: Little, Brown, 1969.

Frankfurter, Marion Denham, and Gardner Jackson, eds. *The Letters of Sacco and Vanzetti.* New York: Viking, 1928.

Grabill, Ethelbert V. *Sacco and Vanzetti in the Scales of Justice.* Boston: The Fort Hill Press, 1927.

Grant, Robert. *Fourscore: An Autobiography.* Boston: Houghton Mifflin, 1934.

Harrison, Henry, ed. *The Sacco-Vanzetti Anthology of Verse.* New York: Henry Harrison, 1927.

Hicks, Granville. *Small Town.* New York: Macmillan, 1946.

Howe, Mark De Wolf, ed. *Holmes-Laski Letters.* Cambridge: Harvard University Press, 1954.

Irving, David. *The Rise and Fall of the Luftwaffe.* Boston: Little, Brown, 1973.

Jackson, Brian. *The Black Flag.* London: Routledge & Kegan Paul, 1981.

James, Henry. *The Bostonians.* London: The Bodley Head, 1967.

Joughin, G. Louis, and Edmund M. Morgan. *The Legacy of Sacco and Vanzetti.* New York: Harcourt Brace, 1948.

Lyons, Eugene. *Assignment in Utopia.* New York: Harcourt Brace, 1937.

Millay, Edna St. Vincent. *Collected Poems.* New York: Harper, 1956.

Montgomery, Robert. *Sacco-Vanzetti: The Murder and the Myth.* New York: Devin-Adair, 1961.

Murphy, Bruce A. *The Brandeis-Frankfurter Connection.* New York: Oxford, 1982.

Murray, Robert K. *Red Scare: A Study in National Hysteria, 1919–1920.* Minneapolis: University of Minnesota Press, 1955.

Musmanno, Michael A. *After Twelve Years.* New York: Knopf, 1939.

Pearson, Edmund L. *Studies in Murder.* New York: Macmillan, 1924.

Porter, Katherine Anne. *The Never-Ending Wrong.* Boston: Atlantic–Little, Brown, 1977.

Radosh, Ronald, and Joyce Milton. *The Rosenberg File: A Search for the Truth.* New York: Holt, Rinehart & Winston, 1983.

Robinson, W. W. *Famous California Trials: Bombs and Bribery.* Los Angeles: Dawson, 1969.

Russell, Francis. *A City in Terror: 1919—The Boston Police Strike.* New York: Viking, 1975.

———. *The Great Interlude: Neglected Events and Persons from the First World War to the Depression.* New York: McGraw-Hill, 1964.

———. *Tragedy in Dedham: The Story of the Sacco-Vanzetti Case.* 50th anniversary edition. New York: McGraw-Hill, 1971.

Scaduto, Anthony. *Scapegoat: The Lonesome Death of Bruno Richard Hauptmann.* New York: Putnam, 1976.

Sherrill, Henry Knox. *William Lawrence: Later Years of a Happy Life.* Cambridge: Harvard University Press, 1943.

Sinclair, Upton. *Boston.* New York: Albert and Charles Boni, 1928.

Thorwald, Juergen. *The Century of the Detective.* New York: Harcourt, Brace & World, 1965.

Transcript of the Record of the Trial of Nicola Sacco and Bartolomeo Vanzetti in the Courts of Massachusetts and Subsequent Proceedings 1920–27. With a supplemental volume on the Bridgewater Case. Prefatory essay by William O. Douglas. Mamaroneck, N.Y.: Appel, 1969.

Trustees of the Boston Public Library. *Sacco-Vanzetti: Developments and Reconsiderations—1979. Conference Proceedings.* Boston: Boston Public Library, 1982.

Vega, Louis M. *L'Increvable Anarchisme.* Paris: 1978.

Yeats, William Butler. *Last Poems and Plays.* New York: Macmillan, 1940.

Young, William, and David E. Kaiser. *Postmortem: New Evidence in the Case of Sacco and Vanzetti.* Amherst: University of Massachusetts Press, 1985.

Zelt, Johannes. *Proletarischer Internationalismus im Kampf um Sacco und Vanzetti.* East Berlin: Dietz Verlag, 1958.

ARTICLES

Bagdikian, Ben H. "New Light on Sacco and Vanzetti." *The New Republic,* July 13, 1963.

Beffel, John Nicholas. "Eels and the Electric Chair." *The New Republic,* December 29, 1920.

Bliven, Naomi. "Accessories After the Fact." *The New Yorker,* December 8, 1962.

Braverman, Shelley. "Were Sacco and Vanzetti Framed?" *Guns Magazine,* May 1963.

Brook, David. "Sacco and Vanzetti Revisited." *Boston Magazine,* October 1971.

Cook, Fred J. "The Missing Fingerprints." *The Nation,* December 22, 1962.

Felicani, Aldino. "Sacco-Vanzetti: A Memoir." *The Nation,* August 14, 1967.

Felix, David. "Apotheosis in Boston: Sacco and Vanzetti from Case to Legend." *Columbia University Forum* VI, Fall 1963.

———. "How Boston Almost Saved Sacco and Vanzetti." *Boston Review,* August 1984.

Foner, Eric. "The Men and the Symbols." *The Nation,* August 20, 1977.

McWilliams, Carey. "Massachusetts Pays Its Debt." *The Nation,* August 20, 1977.

Musmanno, Michael A. "The Sacco-Vanzetti Case: With Critical Analysis of the Book *Tragedy in Dedham* by Francis Russell." *Kansas Law Review,* May 1963.

———. "Tragedy in Dedham: A Final Note," with Francis Russell's reply. *American Heritage,* February 1963.

———. "Was Sacco Guilty?" *The New Republic,* March 2, 1963.

Pernicone, Nunzio. "Carlo Tresca and the Sacco-Vanzetti Case." *Journal of American History,* December 1979.

Rogge, O. John. "Some Further Thoughts on Sacco-Vanzetti." *Bar Bulletin* (New York County Lawyers Association), September–October 1962.

Russell, Francis. "The American Case of the Century." *New England Quarterly,* Winter 1985.

———. "America's Dreyfus Case." *New York Review of Books,* November 5, 1981.

———. "'The Case of the Century' Fifty Years Later." *Harvard Magazine,* July–August 1977.

————. "The End of the Chapter." *National Review*, May 5, 1970.

————. "The End of the Myth." *National Review*, August 19, 1977.

————. "Father and Son." *Metro Boston*, February, 1972.

————. "How I Changed My Mind About the Sacco-Vanzetti Case." *Antioch Review*, Winter 1965–66.

————. "Innocence Betrayed. Was It a Myth?" *Christian Science Monitor*, March 10, 1966.

————. "The Sacco-Vanzetti Myth." *Modern Age*, Summer 1966.

————. "The Second Trial of Sacco and Vanzetti." *Harvard Magazine*, May–June 1978.

————. "Tell Me the Old, Old Story." *National Review*, December 31, 1971.

Sinclair, Upton. "The Fishpeddler and the Shoemaker." *Institute of Social Studies Bulletin* II, Summer 1953.

Index

Abbott, Jack Henry, 34 fn.
Abbott, Leonard, 221
Addams, Jane, 96, 134
Adrower, Giuseppe, 109
Allegra, Pietro, 27 fn.
Allen, R. G., 200
American Heritage, 39–40
Anarchism and anarchists, 2, 13, 14, 22,
    55, 56–57, 66–70, 86, 96, 132, 216
Anderson, Maxwell, 34, 187
Anhalt, Edward, 6
Antioch Review, 39
Atherton, Gertrude, 135
Averich, Paul, 68, 86

Baldwin, Roger, 124, 215
Ballistics
    bullets removed from bodies of guard
        and paymaster, 100
    cartridges found on Sacco, 99
    evidence at trial, 98–102
    fatal bullet fired from Sacco's pistol,
        100, 102, 145–147
    fatal bullet not fired from Sacco's pistol,
        148
    fatal bullet claimed to be substitute,
        153–156
    missing ballistics evidence, 156–157
    Sacco's cartridges and crime-scene
        shells, 99
    Sacco pistol, 61
    shells and cartridges made on same ma-
        chine, 161–162
    shells picked up at crime scene, 48
    switching of pistol barrel, 150–151
    tests with comparison microscope:
        1927, Goddard, 151–152
        1961, Jury, Weller, 158

Ballistics (*cont.*)
        1983, Paul, Robinson, Wilson,
            160–161
    Vanzetti revolver, 61
Barbusse, Henri, 118
Baron, Rosa, 138, 139
Bedard, Alfred, 128
Beffel, John Nicholas, 50, 91
Bell, Daniel, 27 fn.
Best, Marshall, 200
Barone, Bibba, 164, 165
Benkoski, Steve, 166
Berardelli, Alessandro, 46, 47, 48, 49, 109,
        153, 154, 162, 163
Berardelli, Sara, 163
Beston, Henry, 190
Bianchini, Ermano, 184, 188
Biedenkapp, Fred, 117
Bimba, Anthony, 211
Blackwell, Alice Stone, 94, 121, 126
Bliven, Bruce, 202
Boda, Mike, 49, 56, 57, 58, 59, 60, 61, 62, 63,
        64, 73, 85, 103, 104, 171, 172, 226
bombings, 80–83, 105, 140, 199, 211–212
Borden, Lizzie, 207, 208
Borglum, Gutzon, 10, 42
Boston Police Strike, 79
Bradford, Robert, 42
Brandeis, Louis, 205
Braine, John, 187 fn.
Braverman, Shelley, 159
Breed, Wilhelmina, 91
Bridgewater holdup, 44–45
Brini, Beltrando, 88, 183, 191
Brini, LeFavre, 183
Brini, Vincenzo, 75, 76
Brooks, Phillips, 135
Brouillard, Albert, 58

Broun, Heywood, 134, 197, 198
Buckley, William F., Jr., 34 fn.
Buda, Mario, 73; *see also* Boda
Buick getaway car, 45, 46, 48, 54, 58, 167, 170, 171
    route followed, 130–131
Bullard, F. Lauriston, 132
Burke, Frank, 119, 120
Burns, James, 100, 101, 152
Burleson, Albert, 81
Burns, Vincent G., 143
Burns, William J., 178, 211, 212

Callahan, William, 57, 58
Cannon, James, 133
Capen, Samuel, 35, 151
Capone, Al, 188
Carlucci, Paco, 73; *see also* Valdinoce, Carlo
Caruso, Annie, 16
Casement, Roger, 213
Casey, Donald, 171
Cella, Al, 185, 193
Chamberlain, Julius, 169, 170
Chambers, Whittaker, 212
Cheney, Ralph, 144
Chessmann, Caryl, 34 fn., 206
Child, Lydia Maria, 94
Citizen's National Committee, 139
Clark, Francis, 131
Coacci, Feruccio, 50, 55, 56, 57, 58, 62, 63, 64, 80, 110
Coakley, Dan, 20
Coda, Emilio, 25
Codman, John, 93, 121
Collins, John, 156, 159
Colp, Ralph, 2, 3
Committee to Vindicate Sacco and Vanzetti, 10, 42
Communism and Communists, 3–5, 26–27 fn., 79, 96, 118, 132–133, 213
Community Church, 32, 36, 40, 41, 95
Contreras, Carlo, 26 fn.
Cooke, Fred J., 107 fn.
Coolidge, Calvin, 28 fn., 32, 33, 51, 97, 135
Cowley, Malcolm, 143
Creagh, Robert, 226
Crowe, Helen O'Lochlain, 138
cummings, e. e., 198
Curley, James M., 20
Curtis, Oliver, 126, 127
Cutler, John, 34 fn.

Darrow, Clarence, 210, 211, 212
D'Attilio, Robert, 160, 161

Daugherty, Harry, 178
Davis, Angela, 220
Debs, Eugene, 96, 210, 212
Dedham trial, 97–107
    composition of jury, 113
    courtroom guarded, 97
    defendants' fear of arrest, 102, 103
    fairness, 110–117
    identifying witnesses, 98
    Sacco's speech, 105
    verdict, 117
De Falco, Angelina, 14–16, 87, 218, 219, 220, 225–226
    and bribery offer, 14
    sentenced to prison, 16
Defense Committee, 65, 92, 122
De Laurentiis, Dino, 7, 223
demonstrations, 3–4, 117–118, 136
    Boston before executions, 140
    picketing of State House, 137–139
    overseas, 141
Department of Justice, Bureau of Investigation, 1, 79, 80, 171, 173, 182, 193
    and Frankfurter charges of aiding Sacco-Vanzetti prosecution, 173
    and affidavit of Letherman accusing Department, 175
    and affidavit of Weyand, 174
    Hoover demands file summary, 176, 177
    no secrets in files, 182
DePasquale, Mary, 71, 72
Desmond, Walter, 131
De Unamuno, Miguel, 20
Dever, John, 106, 107, 147
Dewey, John, 134, 139
Di Cecca, Tony, 193, 195
Dobson, Jessie, 170, 171
Dobson, William:
    suspected murder-car driver, 170–171, 172
Dolbeare, Harry, 129
Donato, Narciso, 84
Donnaruma, 219
Donovan, Mary, 52, 143
Dos Passos, John, 134, 138, 197–198
Douglas, William, 134, 224
Dowd, John, 176, 177, 179, 180
Dukakis, Michael, 9, 10, 120, 145, 213, 224
    proclaims Sacco-Vanzetti Memorial Day, 8
du Pont, Zara, 138
Dwyer, Norman, 198
Dzerzhinski, Felix, 118

Eastman, Max, 26–28
Eddy, Sherwood, 134

Ehrmann, Herbert, 6, 34, 38, 49, 51, 52,
94, 152, 153, 154, 155, 156, 158,
159, 162, 164, 165, 168, 171, 172,
196, 205 fn.
and Morelli hypothesis for Braintree
crime, 164–168
and bullet substitution, 153
Elder, George Jackson, 205
Elia, Roberto, 83–85
Eliot, T. S., 219
Elizabeth Peabody House, 32, 204
Ensher, Napoleon, 58, 171
Ettor, Joe, 24, 25, 72
Evans, Elizabeth Glendower, 94, 95–96,
97, 106, 121, 124, 125, 183

Fairbanks, Jason, 206–207
Fales, Betsey, 206
Falzini, Luigi, 98, 163
Farmer, Albert, 131
Farrell, James T., 29–31
Fast, Howard, 144
Felicani, Aldino, 12, 13, 15, 28, 31, 40, 41,
42, 51, 70, 80, 90, 190, 216, 223,
226
anger at Dante Sacco, 185
death, 17
defends Moore's memory, 120
and Excelsior Press, 194
and Gruppo Autonomo, 85
possible knowledge of Sacco's guilt, 218
treasurer of Defense Committee, 19, 65
Felix, David, 6, 8, 89–90, 102, 112, 115,
120, 147, 183, 203
Feuerlicht, Roberta, 91, 193
Ferrer, Francisco, 69
Fessenden, Susan, 207
Fitzgerald, John F., 20
Fitzgerald, J. Henry, 100, 101, 148
Fitzmeyer, George, 163
Flynn, Elizabeth Gurley, 24
Flynn, William J., 82, 83
Foss, Eugene, 24
Fraher, Thomas, 48, 49, 162, 163
Fraina, Louis, 79
France, Anatole, 118
Frankfurter, Felix, 9, 33, 37, 38, 111, 135,
173, 196, 202, 203
article stirs world opinion, 133, 204
denounces Thayer's rejection of Ma-
deiros motion, 134
law career, 204
tolerates no dissent, 205
and night of executions, 205
subsidized by Brandeis, 205 fn.
Frankfurter, Marion, 126, 205

Fuller, Alvan T., 1, 2, 7, 38, 39, 42, 135,
136, 168, 197
Furcolo, Foster, 156

Galleani, Luigi, 22, 23, 65, 68, 69, 72, 80,
81 fn., 84, 86, 174, 181
Galante, Carmine, 27 fn.
Gallivan, Jerry, 44, 60
Gambera, Giovanni, 12, 13, 14, 16, 30, 65,
70, 80
arrival in U.S., 64
and Libertarian Club, 64
and Sacco's guilt, 12
and Salsedo's death, 85
and Tresca, 31
visit to Vanzetti, 90
Gambera, Ideale, 11, 18, 217
and Sacco-Vanzetti case, 218, 219, 220,
226
letters on Sacco's guilt, 12, 16
meeting in San Francisco, 218
Gambera, Signorina, 12
Ganley, John, 112
Garrison, William Lloyd, 94
Gerard, George, 112
Giles, Frank, 158
Gill, Augustus, 148, 152
Giovanitti, Arturo, 24, 25, 72, 86
Goddard, Calvin, 151, 152, 156
Goguen, Henry, 157
Gold, Michael, 138
Goldenberg, Harry, 128, 164 fn.
Goldman, Emma, 70, 79
Gompers, Samuel, 212
Gould, Roy, 119, 120
Govoni, Doviglio, 87
Gori, Pietro, 66, 69
Grabill, Ethelbert V., 33
Graham, James, 87, 88
Grant, Robert, 136, 197, 199, 200
Greenslet, Ferris, 10
Gropper, Willie, 138
Grimké, Sara and Angelina, 94
Grossman, James, 5, 6
Guadagni, Felice, 13, 65, 90, 219, 226
Guerin, Daniel, 48, 107

Hamilton, Albert, 150, 156
Hand, Learned, 205
Harding, Warren, 118, 177, 178
Hassam, George, 168, 169, 170, 171,
172
Hassam, Lola, 129
Hatcher, Julian, 159
Hauptmann, Anna, 188
Hauptmann, Bruno Richard, 188

Hauser, Edwin, 113
Hayden, A. H., 82, 85
Haywood, Big Bill, 23, 24, 81, 209, 210, 211, 212
Hayes, James, 120
Hellyer, Henry, 60
Henderson, Jessica, 94
Heron, William, 130
Hibben, Paxton, 138
Hicks, Granville, 137, 198
Hill, Arthur D., 111
Hiss, Alger, 41
Hocking, William Ernest, 135
Holden, Harvey, 198
Holmes, John Haynes, 144
Holmes, Oliver Wendell, 81, 111, 116
Hoover, J. Edgar, 176, 177, 178, 180, 181
Howe, Julia Ward, 94
Hutchinson, Anne, 42

Ienusco, Joseph, 29
Imonde, Joseph "Gyp the Blood," 164, 165
Irving, David, 53

Jack, Cerise Carmen, 94, 125, 187
Jackson, Brian, 9, 185, 216
Jackson, Gardner, 126 fn., 143, 198
James, Edward Holton, 138
James, Henry, 93, 95
Johnson, Ruth, 60, 61
Johnson, Simon, 59, 60, 61
Jones, James, 163
Joughin, G. Louis, 3, 193
Joyce, James, 33
Jury, Frank, 158, 159, 160, 161, 162

Kaiser, David, 213
Katzmann, Frederick G., 13 fn., 14, 16, 21, 36, 37, 38, 39, 62, 63, 88, 93, 97, 100, 102, 103, 104, 105, 106 fn., 109, 147, 151, 152, 153, 155, 175, 179, 193, 194, 197, 213, 226
Katzmann, Percy, 15, 16
Kelley, Clarence, 178
Kelley, George, 109
Kelley, Michael, 72, 78
Kelley, William, 167
Kelliher, Julia, 131
Kennedy, John F., 144
King, Harry, 112
Krieger, Big Bill, 92

La Follette, Robert, 134
La Follette, Suzanne, 24
La Guardia, Fiorello, 28 fn.
Landis, K. M., 81
Laski, Harold, 111, 116, 196

Lawrence, William A., 135
LeBaron, Frank, 57, 60
Lederman, Maurice, 8
Letherman, Lawrence, 173, 175, 178, 179, 180, 182
Levine, Isaac Don, 28, 139
Linn, Clarence, 169, 170
Lippmann, Walter, 134
Lodge, Henry Cabot, 79
Lomasney, Martin, 20
Lopez, Frank, 91
Lothrop, Donald, 40
Lowell, A. Lawrence, 1, 2, 38, 39, 42, 98, 135
  and fate of Sacco and Vanzetti, 197
  and Lowell Committee, 136
  originally thinks Sacco-Vanzetti trial unfair, 135
  satisfied with committee conclusions in after years, 202
  and verdict of committee, 201
Lowell Committee, 104, 152, 168, 197, 214
Lowell, John, 207
Lumpkin, Grace, 138
Lurie, Reuben, 108
Lyons, Eugene, 23, 92, 93, 118–119

Madeiros, Celestino, 126, 164, 166, 167, 168, 171
  confesses to South Braintree holdup, 127
  criminal career, 127
  execution, 140
  and William Thompson, 129
  and Wrentham murder, 128
Madeiros, Mary, 167
Magrath, George, 100, 109, 153, 154
Mailer, Norman, 34 fn.
Malatesta, Enrico, 66
Mancini, Lucia, 13, 14, 65
Mancini, Tony, 164, 165, 166, 167
Mangano, Silvana, 7
Maramaldo, Fabrizio, 19 fn., 20
Margo, 34
Marks, Jeannette, 144
Mencken, H. L., 96, 134
Meredith, Burgess, 34
Merlino, Francesco, 66
Miele, Joe, 168, 169, 172
Millay, Edna St. Vincent, 93, 138, 139
Miller, Edward, 126, 128
Minor, Robert, 22
Monello, Angelo, 12, 226
Monello, Signorina, 12; *see also* Gambera, Signorina
Montaldo, Giuliano, 7, 8, 223
Montgomery, Robert, 5, 17, 26, 88, 90
Mooney, Tom, 114 fn.

Moore, Fred, 3, 15, 24, 29, 30, 96, 97, 99, 100, 105, 106, 113, 116, 118, 119, 120, 121, 124, 151, 171, 193, 194, 203, 214, 215, 219, 223
  and anarchists hiding dynamite, 104
  cocaine addict, 13, 14
  creator of Sacco-Vanzetti case, 22, 90
  death, 122
  early career, 22
  files post-trial motions, 119
  and house on Beacon Hill, 92–93
  and Lawrence strike, 22–23
  leaves case, 122
  offends judge, 115
  and Proctor motion, 120
  and Sacco's guilt, 21
  and verdict, 107
Moors, John F., 96
Morelli, Butsy, 164, 165, 166
Morelli, Fred, 164, 165
Morelli, Joe, 34, 164, 165, 166, 167
Morelli, Mike, 164, 167
Morelli, Patsy, 164, 165
Morgan, Edmund, 10, 88, 89, 90 fn., 110, 152, 168
Morgan, J. P., 81, 105, 106
Morison, Samuel Eliot, 96, 135
Mosmacotelli, Ferdinando, 73; *see also* Sacco, Nicola
Most, Johann, 68, 211
Mott, Lucretia, 94
Moyer, Charles, 209, 210, 211, 212
Mulinari, Enore, 68
Murphy, John, 45
Murray, H. J., 59
Murray, Joseph, 188
Murray, Mary, 188–192; *see also* DePasquale, Mary
Murray, Michael, 16
Murray, Robert, 110
Musmanno, Michael Angelo, 2, 30, 51, 109, 194
  continued belief in innocence of Sacco and Vanzetti, 29
  disputes ballistics evidence, 160
  enters case, 52
  judge at Nuremberg, 53
  and Operation Assault, 19
  speaks to Massachusetts legislative committee, 185
Mussolini, Benito, 23, 92
McAnarney, Jerry, 97, 106, 115, 116, 155
McAnarney, John, 97
McAnarney, Thomas, 97, 104
McCarthy, Joseph, 134
McCullum, Peter, 47, 162
McDevitt, Ray, 166

MacDonald, Paul, 58, 171
McGuinness, James, 161, 162
McManigal, Ortie, 211
MacMechan, Virginia, 94, 125
McNamara, James, 209, 211, 212
McNamara, John, 209, 211, 212
McNiff, Phillip, 17, 18, 90
McWilliams, Carey, 10, 191 fn.

Neal, Shelley, 45, 46, 48, 49, 108, 129
Needham, 35, 56
  and Braintree holdup license plates, 170
  and Bridgewater holdup license plates, 168
  Buick stolen in, 170
  and driver suspect, 170–171
  and Italian colony, 172
Negrini, Bartolomeo, 73; *see also* Vanzetti, Bartolomeo
New England Civil Liberties Committee, 93, 95
Nickerson, Arthur, 89, 90
Nin, Andrés, 26 fn.
Norton, Clem, 20, 21, 41, 193, 194, 223

O'Connor, Edwin, 20
O'Connor, Tom, 20, 40, 41, 42, 53, 55, 185
  boyhood, 50
  blames Stewart for Sacco-Vanzetti arrest, 54
  chief activist with Felicani, Ehrmann, Musmanno, 51
  enters case, 50
  and Committee to Vindicate Sacco and Vanzetti, 19
  and Operation Assault, 19
Orchard, Harry, 210, 211
Orciani, Riccardo, 49, 56, 63, 80, 85, 99, 104, 110, 163, 172
Otis, Harrison Gray, 211

Page, Mabel, 208
Palmer, A. Mitchell, 81, 82–83, 110
Papa, Vittorio, 103, 104
Parker, Seward, 112
Parmenter, Frederick, 46, 47, 49, 129, 163
Paul, Anthony, 160
Peabody, Elizabeth, 95
Pelloux, Regis, 154
Pernicone, Nunzio, 29
  condemns Feuerlicht book, 9
  and Tresca's statement, 30–31
Pettibone, George, 209, 210, 211, 212
Pinkerton Detective Agency, 59, 210
Plunkett, Horace, 201, 202
Pool, Elmer, 131
Popolizio, Giuseppe, 29

Porter, Katherine Anne, 94–95
  and August death week, 8
  and State House picket line, 138–139
Pound, Roscoe, 135, 205
Powers, Leland, 82, 85
Proctor, William, 117, 120, 155, 213
  affidavit for new trial, 146
  dispute with district attorney over court
    fee, 145
  equivocates on ballistics evidence, 101
  and fatal bullet, 145
  lack of competence, 102
  Proctor-Hamilton Motion for new trial,
    146
Puffer, Clarence, 56

Quintiliano, Luigi, 85

Ramuglia, Anthony, 109–110, 225
Rantoul, Louise, 94
Rapp, Henry, 108
Rapport, Beatrice Tresca, 29
Reardon, Paul, 155
Recchi, Carlo, 83
Red Scare, 110
Reich, Henry, Jr., 143
Rexroth, Kenneth, 184
Riordan, Robert, 115
Robinson, Marshall, 160, 161
Robinson, Merton, 149
Roche, George, 159, 161
Roche, John, 28–29
Rockefeller, John D., 81, 105, 106
Rockefeller, John D., Jr., 106 fn.
Rockwell, Norman, 184
Rolland, Romain, 118
Roosevelt, Eleanor, 42
Roosevelt, Franklin D., 81
Root, Inspector, 57
Rorty, James, 5, 26, 28, 29, 138, 144
Rose, Reginald, 223
Rosenberg, Julius and Ethel, 41, 212–213,
  216
Rossi, Paul, 164

Sacco, Dante, 183–190, 192
Sacco, Inez, 184
Sacco, Mildred, 189
Sacco, Nicola:
  accuses judge after sentencing, 214
  arrives in U.S., 70
  claims to have been in Boston on crime
    date, 109
  Colt and cartridges at his arrest, 61
  could have saved Vanzetti, 216
  denounces Moore, 121–122
  discharges Thompson, 214
  flees to Mexico, 77

Sacco, Nicola (*cont.*)
  guilt, 3, 12
  Italian background, 71
  letter to son, 186
  marriage, 72
  and Milford, 71
  psychotic episode, 214
  soldier of revolution, 216
  studies English, 125
  suicide attempt, 121, 214
  and Three-K factory, 78
Sacco, Rosina, 72, 73, 171, 184, 187, 188,
  189
Sacco, Spenser, 8, 185, 192, 194–195
Sacco-Vanzetti:
  arrest, 61
  apotheosis, 143–144
  disposal of ashes, 18
  dynamite, 104
  execution, 141
  funeral procession, 142–143
  letters, 34
  letters edited, 26
  lies at their arrest, 102
  mental breakdowns, 3
  militants, 16
Salomone, William, 17
Salsedo, Andrea:
  confesses to printing anarchist pam-
    phlet, 83
  death, 84, 85
Sands, Eliot, 155
Sartori, Julia, 200
Sayre, Francis, 135
Schlesinger, Arthur, 126 fn., 135
Shahn, Ben, 144
Shanks, Edward, 222
Sheels, Bessie May, 114
Shields, Art, 91
Sibley, Frank, 113, 114, 115
Simmons, Edward, 112, 147
Sinclair, Upton, 5, 21, 22, 95, 104, 105,
  106 fn., 124, 183, 215
Sisitsky, Alan, 8
Smith, Edgar, 34 fn.
Squires, Francis, 15, 16, 128
Stein, Gertrude, 95
Steunenberg, Frank, 209, 210
Stewart, Michael, 54, 55, 57, 58, 59, 61,
  109, 173
Stone, Lucy, 94, 207
Stong, Phil, 222
Stratton, Samuel, 136, 197

Tarbell, Ida, 135, 139
Taylor, Daniel, 145
Taylor, Fred, 169, 170
Taylor, Telford, 53

Thayer, Lucien, 113
Thayer, Webster, 35, 38, 39, 87, 147, 150,
    151, 182, 193, 197, 199, 215
  bombing of house, 105
  charge to jury at Dedham, 37
  charge to jury at Plymouth, 89
  death threats, 96–97
  denies Madeiros motion, 131–132
  and fairness, 111–116
Thomas, Norman, 28, 30, 121, 134
Thompson, William, 50, 128, 129, 131,
    146, 151, 152, 153, 164, 167, 173,
    178, 180, 182, 196, 199, 221
  at trial opening, 115
  attacks Thayer's prejudice, 116
Thoreau, Henry, 70
Timilty, Diamond Jim, 20
Totty, Warren, 170, 171
Tracey, William, 129
Tresca, Carlo, 3, 22, 28, 29, 70, 72, 80,
    194, 218
  admits Sacco's guilt, 27–31
  death, 26
  early life, 23
  meets Gambera, 31
  sends Moore to take over Sacco-Van-
    zetti defense, 25
Tucker, Charles, 208, 209
Turner, William, 149, 153

Vahey, John, 87, 88, 89, 90, 208
Van Amburgh, Charles, 100, 145, 149, 156
Van Amburgh, Charles, Jr., 156, 157, 160
Valdinoce, Carlo, 73, 80, 83, 85
Vanzetti, Bartolomeo:
  boyhood in Italy, 73
  and Brinis in Plymouth, 75–76
  changes revolver testimony, 98
  collapse of alibi of collecting literature,
    103
  death of mother and leaving for the
    U.S., 74
  eulogy of Sacco, 221–222
  in Mexico, 77

Vanzetti, Bartolomeo (*cont.*)
  knowledge of Bridgewater holdup, 90
  letter to Dante Sacco, 186–187
  love of nature, 125
  obsessive interludes, 214–215
  Plymouth trial, 24
  reading and writing in jail, 126
  refuses to take stand at Plymouth, 88
  returns to Plymouth to peddle fish, 78
  speech to court on sentencing, 214
  statement to Stong, 222
  studies English, 155
  wanderings, 78
  work in New York, 75
Vanzètti, Luigia, 25
Vanzetti, Vincenzina, 8, 17
Vidale, Vittorio, 26 fn.
Villard, Oswald Garrison, 139
von Zahn, Peter, 223

Warner, Arthur, 114
Wayman, Dorothy, 114
Weiss, Feri, 174
Weller, Jac, 157, 158, 159, 160, 161
Wells, H. G., 34
West, William J., 174, 175, 176, 177, 180,
    181
Weyand, Fred, 173, 174, 175, 178, 179,
    182
Whitehead, Alfred North, 188
Wieck, David, 85
Williams, J. A., 213
Williams, Harold, 100, 101, 102, 146, 147,
    151, 153, 155, 175, 213
Wilson, George, 160, 161
Wise, Stephen, 135
Wood, Clement, 143

Yeats, W. B., 213
Young, William, 213

Zagroff, Sergei, 14
Zelt, Johannes, 3, 4, 5